THE COMPLETE IDIOT'S GUIDE TO

HTML5 and CSS3

by Joe Kraynak

ALPHA

A member of Penguin Group (USA) Inc.

To Google, my muse and oracle.

ALPHA BOOKS

Published by the Penguin Group

Penguin Group (USA) Inc., 375 Hudson Street, New York, New York 10014, USA

Penguin Group (Canada), 90 Eglinton Avenue East, Suite 700, Toronto, Ontario M4P 2Y3, Canada (a division of Pearson Penguin Canada Inc.)

Penguin Books Ltd., 80 Strand, London WC2R 0RL, England

Penguin Ireland, 25 St. Stephen's Green, Dublin 2, Ireland (a division of Penguin Books Ltd.)

Penguin Group (Australia), 250 Camberwell Road, Camberwell, Victoria 3124, Australia (a division of Pearson Australia Group Pty. Ltd.)

Penguin Books India Pvt. Ltd., 11 Community Centre, Panchsheel Park, New Delhi—110 017, India

Penguin Group (NZ), 67 Apollo Drive, Rosedale, North Shore, Auckland 1311, New Zealand (a division of Pearson New Zealand Ltd.)

Penguin Books (South Africa) (Pty.) Ltd., 24 Sturdee Avenue, Rosebank, Johannesburg 2196, South Africa

Penguin Books Ltd., Registered Offices: 80 Strand, London WC2R 0RL, England

International Standard Book Number: 978-1-61564-084-3
Library of Congress Catalog Card Number: 2010917068

13 12 11   8 7 6 5 4 3 2 1

Interpretation of the printing code: The rightmost number of the first series of numbers is the year of the book's printing; the rightmost number of the second series of numbers is the number of the book's printing. For example, a printing code of 11-1 shows that the first printing occurred in 2011.

Printed in the United States of America

Note: This publication contains the opinions and ideas of its author. It is intended to provide helpful and informative material on the subject matter covered. It is sold with the understanding that the author and publisher are not engaged in rendering professional services in the book. If the reader requires personal assistance or advice, a competent professional should be consulted.

The author and publisher specifically disclaim any responsibility for any liability, loss, or risk, personal or otherwise, which is incurred as a consequence, directly or indirectly, of the use and application of any of the contents of this book.

Most Alpha books are available at special quantity discounts for bulk purchases for sales promotions, premiums, fund-raising, or educational use. Special books, or book excerpts, can also be created to fit specific needs.

For details, write: Special Markets, Alpha Books, 375 Hudson Street, New York, NY 10014.

Publisher: *Marie Butler-Knight*

Associate Publisher: *Mike Sanders*

Executive Managing Editor: *Billy Fields*

Senior Development Editor: *Christy Wagner*

Production Editor: *Kayla Dugger*

Copy Editor: *Christine Hackerd*

Cover Designer: *William Thomas*

Book Designers: *William Thomas, Rebecca Batchelor*

Indexer: *Brad Herriman*

Layout: *Brian Massey*

Proofreader: *Laura Caddell*

Contents

Appendixes

Introduction

The World Wide Web is an incredible place where you can explore a seemingly infinite stash of media on demand 24/7. Perhaps even more amazing is that most of the content consists of text-only files—hypertext markup language (HTML) files, which contain most of the content, and cascading style sheets (CSS), which format all that content. Master these two web languages, and you're well on your way to becoming a world-class developer.

HTML and CSS have been around for quite a while and have always provided a solid foundation for web development. The good news is they're about to get a whole lot better. During the writing of this book, the World Wide Web Consortium (W3C) was working on new specifications—HTML5 and CSS3—that introduce a number of features designed to improve the appearance of web pages and make them more dynamic and interactive.

By the time you read this, HTML5 and CSS3 may be the official specifications, but you don't need to wait for the new specification to be finalized before you start implementing these new features. You can and should begin right now, and *The Complete Idiot's Guide to HTML5 and CSS3* is here to help!

What You Learn in This Book

This book assumes no prior knowledge of HTML and CSS. In fact, it assumes no prior knowledge of web development. This book makes one big assumption: that you're starting where I started several years ago—from square one. You want to build a website, but you really don't know where to begin. Perhaps you think you need to learn how to use an HTML editor (you don't). Maybe you think you need to build the site on your computer and then upload the files (you don't). Perhaps you're unaware of web development tools that can greatly simplify the process.

Although this book focuses primarily on HTML5 and CSS3, it presents these topics in the context of building a website. When you're first getting started, building a site from scratch using only HTML and CSS can be overwhelming. You're usually better off starting with a content management system (CMS), such as WordPress, and a predesigned theme. You can then use your knowledge of HTML and CSS to customize your site instead of starting from scratch. This approach gets your site up and running as quickly as possible, and allows you to learn at a more comfortable pace.

The Complete Idiot's Guide to HTML5 and CSS3 covers a lot of ground. To make all this material more manageable, chapters are grouped into the following five parts, along with several appendixes:

Part 1, Getting Started with HTML and CSS, brings you up to speed on the basics of building a website and using HTML5 and CSS3 to do it. Here you discover how to get started with a web hosting service, how to exchange files between your computer and your web server, and how to use a CMS to build and maintain a site using web-based tools instead of a complicated HTML editor.

Part 2, Authoring Pages and Posts with HTML, shows you how to use HTML tags to build web pages from the ground up. Chapter 4 brings you up to speed on the fundamentals of HTML, introduces you to new elements in HTML5, and leads you through the process of creating a framework for a web page that functions as a container for all the other HTML elements on the page. The remaining chapters show you how to add elements, including headings, paragraphs, lists, quotes, images, links, and video.

Part 3, Formatting and Layout with CSS Styles, shows you how to make all those pages you built in Part 2 look pretty. Chapter 10 builds a strong foundation for everything else in this part, explaining how to create style rules and use selectors to specify which HTML elements the styles apply to. Chapter 11 shows you how to take a shortcut by starting with a theme, and the remaining chapters cover specific CSS topics, including formatting text, adding colors, customizing backgrounds, creating drop-shadows, and using CSS3 to create nifty animation effects without knowing anything about programming.

In **Part 4, Making Your Pages More Dynamic and Interactive,** you discover the basics of using forms to collect data and how to use jQuery to dynamically change a page's contents and/or appearance in response to a user's actions. Chapter 23 features a demonstration of HTML5's new canvas element, to give you a general understanding of how the canvas functions.

Part 5, Testing and Fine-Tuning Your Site, offers guidance on how to test your site in multiple browsers, make it a more attractive target for search engines, and optimize its performance. While the other parts in this book focus primarily on how your site looks, Part 5 focuses on how it functions.

In the back, several appendixes serve as your handy reference to HTML tags and CSS style properties and values. When you know what you're doing and just need to look up the exact code required to do it, this is the place to turn. I've also included a glossary, where you can find definitions for some of the more perplexing HTML and CSS jargon and acronyms.

Conventions Used in This Book

I use the following conventions in this book to make it easier to understand:

- Commands or options you click appear **bold**.

- HTML elements are referenced by their opening tags; for example, <p> for paragraph and <img> for image.

- CSS selectors, properties, and values appear in *italics*.

- HTML and CSS source code appear in computer font, as follows. Just type it exactly as shown:

```
body {background:url(file://localhost/D:/Data/CIGHTML/
    ➥ SourceCode/ljubljana.jpg); background-position:center top;
    ➥ background-repeat:no-repeat; }
```

Extras

A plethora of sidebars and other icons offer additional information about what you've just read. Here's what to look for:

DEFINITION

Web developers love jargon and cryptic acronyms, including HTML, CSS, and W3C. When a term baffles you or an acronym annoys you, look here for a plain-English definition.

WHOA!

Before you even think about clicking that button, check out these sidebars for precautionary notes. Chances are, I've made the same mistake myself, so learn from my mistakes instead of yours.

INSIDE TIP

When you've been building and formatting web pages for as long as I have, you learn better ways to perform the same tasks and avoid common pitfalls. To share in that knowledge, check out the Inside Tips.

NOTE

These fun sidebars offer interesting facts and background information.

Next to some paragraphs, you'll see icons like these:

This icon indicates that the text covers information new to HTML5.

And this icon indicates that information new to CSS3 is discussed.

Online Bonus

We realize typing source code can be a drag, so if you want to work with some of the examples presented in this book, head to idiotsguides.com/html5, where you can download some source code to play around with. It's always easier to customize code than start from scratch!

Acknowledgments

Crafting a book is a collaborative effort requiring a team of talented, dedicated professionals. I owe special thanks to Mike Sanders for choosing me to author this book, and for handling the assorted details to get this book in gear. Thanks to Christy Wagner for guiding the content of this book, keeping it focused on new users, fixing all my typos, and fine-tuning the content. Thanks to Kayla Dugger for shepherding the manuscript (and art) through production, and to the Alpha Books production team for transforming a collection of electronic files into such an attractive book. I also owe special thanks to my agent, Neil Salkind, for his wisdom and guidance, and to the rest of the staff at Studio B for expertly managing the minor details of my career (like making sure I get paid).

Special Thanks to the Technical Reviewer

The Complete Idiot's Guide to HTML5 and CSS3 was reviewed by an expert who double-checked the accuracy of what you'll learn here, to help us ensure that this book gives you everything you need to know about building quality web pages using HTML5 and CSS3. Special thanks are extended to Josh Hill.

Trademarks

All terms mentioned in this book that are known to be or are suspected of being trademarks or service marks have been appropriately capitalized. Alpha Books and Penguin Group (USA) Inc. cannot attest to the accuracy of this information. Use of a term in this book should not be regarded as affecting the validity of any trademark or service mark.

Getting Started with HTML and CSS

In the old days, you'd build your website on your computer using an HTML editor or a plain text editor such as Notepad. Then, you'd upload your pages to your web server.

By today's standards, that process is outmoded. Now you can install a content management system (CMS) on your web server and have a site up and running in a matter of minutes. You can then log in to your site online to customize its appearance and layout with HTML and CSS.

In the past, getting started with HTML and CSS meant installing an HTML editor and learning how to use it. Today, getting started means having a web hosting account and knowing how to use it to get your site up and running. Part 1 shows you how.

In addition, this part helps you wrap your brain around HTML and CSS, so you have a framework for understanding what you're about to learn in the remaining chapters.

Laying the Groundwork

In This Chapter

- Choosing a path to your web presence
- Selecting a web hosting service and setting up an account
- Deciding on the right domain name
- Checking out your hosting service's control panel
- Uploading files to the web … when the time comes

Before you even think about HTML or CSS, you need to choose the place on the web where your site will ultimately reside. This may seem a little premature. After all, you haven't even created your site yet! If you're like most users, however, you'll actually create your site online using some sort of content management system (CMS), and your choice of where to host your site may determine which CMS you use for creating and managing your site.

This chapter helps you explore your options, choose a web hosting service, register your own domain name, get your own @yourdomain.com e-mail address, and transfer files between your computer and your hosting service account. By the end of this chapter, you'll have a solid foundation on which to build your site.

Exploring Your Website Hosting Options

Regardless of how you choose to build your site, it eventually needs a place on the web to call home. This is what a hosting service is all about. The hosting service provides access to a web server where all the documents, images, audio, video, and other content that comprise a website reside. The site's address is a domain name of your choosing, such as yoursite.com, and every component of the site has its own uniform resource locator (URL), such as http://yoursite.com/images/myphoto.jpg.

Whenever someone uses a web browser to open a page on the site by entering its address or clicking a link to it, the web server sends the page and all the components that comprise the page to the user's web browser, which then displays the page. Without a web server, nobody can access your site.

You can use any one of numerous hosting services to host your site, but they generally break down into the following four types:

- Free hosted website
- Free hosted blog
- General-purpose hosting service
- Niche hosting service

The following sections cover these different types of hosting services in greater detail.

Free Hosted Websites

A free hosting service typically provides a CMS that enables you to set up and maintain a basic site with a limited number of pages. The hosting service typically provides tools to simplify the process of designing and building the site, and may even offer a wizard that leads you through the process of choosing a design and entering content. You won't deal much with HTML or CSS.

One of the most popular free hosting services is Google Sites (sites.google.com). With Google Sites, you start by choosing a design template, giving your site a name, and specifying a site URL that starts with http://sites.google.com, as shown in Figure 1.1.

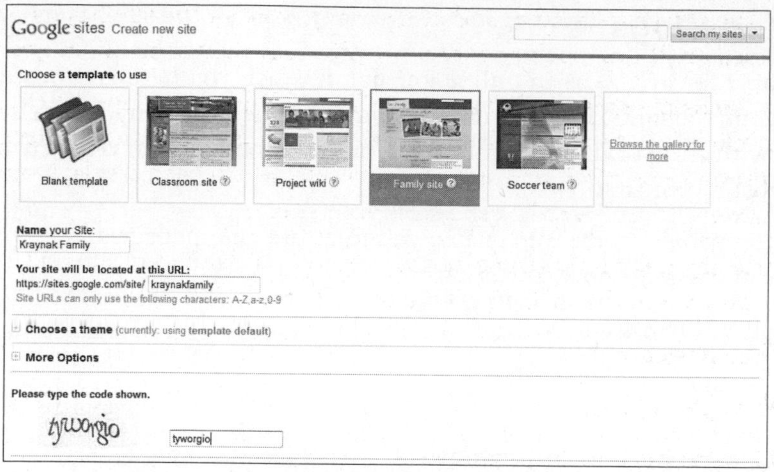

Figure 1.1: *You can create a free hosted website at Google Sites.*

Free hosted websites typically have a few drawbacks, including the following:

- The site address usually starts with the domain name of the hosting service. This makes your site address difficult for visitors to recognize and remember.

- The hosting service may display banners and/or advertisements on your site, which can negatively affect your site's credibility.

- The number of pages and amount of storage space for files may be severely limited.

- Search engines may ignore free sites or at least not give them a very high search ranking.

- You may be unable to add special features, such as an online store, blog, chat rooms, and discussion areas.

- You don't get a branded e-mail address, such as yourname@yoursite.com.

- Technical support may be limited or nonexistent.

- Hosting may not be free forever. Most free hosting is actually a free trial, although I anticipate Google Sites will remain free.

- If you later choose to move your site to its own domain, you can lose traction with search engines. You're better off starting your site on its own domain.

Free Hosted Blogs

A *blog*, short for *web log*, is an online journal in which you regularly post content to express your thoughts, insights, desires, announcements, or anything else you'd like to share with the world. Your posts are typically arranged in reverse chronological order (most recent first).

Several companies on the web enable you to create and manage a blog for free. Here are a few of the most popular options:

- WordPress.com
- Blogger.com
- LiveJournal.com
- Xanga.com

Free hosted blogs have many of the same drawbacks as free hosted websites, but they also share one significant benefit: the blogging software is updated regularly for you, so you're always working with the latest, greatest version of the *blogging platform*. If you set up your own blog, *you* need to update the software—not a huge deal, but it does require some time and attention.

> **DEFINITION**
>
> A **blogging platform** is software that typically resides online and enables you to create, design, and manage your blog.

General-Purpose Hosting Services

A general-purpose hosting service provides the tools and services you need to register your own domain name, build and manage a custom site, and set up your own branded e-mail accounts.

By *general-purpose hosting service*, I mean a service that's not designed for specific professions, such as real estate, medical, or law. It's entirely up to you to determine how the site looks, what it offers, and how it functions. The service provides you with access to the tools you need to create and manage your site and a place for your site to call home.

I use a general-purpose hosting service for all my sites and client sites, and many other web developers do the same. A general-purpose hosting service offers the following benefits:

- Your site has its own, unique domain name. As long as you pay the annual registration, you own that domain name.

- You choose whether your site contains advertisements, how many, and where they appear. Better yet, if you sell advertising space, *you* keep all the money.

- Most services offer unlimited storage, so your site can be as big and complex as you want it to be. You can also grow your site later with a blog, chat room, online store, discussion areas, and so on.

- Most services offer hundreds or even thousands of branded e-mail addresses, so everyone in your home or business can have an e-mail address ending in @yoursite.com.

- Technical support is typically included, but how comprehensive it is varies among hosting services.

- The monthly fee is typically very affordable, because so many good hosting services are competing for your business.

In short, a general-purpose hosting service gives you more freedom and power to establish an Internet presence and even build a brand presence.

Niche Design/Hosting Services

Niche design/hosting services are available for many businesses and professions, so if you're an owner-operator of your own business—such as a medical or dental office, real estate firm, credit union, restaurant, or accounting or law firm—you may want to look into a niche service that caters to your particular business type.

Because the niche design/hosting services have experience in your profession or industry, they can offer guidance on how to make and keep your site competitive. They also know what your site requires in terms of security and privacy features, online forms to collect data, and standard ways of presenting information. For example, firms that specialize in hosting real estate websites may already have the infrastructure in place to retrieve local real estate listings and feed them to a specific page.

Niche design/hosting services typically offer turnkey solutions, so if you choose this option, you probably won't be doing much of the HTML and CSS required to design and maintain your site. But still, knowing the basics can come in handy for when you must update content or post blog entries.

To find a niche service, search the web for your profession or business type followed by "web design" (without the quotes); for example, you might search for "doctor office web design."

Choosing a Web Hosting Service

I encourage you to go with a full-featured, well-established hosting service that has a solid reputation, such as Bluehost (bluehost.com), HostGator (HostGator.com), InMotion (inmotionhosting.com), or iPage (iPage.com). You can Google "web hosting" and find links to oodles of other hosting services.

Before you sign up with a service, check reviews and ratings at websites like Upperhost (upperhost.com) or Hosting Review (hosting-review.com), where reviews are less likely to be biased and consumers are allowed to weigh in. Some review sites are more interested in selling services and collecting affiliate commissions than in providing honest reviews and ratings. Also, visit each hosting service's help area to see how helpful it really is.

Creating an Account ... and Paying for It

When you've finally chosen a web hosting service, it's time to create an account. Assuming you've purchased anything on the web, this should be a snap. All you do is click the link to sign up and then follow the on-screen instructions and cues to enter your billing information and credit card number.

INSIDE TIP

Prior to opening an account, check whether the hosting service offers any special deals, such as a free domain registration, and do what's necessary to claim that special offering. If you sign up without getting the special offer, call the service and explain what happened. They should be able and willing to credit your account.

Becoming Master of Your Own Domain (Name)

Your domain name, such as www.yoursite.com, is your address on the web. You can use it with or without the www. as your site address, add *yourname@* to the beginning of it and use it as an e-mail address, add *ftp* to the beginning to upload files to the file transfer protocol (FTP) server, add *blog* to the beginning to use it as your blog address, and much more. (For additional details about FTP, see "Ya Gotta Know How to FTP" later in this chapter.)

In the following sections, you discover how to come up with a good domain name, register it, and add subdomains to organize the different content areas of your site.

Conjuring Up a Good Domain Name

You should spend about as much time naming your domain as you would spend naming a baby. This name is going to accompany your website through its foreseeable existence, so you want something you're going to be happy with for a long time to come. Be sure the domain name you choose has the following qualities:

- **Short:** Users don't like to type in a lengthy address to get where they're going.

- **Unique:** Nothing's worse than having a domain name that's commonly mistaken for another name.

- **Recognizable and memorable:** Users shouldn't need to wrack their brains trying to recall your domain name.

- **Phonetic:** The name should be easy to pronounce and spell.

- **Descriptive and keyword optimized:** Whatever you want your site to be known for should be in your domain name.

- **Symbol free:** Stick to letters and perhaps numbers.

- **Common extension:** .com and .net are the two most common extensions, and .com is the preferable of those two. If you're creating a government site, go with .gov. For a nonprofit organization, use .org.

You may want to formulate three or four possibilities, just in case someone has already claimed your first choice.

Registering Your Domain Name

With your domain name list in hand, log in to your web hosting account, perform a domain name search, and (assuming somebody hasn't already claimed the domain) register your domain name. The process is pretty easy—you log in to your hosting account, click the option to register a domain, and then follow the onscreen instructions, as shown in Figure 1.2.

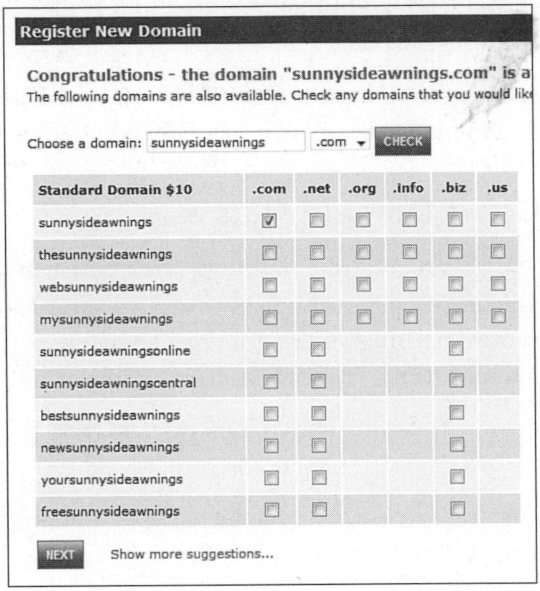

Figure 1.2: *Check the domain status and then register the domain.*

Most services offer an auto-renew option, so you don't have to worry about renewing your registration when it expires. I strongly recommend using auto-renew so you don't lose your domain to someone. Also, if you get a new credit card number, be sure to update your account information; otherwise, you may lose your domain due to nonpayment.

Branching Out with Subdomains

When you register one domain, you gain access to countless *subdomains*, such as blog. yoursite.com, shop.yoursite.com, and chat.yoursite.com. These subdomains enable you to make your site modular while still building brand presence for your top-level domain—yoursite.com.

DEFINITION

A **subdomain** is a domain within a domain. It has the same domain name and extension but adds a prefix.

The subdomain simply provides a URL that points to a separate folder on your account. For example, if you create the subdomain shop.yoursite.com, you can point it to the folder yoursite.com/shop. Whenever a user enters shop.yoursite.com, they'll be accessing files stored in yoursite.com/shop.

Creating subdomains is a snap. Log in to your hosting service and click the option for subdomains. Click in the **Subdomain** box and type the prefix for the subdomain you want to use. In the **Document Root** box, type a name for the folder in which the subdomain's files will be stored. Click the **Create** button to create the subdomain (see Figure 1.3).

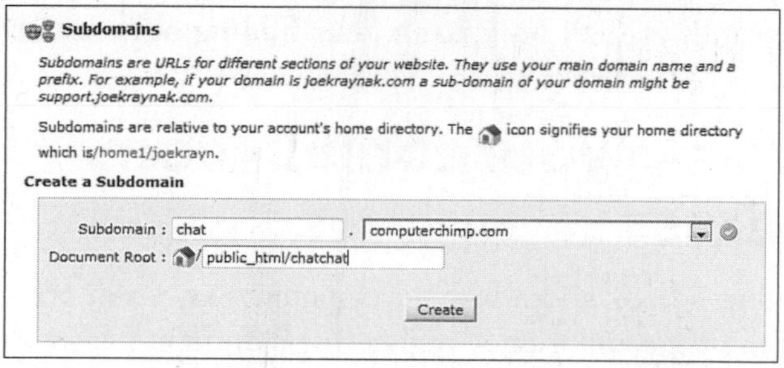

Subdomains

Subdomains are URLs for different sections of your website. They use your main domain name and a prefix. For example, if your domain is joekraynak.com a sub-domain of your domain might be support.joekraynak.com.

Subdomains are relative to your account's home directory. The 🏠 icon signifies your home directory which is/home1/joekrayn.

Create a Subdomain

Subdomain : chat . computerchimp.com

Document Root : 🏠/ public_html/chatchat

Create

Figure 1.3: *Creating a subdomain is easy.*

Poking Around in Your Hosting Service's Control Panel

Almost all web hosting services contain a control panel that functions as a gateway to everything the service offers. Figure 1.4 shows a portion of the Bluehost Control Panel.

The control panel provides the tools you use to build and manage your site. You can manage your account and billing information, change your password, access the help system, configure e-mail accounts, transfer files to and from the server, manage your domains, and install software and services.

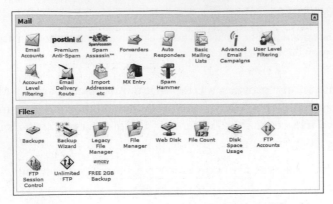

Figure 1.4: *Sample web hosting service control panel.*

Poke around in the control panel to see what your hosting service has to offer. Some services provide online help or videos to get you up to speed on their features. It's usually worth spending a half hour to an hour finding out what's available.

Getting Your @yourdomain.com E-Mail Address

Covering e-mail in a book about web development may seem off topic, but if you're going to spend the time and money registering a domain name, I want to be sure you make the most of that name. In all likelihood, your web hosting account includes access to a mail server to handle incoming and outgoing messages. With most services, you can set up e-mail accounts for hundreds or even thousands of users, each with a unique e-mail address that includes @yourdomain.com.

The process for setting up e-mail accounts varies according to the hosting service, but you can usually access e-mail accounts through an option on the control panel. This displays a screen like the one shown in Figure 1.5, where you can create a new account with a unique e-mail address and password, and specify the maximum storage space for each account.

Typically, you access your e-mail account via the web by going to mail.yoursite.com and logging in with your e-mail address and password. If you use a separate e-mail client such as Windows Live Mail or Outlook to send and receive messages, you should be able to find instructions in the help system that contain the settings you need to add your account.

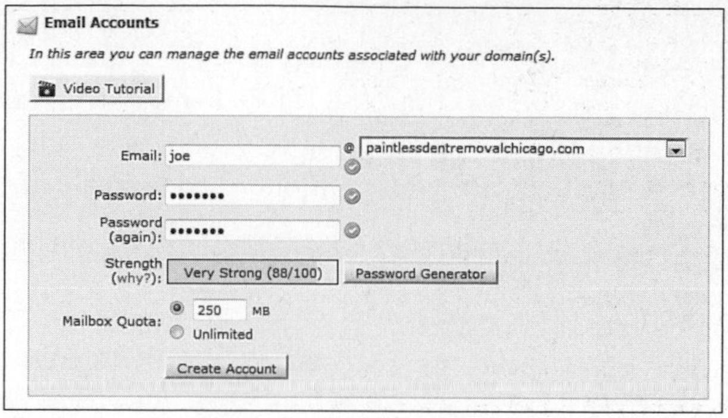

Figure 1.5: *Create at least one e-mail account for yourself.*

Ya Gotta Know How to FTP

FTP is a means of transferring files from your personal computer to your web server and vice versa. If you're using a CMS to create and manage your site, you don't need to know a whole lot about FTP, but eventually, you'll encounter a situation in which you need to use FTP to perform a specific task or troubleshoot your site.

FTP isn't very complicated. After establishing a connection between your computer and your FTP server, it's as easy as opening, copying, and moving files from one folder to another on your own computer.

Doing It Through Your Hosting Service

Your hosting service is likely to provide an FTP client you can use to transfer files between your account and your computer. This is usually the most hassle-free option because you don't have to download and install additional software.

Log in to your account, access the control panel, and click the FTP option, as shown in Figure 1.6. (The appearance and name of the FTP option may vary among different hosting services.)

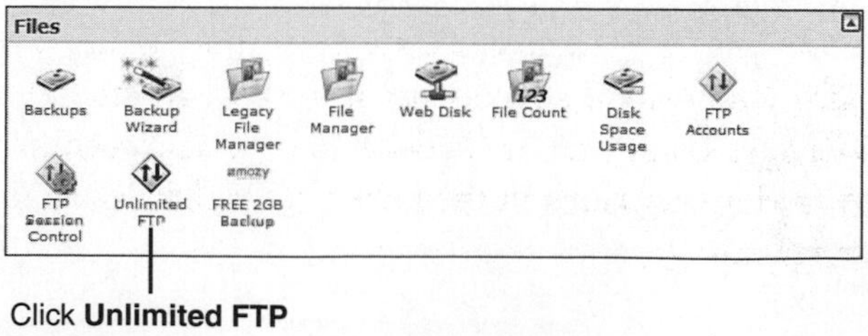

Click **Unlimited FTP**

Figure 1.6: *Run your hosting provider's FTP client.*

The FTP client appears, as shown in Figure 1.7. On the left, the FTP client displays disk drives, folders, and files on your computer. On the right are folders and files for your hosting service account. Using the FTP client, you can create, rename, and delete folders; obtain information about a folder or file; view selected files; and drag and drop folders and files between your computer and your hosting account.

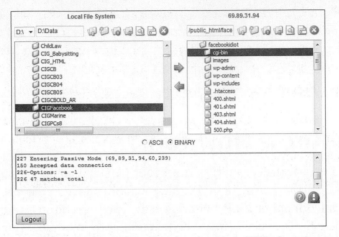

Figure 1.7: *A typical hosting provider's FTP client.*

Your hosting service may also offer a more robust file management program, typically named something like File Manager. Figure 1.8 shows Bluehost's File Manager. The file manager enables you to do everything you can do with the FTP client and then some, including opening and editing files. You can upload and download files using the file manager, although the two-paned layout of the FTP client makes file transfer easier.

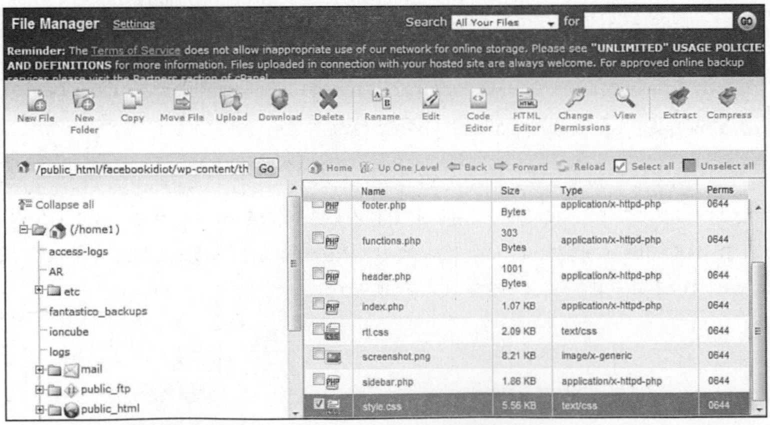

Figure 1.8: *You can do more with a file manager.*

Opting for a Dedicated FTP Client

Although I often use my hosting provider's FTP client, I usually use a dedicated client that's installed on my computer. This requires you to download and install a client and set it up to access your hosting account, but it simplifies the process of logging in to your hosting account.

You can find plenty of freeware and shareware (try before you buy) FTP clients. My favorite is FileZilla, which you can download and install from filezilla-project.org. After downloading and installing the program, run it and click **File, Site Manager**. Click the **New Site** button, and enter the details required to log on to your site:

- **FTP address:** This is usually ftp.yoursitename.com.

- **Port number:** You may be able to leave this blank. If that doesn't work, try **21**. And if that doesn't work, consult your hosting service's help system or contact technical support.

- **Server type:** Choose **FTP** or **File Transfer Protocol**.

- **Logon type:** Choose **Normal**.

- **Username:** This is the name you chose or the hosting service assigned to you. If you're not sure, check the control panel or access your account information from the control panel to find out.

- **Password:** Enter the password you use to log in to your hosting account.

INSIDE TIP

You can create separate FTP accounts to enable other individuals to upload and download files. In most cases, you should restrict access to a specific folder, so only you have access to your root directory. Otherwise, someone else can do a lot of damage and even wipe out your site.

Navigating Folders on Your Server

However you choose to FTP, you navigate folders on the server just as you do on your computer: double-click a folder to open it. To move back to a previous folder, click the **Up one folder** icon, as shown in Figure 1.9. You can also type the path to a folder, above the folder list, to go directly to it.

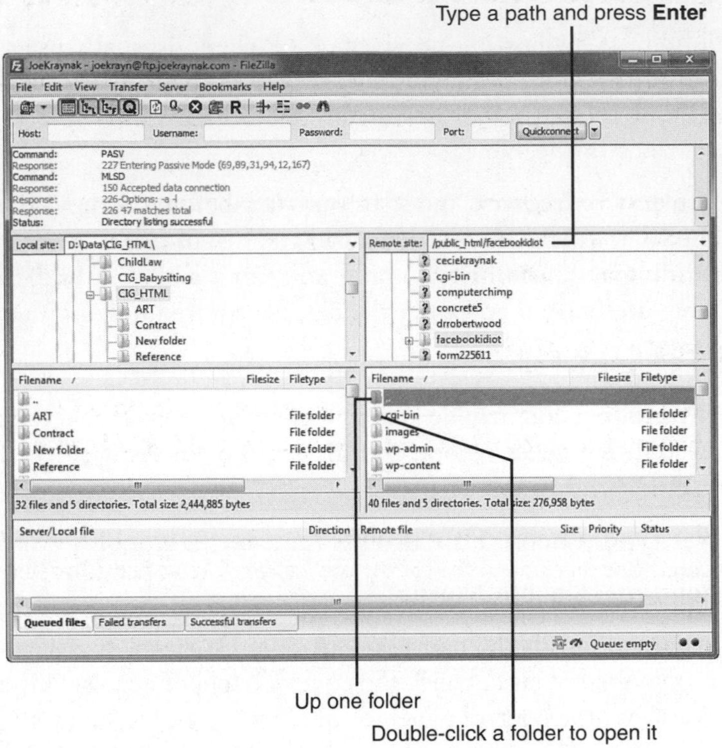

Type a path and press **Enter**

Up one folder

Double-click a folder to open it

Figure 1.9: *Navigating folders in FileZilla.*

You'll see plenty of folders, but the one you'll be working with most is named public_html. When the time comes to publish your site, you'll upload the files that comprise your site to the public_html folder or create a subfolder inside the public_html folder and upload files to that folder. This makes the files that comprise your site publicly accessible on the web.

FTP's Ups and Downs: Uploading and Downloading Files

Now that you know how to navigate folders, uploading and downloading files is a snap:

1. Display the file or folder you want to copy in one pane.

2. Open the destination folder in the other pane.

3. Drag the file or folder from its source to the destination, and release the mouse button.

4. If a dialog box pops up informing you you're about to overwrite a file of the same name, click **Cancel** to abort or **OK** or **Yes** to proceed.

Depending on your FTP client, you may be able to initiate an upload or download operation by selecting the file(s) or folder(s), right-clicking one of the selected items, and choosing **Upload** or **Download**.

Digging Up Hidden Files

If you ever need to edit a file and can't find it where it's supposed to be, the file may be hidden. Hosting providers often hide files that should be edited only by advanced users.

To view hidden files, head to your hosting account control panel, and look for an icon in the **Advanced** area named something like **Index Manager**. Double-click the icon to display options for accessing files and folders. Click the option to show hidden files, and then click the **OK** or **Go** button to make the change.

The Least You Need to Know

- To have the most control over your website, opt for a general-purpose hosting service, such as Bluehost, InMotion, or iPage.
- Create an account and register a domain with the hosting service of your choice.
- After logging in to your hosting account, you can access most features your service offers through its control panel.
- Take full advantage of your hosting account by creating and using one or more e-mail accounts.
- FTP enables you to exchange files and folders between your computer and your hosting account.
- Consider using a dedicated FTP client, such as FileZilla, instead of or in addition to the FTP client your hosting service provides.
- You can use FTP to publish your site by uploading the files that comprise your site to the public_html folder or one of its subfolders … but there are easier ways, as you'll see in Chapter 3.

Grasping HTML and CSS Basics

In This Chapter

- Introducing HTML, XHTML, and other MLs
- Wrapping your brain around all you can do with HTML
- Understanding how CSS fits in
- Getting up to speed on changes in HTML5 and CSS3

Throughout this book, you're going to pay a lot of attention to details—the many individual "codes" that comprise HTML and CSS. This chapter ignores the details to provide the big picture of HTML, CSS, and how they work together in helping a web browser display a web page as it's meant to appear. This big-picture view provides a framework on which to hang all the details.

Near the end of the chapter, you discover an overview of the new features being introduced in HTML5 and CSS3—new standards in development during the time this book was being written.

What Is HTML, Anyway?

HTML (*HyperText Markup Language*) is the ugliness behind every web page that enables browsers to display the page in all its glory. To see what I mean by this, use your browser to display a web page you think looks pretty good and then view its source code. To view the source code in Internet Explorer, for example, click **Page**, **View Source**. Figure 2.1 pulls the mask off source code.

```
</head>
<body class="custom">
<div id="container">
<div id="page">
        <div id="header">
                <p id="logo"><a href="http://joekraynak.com">Joe Kraynak</a></p>
                <h1 id="tagline">Freelance Writer</h1>
        </div>
<ul class="menu">
<li class="tab tab-home current"><a href="http://joekraynak.com" rel="nofollow">Home</a></li>
<li class="tab tab-1"><a href="http://joekraynak.com/about" title="About">About</a></li>
<li class="tab tab-2"><a href="http://joekraynak.com/affordablecustom-web-design" title="Web Design">Web Design</a></li>
<li class="tab tab-3"><a href="http://joekraynak.com/recent-books" title="Relatively Recent Books">Books</a></li>
<li class="tab tab-4"><a href="http://joekraynak.com/testimonials" title="Testimonials">Testimonials</a></li>
<li class="tab tab-5"><a href="http://joekraynak.com/contact-me" title="Contact Me">Contact Me</a></li>
<li class="tab tab-6"><a href="http://joekraynak.com/hire-me" title="Services/Rates">Services</a></li>
<li class="tab tab-7"><a href="http://joekraynak.com/payments" title="Pay Me">Pay Me</a></li>
</ul>
        <div id="content_box">
                <div id="content" class="hfeed">
                        <div class="post-1129 post type-post hentry category-economy category-politics tag-economy
post_box top" id="post-1129">
                                <div class="headline_area">
                                        <h2 class="entry-title"><a href="http://joekraynak.com/politics/real-
redistribution-of-wealth.html" rel="bookmark" title="Permanent link to The Real Redistribution of Wealth in the U.S.">The
Real Redistribution of Wealth in the U.S.</a></h2>
                                </div>
                                <div class="format_text entry-content">
<p>I&#8217;ve heard and read a great deal about the redistribution of wealth being initiated by the Obama administration
and the democrats in general. Supposedly, the policy is intended to take money from the rich and give it to the
poor&#8230; like Robin Hood. I really don&#8217;t have much of a problem with that. I think the rich are too rich in the
U.S. and the poor and middle class (whatever that is nowadays) are too poor.</p>
<p>What bothers me is that the redistribution of wealth that&#8217;s actually occurring in the U.S. is moving money from
the moral to the immoral, from taxpayers to tax dodgers, from the industrious to corporations to bloated government to the
indolent. It&#8217;s bipartisan, so Obama and his ilk are not solely to blame, and it&#8217;s not limited to the two major
political parties. The root problem is one of morality, ethics. Our country has lost its moral compass. William Bennett is
right.</p>
```

Figure 2.1: *Source code isn't pretty.*

DEFINITION

HTML stands for **HyperText Markup Language**—a collection of standard tags and rules for identifying web content in a way that enables web browsers to render web pages properly. The *hyper* in *HyperText* refers to the fact that web pages typically contain interactive links that connect to other content on the same or different sites.

The Language of the Web

Every language consists of vocabulary and *syntax*—grammar rules that govern the arrangement of words in sentences and phrases. In HTML, the vocabulary consists of *tags*, and the syntax consists of rules on how those tags must be used.

Tags come in two types: paired and unpaired. With *paired tags*, an opening tag marks the beginning of an element, and a closing tag marks the end. For example, <b>**Displays text as bold**</b>. An *unpaired tag* flies solo, opening and closing the element within a single tag, such as <img /> for inserting an image.

HTML syntax is pretty lax. You can type tags in upper- or lowercase: <strong> and <STRONG> are both acceptable. When using unpaired tags, you don't need to close the tag; for example, <img> or <img /> are both acceptable. When nesting tags, you can open and close them in any order that works:

Correct: <p><strong>**Paragraph in Bold**</strong></p>

Acceptable: <p><strong>**Paragraph in Bold**</p></strong>

XHTML syntax is another story, as you'll see in the following section.

XHTML—HTML's Button-Down Cousin

XHTML is HTML that follows a stricter syntax. The most important rules are to type tags all in lowercase, close all tags (even unpaired tags), and (when nesting tags) insert closing tags in the reverse order of the opening tags. Here's an example of incorrect versus correct nesting:

Incorrect: <p><strong>**Paragraph in Bold**</p></strong>

Correct: <p><strong>**Paragraph in Bold**</strong></p>

Chapter 4 introduces you to more tags and the XHTML rules for their proper use.

Adding Details with Attributes

You can add instructions to tags through the use of *attributes*. Here's an example:

```
<img src="http://joekraynak.com/images/kindle.jpg" />
```

This <img /> tag includes the attribute src="http://joekraynak.com/images/kindle.jpg", which tells the browser where the image is stored.

Chapter 4 goes into a little more detail about attributes. In addition, as later chapters introduce specific HTML elements, you'll find guidance on using common attributes that apply to each element.

An Evolving Language

HTML is an ever-evolving language that attempts to keep pace with technology and user needs. Because of this, new tags and attributes are often added, and old, obsolete ones are deprecated (meaning they are dropped from the language). HTML5 introduces numerous new tags, which you'll learn more about near the end of this chapter as well as throughout the book.

Over the years, many tags and attributes have been deprecated, especially *presentation tags* and *attributes*, including the following:

<center> for centering elements on a page

<font> for specifying font, color, and text size

<strike> to display ~~strikethrough~~ text

<u> to <u>underline</u> text

color attribute

border attribute

height attribute

width attribute

Most browsers can still handle these deprecated items, but you should still try to avoid using them. Most items are deprecated for good reason, usually because cascading style sheets (CSS) can do the same job better.

> **DEFINITION**
>
> **Presentation tags** and **attributes** primarily control the appearance of an element.

Other MLs You Might Like to Meet

As you gain experience with HTML and XHTML and perform your own research to learn more, you may encounter other MLs—markup or meta languages.

XML is one of the most common and is actually where the *X* in *X*HTML comes from. Anyone can use XML to build their own markup language, complete with custom tags for identifying different elements in a document. XML is commonly used, for example, to tag different types of data, so database programs can extract data from documents and reorganize and use that data in different ways. XHTML is actually an XML that contains a fixed and well-defined set of tags.

You may also encounter mentions of *SGML* (Standard Generalized Markup Language). SGML is a set of rules that govern the creation of markup languages. XML is actually a simplified version of SGML developed specifically for marking up online documents.

Checking Out All You Can Do with HTML

The primary role of HTML is to help web browsers determine what they're dealing with—a paragraph, a heading, an image, a bulleted or numbered list, a link—you name it. Once the browser knows what the element is, it can figure out how to display that element and where to position it on the page. This is why the same web page may look different in different browsers.

As you'll discover later in this chapter, you can use CSS to gain more control over how a browser displays the elements that comprise a web page.

Structuring Web Pages

HTML features a number of tags for structuring web pages, including the following:

<head> for essential items the user won't see

<title> for the title of the page

<body> to indicate the page content the user will see

<header> to indicate content that typically appears at the top of every page

<nav> to indicate the primary navigation area

<h1> to <h6> for headings

<article> for running text that typically appears below a heading

<section> to create sections within articles

<aside> to mark text that's not necessary in understanding a given section or article

<footer> to indicate content that typically appears at the bottom of every page

Creating Headings

You use headings on a web page for the same purpose as you use them in any document—to provide a descriptive label for the text that follows it. HTML features six heading levels: <h1>, <h2>, <h3>, <h4>, <h5>, and <h6>. The different heading levels serve two purposes:

- They help in structuring a document by providing a way to create a hierarchical table of contents with headings and subheadings.

- They provide visual cues to readers on whether a heading introduces a primary section or a subsection.

Unless you specify otherwise, heading sizes decrease from <h1> (largest) down to <h6> (smallest).

Creating Paragraphs

Technically speaking, you don't really need the <p> tag to divide text into paragraphs. You can simply press the **Enter** key twice at the end of a paragraph to create space preceding the next paragraph.

Using the <p> tag, however, enables you to use CSS to apply detailed formatting to the <p> elements in a document. For example, you can adjust the space between paragraphs by a couple pixels to create just the effect you're looking for.

Formatting Text: Bold and Italic

HTML shies away from formatting because you can format much more easily and make global formatting changes through the use of CSS. However, HTML has a couple tags primarily used to change the appearance of text:

<b> bold

<i> italic

<sub> subscript

<sup> superscript

Creating Lists

On the web, lists rule. They help break densely packed paragraphs into easily digestible tidbits, provide step-by-step instructions, present outlines for documents, and are often used to build navigation into a site.

With HTML, you can create both ordered (numbered) and unordered (bulleted) lists. See Chapter 5 for details.

Linking to Other Pages and Sites

Hyperlinks (or *links* for short) put the "Hyper" in HTML. They enable you to create navigation bars for your site, link from one page on your site to another, and link out to other sites and resources.

You can transform any text or image into a link simply by bracketing it with the paired tags <a> and </a>. Chapter 6 shows you how.

Inserting Images

Photos, illustrations, and other graphics make the web a more interesting, engaging, and informative place to hang out. With HTML, you can easily add images to your documents.

You simply upload the document to your hosting account, as explained in Chapter 1, and use the <img /> tag to pull the image into a web page wherever you want it to appear. See Chapter 7 for details.

Embedding Video

If you have video clips you'd like to place on your site or you want to share a YouTube video with people who visit your site, you can add an HTML <embed> or HTML5 <video> tag where you want the video to appear, along with an attribute linking to the video. When someone opens the page in a browser, the browser fetches the video and plays it, as shown in Figure 2.2. See Chapter 8 for details on how to embed video on a web page.

Figure 2.2: *HTML enables you to embed video on pages.*

Adding Audio

You've been to websites where music starts playing or someone starts talking to you as soon as the page appears. That's HTML talking. With HTML, you can link to audio files, so users click links to play them, or embed them on pages, so they play automatically when the page appears. Chapter 8 shows you how.

Creating Tables to Align Text

Whenever you need to align text in columns and rows, consider using a table. With HTML, you can format text in tables, create column headings, and even have a column heading span two or more columns. Figure 2.3 shows a table created with HTML in action. See Chapter 9 for details on creating tables and Chapter 19 for using CSS to format tables.

Fruits	Vegetables	Nuts	Grains
Apples	Lettuce	Cashews	Rice
Bananas	Carrots	Walnuts	Corn
Oranges	Onions	Pecans	Wheat

Figure 2.3: *You can create tables in HTML.*

Collecting Data via Forms

Web-based forms enable users to place orders on shopping sites, register for newsletters and seminars, apply for jobs, request prescription refills, and much more. Most of these forms are created using HTML form tags. The actual processing and transmission of data requires additional behind-the-scenes technology, but the form tags are responsible for creating the fill-in-the-blank forms, as shown in Figure 2.4. For more about forms, check out Chapter 21.

. Appointment Request

Please fill out the form below to request an appointment. Carol will get back to you available times based on the information you provide.

Online forms are provided as a convenience for patients who choose to use them, but these forms are not secure. Secure forms are currently in development. If you do not feel comfortable entering your information online, you can print a paper copy of the form and either fax it to our office at ▮▮ ▮▮▮▮ ▮▮▮▮ or bring it to your next appointment.

The fields marked with (*) are required fields.

	Patient Name *	
	Date of Birth *	
	Please indicate if you need 30 minutes, 45 minutes, 1 hour, a 90 minute child intake or a 60 minute adult intake. *	○ 30 Minutes ○ 45 Minutes ○ 1 Hour ○ 90-Minute Child Intake ○ 60-Minute Adult Intake
	When do you need this appointment? *	

Figure 2.4: *HTML forms enable users to enter information on your site.*

Adding Style and Grace with CSS

A plain-Jane HTML page is clunky and unattractive—all substance and no flavor, no color, no spice. Add *CSS*, and you immediately transform a site from an ugly duckling into a stunning swan. Figure 2.5 shows a site before and after being formatted with CSS.

DEFINITION

CSS is short for *Cascading Style Sheets,* a set of formatting rules for controlling the appearance and layout of HTML documents. CSS enables web developers like you to separate web content from formatting, to facilitate the process of changing the design without having to change settings on every single web page.

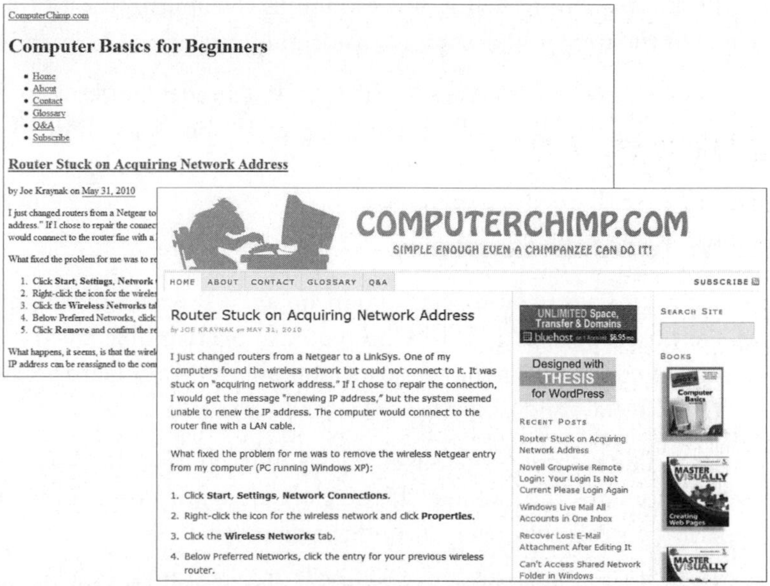

Figure 2.5: *CSS formatting brings a site to life.*

CSS targets HTML elements and applies formatting to those elements. You can apply whatever formatting you want. For example, you can have all your <h1> headings appear in 24-point font, blue, italics by using the following CSS style rule:

```
h1 {font-size:24px;
    font-style:italic;
    color:blue; }
```

The h1 targets the <h1> tag, and the rest of the style rule—the part between the curly brackets—indicates the formatting to apply.

Best of all, CSS enables you to keep the content and formatting of your site separate, so if you decide later to make those 24-point <h1> headings 22-point instead, all you do is change the *font-size* property from 24 to 22 in your CSS file, and the change is made to *all* the <h1> headings on *all* the pages on your site.

Putting Stuff in Boxes

In a desktop publishing program, every element that makes up a page is in a box, including text. This gives you more control over arranging and positioning items on a page—more control than you have in a typical word processor.

CSS follows the same model. It enables you to use boxes to structure pages and position elements on a page. You can even add borders and background shading to your boxes in any color and shade imaginable. You control the position of each box, its dimensions, how surrounding text wraps around it, the appearance of the border, the distance between the border and content inside and outside the box, and more.

In Chapter 16, you discover more about the CSS box model and how to use it to add boxes, borders, backgrounds, and buttons. Chapter 18 shows you how to use boxes to control page layout.

Adding Space Around Stuff

Sometimes you want objects on a page to butt up against each other or even overlap, but most of the time, you don't. With CSS, you can overlap objects—or not—and you have complete control over the space around objects. CSS features two properties that control the space around objects:

- **Margin:** The *margin* property enables you to control the space outside the box that contains the element. If the element is not inside a box, the *margin* property controls the space around the element.

- **Padding:** The *padding* property controls the space between the element inside the box and the box that surrounds it.

Making Stuff Bigger or Smaller

Unless you specify otherwise, the browser decides how large or small each element is to appear. With CSS, you gain more control over the size of elements, including images, column widths, box dimensions, margins, padding, and font sizes.

Chapter 10 shows you how to specify dimensions in CSS using various units, including pixels and percentages. The remaining chapters in Part 3 provide plenty of examples for specifying dimensions.

Giving Your Text a Facelift

CSS gives you complete control over font style, size, color, and alignment. With CSS3, you can even add drop-shadows to create an awesome three-dimensional effect. You also have control over the appearance of links and can make the appearance change when a user moves the mouse pointer over a link or after a user visits the page the link points to.

For more about text formatting, see Chapter 12. To control the appearance of links, head to Chapter 15.

Adding a Splash of Color

Proper use of color improves not only the appearance of a site but also its functionality. Colorful headings, for example, provide visual cues to readers about how the content is organized. Color can also set a tone for the site and communicate with users on an emotional level. While HTML is all black and white, CSS enables you to apply color to HTML elements.

Chapter 13 goes beyond showing you how to add color to elements using CSS. It explains color theory, reveals common color associations, and shows you how to create an attractive color scheme and find the right codes for the colors you want to use. This book also contains a color insert with additional information and examples.

Adding Colorful Backgrounds and Borders

Boxes are a nice touch, but you can really bring those boxes to life by adding borders and background shading in the colors of your choice. See Chapter 16 for details.

The Next Generation: Stepping Up to HTML5 and CSS3

During the writing of this book, the HTML and CSS standards were undergoing some major revisions. As you're reading this, those standards may or may not be official. However, most web browsers recognize at least some of the new HTML elements and CSS properties, so you need to be aware of these new and improved standards and perhaps begin to use them when creating web pages.

The following sections provide brief overviews of what's new in HTML5 and CSS3. Throughout this book, you learn more about individual elements introduced in HTML5 and properties introduced in CSS3. Just look for the HTML5 and CSS3 icons used to flag these new standards.

What's New in HTML5

HTML5 introduces several improvements over earlier standards, providing better ways to structure documents and make them more animated and interactive:

Simple document type declaration (DTD): As explained in Chapter 4, at the top of every web page is a document type declaration (DTD) indicating that the page is written in HTML. HTML5 uses a very simple DTD:

> **Former DTD:** <!DOCTYPE HTML PUBLIC "-//W3C//DTD HTML 4.01//EN" "http://www.w3.org/TR/html4/strict.dtd">

> **New DTD:** <!DOCTYPE html>

New structure tags: Several new structure tags, including <header>, <footer>, <article>, and <aside>, provide additional ways to target elements for CSS formatting while making web content more accessible.

<audio> and <video> tags: These tags simplify the process of placing audio and video content on sites and enable you to add text, such as the transcript of a video for the visually impaired.

<canvas> tag: The <canvas> tag enables you to create a container for animated and interactive 2D content, such as games and presentations.

Context menus: Context menus make a site more interactive without taking up space, giving users on-demand access to more options.

New inline elements: Several new inline elements enable you to insert special content, including progress bars, meters, and time. The <mark> tag enables you to identify text that's highlighted in some way (via CSS, of course).

New form input types: In addition to text boxes, check boxes, option buttons, and lists, HTML5 includes more than a dozen new form input types, including date, time, e-mail, and url.

New interactive elements: To make web pages more interactive, HTML introduces the following three new elements:

> *<details>* allows you to add information about an element that can be displayed when a mouse pointer is over the element, sort of like a tooltip.

<data grid> enables you to create an interactive table, so users can select rows or columns and edit or sort data, for example.

<menu> was deprecated (dropped) but is now back in HTML5. You can use it to create toolbars or context menus.

Optional http:// for links: When tagging links, you used to need to include the http:// at the beginning of a web address. In HTML5, you don't.

Old way: <a href="http://samplesite.com">This is a link</a>

New way: <a href="samplesite.com">This is a link</a>

Optional quotation marks for attributes: With HTML5, quotation marks around attributes are necessary only when the attribute contains a space. Otherwise, the quotation marks are optional; <a href="samplesite.com"> and <a href=samplesite.com> both work in browsers that support HTML5. The safest option is to establish a habit of using the quotation marks.

New async attribute: This tells the browser not to wait until a particular script loads before displaying other elements on the page, thus eliminating delays often caused by scripts.

Deprecated elements: HTML5 no longer includes elements deemed obsolete, including frames, center, acronym, and underline. Believe me, this is no great loss, and this book doesn't cover them.

Deprecated attributes: HTML5 no longer uses exclusively presentation (formatting) attributes that can be better handled by CSS, including align, background, border, height, and width, to name a few.

What's New in CSS3

HTML isn't the only standard undergoing a major overhaul. CSS is moving up from CSS2 to CSS3. Following are some of the changes under consideration during the writing of this book:

Newspaper columns: CSS has always been great for displaying text in rows and columns, but now you can use it to create newspaper columns.

New box properties: New box properties enable you to do some pretty cool things with boxes, including adding a drop-shadow to create a 3D effect and controlling the display of text that exceeds the size of the box it's in.

New border properties: New border properties enable you to create rounded borders, use an image to create the border, and use multiple border colors.

New background properties: New background properties provide more control over the position and size of background image(s) and enable you to use more than one background image in a box.

More color options: CSS has always featured ways to add color to HTML elements, but with CSS3, you can mix your own colors using hue, saturation, lightness (HSL); HSL plus alpha (HSLA); or red, green, blue, plus alpha (RGBA) color values. (The alpha channel enables you to control the opacity or transparency of a color.)

Opacity/transparency: In addition to controlling the opacity of a color to make it more or less transparent, CSS enables you to control the opacity of other HTML elements, including headings, paragraph text, and images.

Text shadow: If your text looks a little flat to you, consider adding a text shadow effect to make the text appear as though it's floating above the page.

Text overflow: When a box is too small to display all the text it contains, this property displays an ellipsis or arrow indicating more text is included but not shown.

Word wrap: This property enables you to break long words between two lines so the word stays inside its box. Without the *word wrap* property, a string of text wider than the box it's in flows out over the right side of the box.

@fontface: The *@fontface* property gives you more fonts to work with. Using this property, you can use any licensed TrueType or OpenType font by specifying the source location.

Nav: The nav properties enable you to specify keyboard navigation for your site. For instance, you can specify that when a certain key is pressed, such as the Tab key, the next option (down or to the right) is highlighted.

Media queries: The *media queries* property enables you to apply different styles based on the device that's accessing your site. For example, a user accessing your site via a standard computer may get the big version of the site, while someone with an iPhone gets a shrinked-down version. You don't need to create two or more different sites to accommodate various devices.

Support for speech synthesis: You can style text in a way that a browser that supports speech synthesis can "read" the text out loud to the user.

WHOA!

Browser support for the latest HTML and CSS standards varies. Always test your site in several of the most popular browsers to ensure most people surfing the web can easily navigate your site and access its content. See Chapter 24 for more about testing your site in different browsers. There you will also find guidance on how to begin implementing the new standards before browsers fully support them.

The Least You Need to Know

- HTML tags identify the nature of different elements, whereas CSS applies the formatting to those elements.
- To properly use HTML paired tags, insert the opening tag at the beginning of the element and the closing tag at the end.
- XHTML is simply HTML with a stricter set of rules to follow.
- By formatting with CSS, you can make changes in a single style sheet that change the formatting for all the pages on your site.
- HTML5 and CSS3 introduce plenty of new features, but web browsers may be slow to support the new features.

Making Your Job Easier with a CMS

In This Chapter

- Choosing a web page creation and editing program
- Checking out your hosting service's authoring tools
- Opting for a CMS
- Installing your CMS and logging in
- Choosing an attractive theme for your site
- Populating your site with content

Everyone who designs sites and publishes web content has his or her favorite tools to use. Because of this, nobody can really provide step-by-step instructions on how to create a website without focusing on a specific toolset.

In this chapter, I introduce you to various options while strongly recommending you use a content management system (CMS). Then I show you how to install a CMS, log in, and perform a few basic tasks, including choosing a theme and posting content to your site.

After you have your site up and running, you can tweak the HTML and CSS to customize it.

Sampling Web Page Authoring Options

Numerous tools are available for designing sites and creating and editing content. If you want to go old school, for example, you can create your entire site in a text editor or word processor and upload the files that comprise your site to your hosting account via FTP. To make your job easier, you can use a professional web design program such as Dreamweaver, a dedicated HTML editor such as CoffeeCup, or create your website and publish content directly online using a CMS. The following sections help you choose the right approach for you.

Going Old School with a Plain Text Editor

You don't need a fancy program to create web pages in HTML. You don't even need a word processor. A lowly text editor, such as Windows Notepad or Mac OS TextEdit, is all you need. Using a text editor, you type in all your content and then mark it up by typing each and every opening and closing HTML tag, as shown in Figure 3.1.

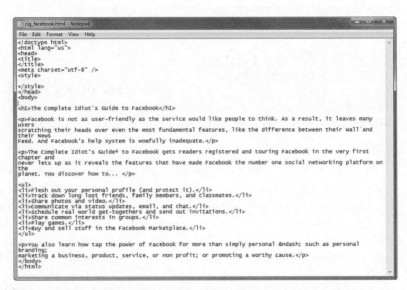

Figure 3.1: *You can create web pages using a plain text editor.*

The good thing about creating web pages in a plain text editor is that your source code remains very clean. Some of the fancier web authoring programs clutter the source code with a lot of useless tags.

Typing source code in a plain text editor does have some drawbacks:

- You have to type each code manually.

- You have to switch back and forth between the plain text editor and your web browser to see what your page will actually look like.

- It's easy to make a typo or omit a closing tag, which can really mess up a page when it's open in a web browser.

- Troubleshooting problems in the code can be a nightmare.

> **WHOA!**
>
> You can use a word processor instead of a plain text editor. Be sure not to use any of the word processor's formatting (such as bulleted or numbered lists). Also, save the document in a plain text format with the filename extension .htm or .html. Use straight quotes and apostrophes—not the fancy "smart" or curly ones. If you want to include any signs or symbols, such as an en dash, use an HTML character entity rather than letting the word processor insert it. (See Chapter 4 and Appendix D for more about inserting HTML character entities.)

Stepping Up to an HTML Editor

HTML editors are designed specifically for authoring and editing HTML source code. Using an HTML editor, you create and format web pages on your computer and then upload the files to your hosting provider's web server. HTML editors come in two flavors:

- **Visual HTML/CSS editor:** A visual or WYSIWYG (What You See Is What You Get) HTML editor enables you to create and edit web pages just as easily as you create and format documents in a word processing or desktop publishing program. The editor handles the HTML source code behind the scenes. With a visual editor, you usually have the option to work in visual mode or edit the source code directly.

- **Code editor:** With a code editor, you work directly with the source code, but the editor typically provides buttons you can click to insert tags rather than type them.

An HTML editor offers several advantages over a plain text editor:

- You don't have to type tags. You either enter formatting commands and the editor creates the source code for you (visual editor), or you insert tags with the click of a button (code editor).

- The editor ensures all your tags are closed and your source code is in the proper syntax.

- Your lines of source code appear numbered and perhaps color-coded, simplifying the process of troubleshooting later.

Although HTML editors are useful for creating HTML source code, they're typically less well equipped to handle CSS. Most, like KompoZer, include tools for creating and managing CSS styles, but you still need to create the style rules yourself—the WYSIWYG view doesn't enable you to create styles by changing an element's formatting. For features like that, you need a professional-strength website design and development program.

Going All Out with a Professional Program

If you're willing to part with a chunk of change, you can opt for a professional website design and development program, such as Adobe Dreamweaver—$399 for the full version last I checked. Microsoft Expression Studio 4 Web Professional is another option, retailing for about $149.

With a professional web design program, you can focus solely on the look and feel of your site. You cut and paste, drag and drop, and format your pages using various toolbar options, and the program creates the HTML source code and CSS styles for you. A professional program also gives you the luxury of creating sites offline and the tools to publish your site when it's ready to go live.

It's still good to know HTML and CSS. If you run into trouble, you may need to tweak your source code and styles.

Doing It All Online with a CMS

With a *CMS*, you can design and build a site, add content, and publish your site all online. In addition, you can collaborate on website design and content development with others located anywhere in the world because each person can log in to the CMS independently via the web.

Popular CMSs include WordPress, concrete5, Joomla!, Drupal, and MODx. I like WordPress, but Joomla! is very popular, and concrete5 is definitely worth checking out.

DEFINITION

A **CMS** is a collection of applications, databases, and processes that store a site's data and settings and serve up that data on demand. As you change CMS settings, install plug-ins, and add content, everything is stored in one of the CMS's databases. Your site has no bona fide web pages; when a visitor accesses a page or post (by clicking a link or typing its address), the CMS extracts everything it needs from the databases, constructs the page or post, and serves it to the browser almost instantly. This ensures that any changes you make to your site, a post, or a page are reflected immediately on your pages and posts.

Using a Blogging Platform as Your CMS

A blogging platform, such as WordPress, is perfectly suitable for creating and managing a website, blog, or combination website/blog. I create and manage sites for myself, my friends, and my clients exclusively with WordPress and primarily use HTML to fix problems and CSS to tweak the design of any templates I use.

WordPress offers many advantages:

- It's free.
- It's easy to install, use, and upgrade. In a matter of minutes, you can have your site up and running.
- Posting fresh content is as easy as creating a document in a word processing program and clicking a button. You can even post content via e-mail.
- It's available through almost all web hosting services.
- Numerous free CSS *themes* are available, so you don't have to design your site from scratch. You can tweak the theme's CSS to customize your design.
- It's flexible. You can create a blog and add website components later or vice versa.
- Search engines love it, and plenty of search engine optimization (SEO) tools are available for it.
- Widgets enable you to accessorize your site with modular components.
- Plenty of plug-ins are available for enhancing your site with new tools and features.
- It's widely used, so you can find plenty of help on the web if you run into problems.

DEFINITION

A **theme** contains styles that control the appearance and layout of web pages and everything on those pages. You can totally change the appearance and layout of a site simply by choosing a different theme.

Checking Out What Your Hosting Provider Offers

Almost all hosting service providers, especially the most popular ones, offer multiple CMSs. Bluehost, for example, features its own Page Wizard Site Builder along with access to CMSs, including WordPress, Joomla!, Drupal, concrete5, and MODx. It also offers photo galleries, including Zenphoto and Coppermine; e-commerce management software for creating and managing an online store; form builders; and additional tools for adding discussion forums, live chat, and social networking components to your site.

To see what your web hosting service provides, log in to your account and poke around in the control panel, as explained in Chapter 1. See if the control panel has a group of icons labeled "Software," or something similar. Many hosting services include an icon named SimpleScripts or Fantastico De Luxe—if you see such an icon, click it to see available tools. Figure 3.2 shows icons for available web development tools on Bluehost via SimpleScripts.

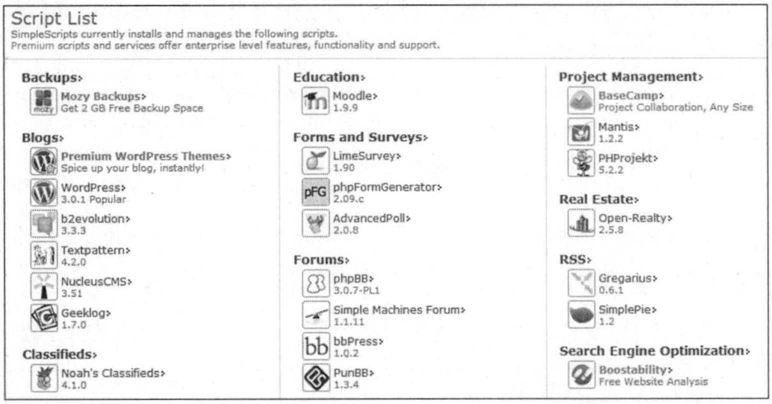

Figure 3.2: *CMSs and other tools are available through Bluehost's SimpleScripts.*

Best of all, you can use SimpleScripts or Fantastico De Luxe to install the CMS or other software of your choice for free. All you do is click the icon for the CMS you want and follow the on-screen instructions to complete the installation. If given the choice, choose to customize the installation or set advanced options, so you can name your site and choose a username and password now rather than later.

INSIDE TIP

For security purposes, consider installing your CMS in a separate folder rather than in the root directory of your site. Give the folder some obscure name that doesn't reflect your site's name or address. Otherwise, anyone can access your login screen simply by going to www.yoursitename.com/wp-login.php and try to log in. By installing the CMS into a separate folder, such as xk-17, people will need to know the folder name to access the login screen. The address of your site will still be www.yoursitename.com, but the CMS files will be stored in a separate folder. It's not air-tight security, but it helps.

When the installation is complete, you're presented with details on where the software is installed and how to log in to your CMS, as shown in Figure 3.3. You may receive an e-mail message with your username and password for logging in. You can then log in and change your username and/or password.

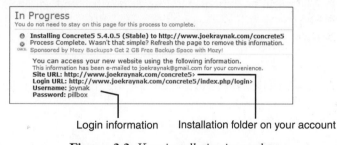

Login information   Installation folder on your account

Figure 3.3: *Your installation is complete.*

Logging In and Out of Your CMS

Your CMS is now on your hosting service provider's web server, where you can log in and start fiddling with your site. Use your browser to go to the address of your login page specified at the end of the installation process. Type your username and password in the appropriate boxes, and click the **Sign In** button to sign in, as shown in Figure 3.4.

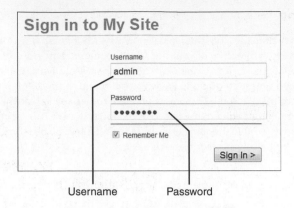

Figure 3.4: *Log in to your CMS.*

In most cases, you're presented with a dashboard that enables you to post content to your site, choose a different theme, add functionality, and adjust various settings. Dashboards differ a great deal among CMSs, so you'll need to poke around on your own, consult online documentation, or purchase a separate book for the CMS you choose.

The dashboard also includes a link or button for logging out when you're done working on your site.

Giving Your Site a Makeover with a Different Theme

CMSs come with a default theme that typically makes your site look fairly bland, but additional themes are usually available and often free. Look for an option on your CMS's dashboard for Appearance or Themes, click the option, and follow the trail of links to check out additional themes. You can usually install and activate a theme directly from the dashboard, as shown in Figure 3.5, but you may need to upload thet theme folder and files via FTP, as explained in Chapter 1.

For more about choosing, activating, and personalizing a theme, see Chapter 11.

Current theme   Install new themes

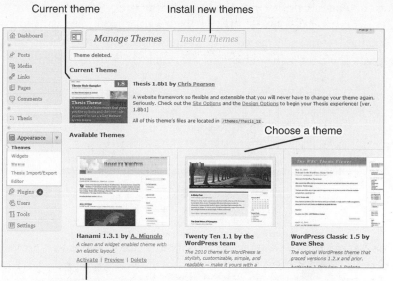

Activate a theme

Figure 3.5: *A theme controls the look and layout of the site.*

Adding Content to Your Site

Now for the easy part—adding content. This is where CMS shines. Content varies depending on whether you're creating static content or something more interactive for a blog:

- **Pages:** Pages are static and usually reachable via the main navigation on your site, such as an About or Contact Us page. If you're creating a website, your website will consist of one or more pages.

- **Posts:** Posts appear in reverse chronological order on a blog's home page and typically enable visitors to post comments. As such, posts tend to be more dynamic and interactive.

Although posts and pages differ, the process for creating them is basically the same. You choose what you want to create—post or page—and are greeted with a screen for composing the post or page, as shown in Figure 3.6. The CMS typically allows you to enter and edit content in visual mode or HTML mode (if you prefer dealing directly with the source code).

You name the page or post, enter the desired content (including one or more images), and apply formatting if you wish. If you write a post, you may want to assign it to a specific category and add tags that describe what the post is about. When you're ready to place the post or page on your site, click the **Publish** button.

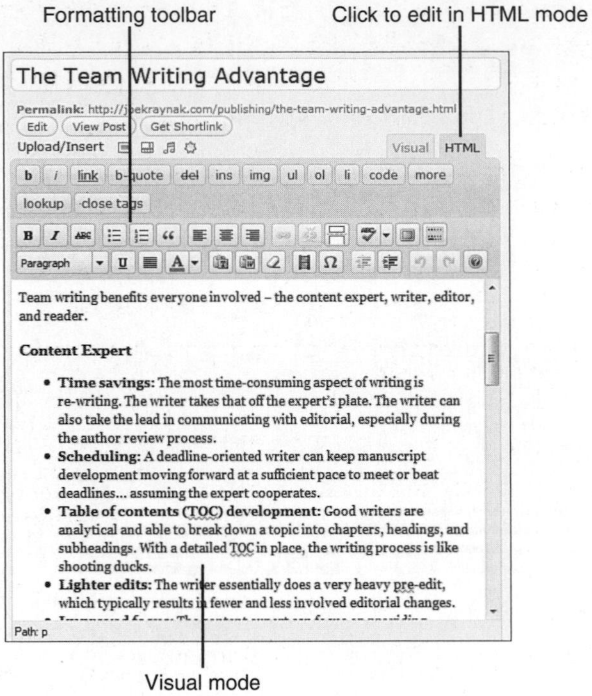

Figure 3.6: *Add content to your site.*

Sometimes, you *must* edit in HTML mode. For example, you can place a YouTube video on your site by copying an embed code for the YouTube video and pasting it into a page or post. When pasting the code, you must be in HTML mode, or it won't work. See Chapter 8 for details on embedding video.

Exploring Other CMS Features, Options, and Settings

Typically, as soon as you install a CMS, your website is up and running. It may not look like much, but if you type its address into a browser, you'll get something more than a message telling you your page can't be found.

Before you spend much time creating pages or posts or tweaking the CSS files that control the design, you may want to change some settings, add widgets to your site, and install plug-ins to personalize and enhance your site. In the following sections, I show you what I do after installing a CMS—WordPress specifically.

Giving Your Site a Site Title and Tagline

Every site needs a catchy name and a tagline that briefly describes what the site is all about. To add a site title and tagline in WordPress, log in to WordPress, scroll down to Settings (the left side of the dashboard), and click **General**. (You may need to click **Settings** if the Settings menu options aren't visible.)

Drag over the text in the **Site Title** box, and type the title you want to use for your site. Click in the **Tagline** box, and type a brief description of what your site will be all about (see Figure 3.7). Scroll down the page, and click **Save Changes**.

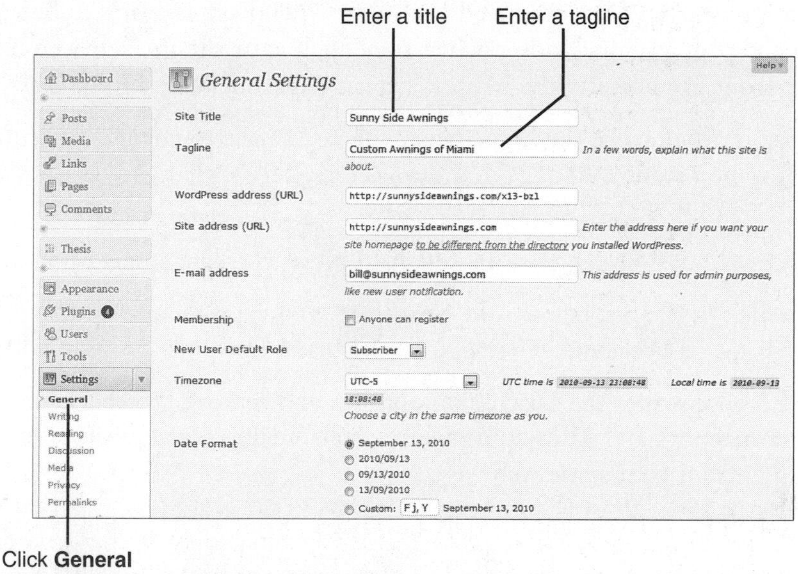

Figure 3.7: *Give your site a title and tagline.*

Specifying Your Site Address

While you're tinkering with the General Settings, check the **Site address (URL)** box. This is the address you and others type in a browser to access the site.

WHOA!

Do NOT change the WordPress address (URL). This is the address of the folder that contains the WordPress files and where you go to log in. If you change this setting, you can't log in to WordPress to change it back. Regaining access to your site is possible, but it's a BIG hassle.

Your Site address (URL) can be the address of the folder in which you installed your CMS, but you can use a different address. For example, you can install your CMS in www.yoursite.com/xk17 but change the Site address (URL) to www.yoursite.com or blog.yoursite.com so visitors don't have to type the /xk17 to access your site.

If you assign the blog a different address, scroll down the page and click **Save Changes**.

Choosing Your Front Page Preference

If you're using a blogging platform such as WordPress exclusively to create and maintain a blog, you can skip this section. Your front page is your only page, and it's the page that displays your recent blog posts in reverse chronological order.

If, however, you're using a blogging platform to create and maintain a website or a combination website/blog, you need to decide which page is going to be your front page, or the page visitors land on when they open your site in their web browsers. Will the front page display the blog or a static page, such as a Home page?

If the blog is going to be the home page, you don't have to change anything. If, however, you want a static web page to greet visitors, here's what you do (in WordPress, that is):

1. On the dashboard, click **Pages**, **Add New** to create a new page.

2. Click in the box below Add New Page, and type a name for the page, such as Home or Welcome. The page can be blank for now—you can add stuff later.

3. Scroll down to the Discussion options, and remove the checks next to **Allow comments** and **Allow pings**. You probably don't want visitors posting comments on your static web pages.

4. Click **Publish** to publish your new page.

5. If your site is going to include a blog, repeat steps 1 through 4 to create a separate page for your blog. Name it something like Blog or My Blog.

6. Scroll down to the Settings group (bottom left on the dashboard) and click **Reading**.

7. Under Front page displays, click **A static page** and then open the **Front page** list and click the page you created in step 1 (see Figure 3.8).

8. If you created a separate page for your blog in step 5, open the **Posts page** list and choose the page you created for your blog.

9. Click **Save Changes**. Your site now has a static home page and, if you created a blog page, a separate page for your blog posts.

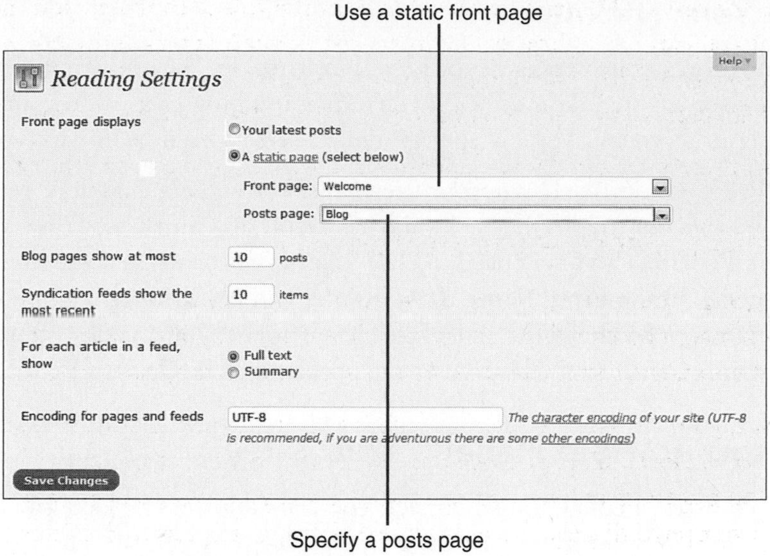

Use a static front page

Specify a posts page

Figure 3.8: *In WordPress, you can have a static front page.*

Entering a Permalinks Preference

In a CMS, pages or posts are numbered. Unless you specify otherwise, when someone opens a post, the post's number (instead of its name) appears in the address; for example, www.yoursite.com/?p=123. To have the post or page title appear instead, change the permalinks option.

In WordPress, log in to the dashboard, scroll down to Settings (lower left), and click **Permalinks**. Click **Custom Structure** and then click in the **Custom Structure** box and type the following:

```
/%category%/%postname%.html
```

This tells WordPress to include the post or page category and name, followed by .html in the address. If you add a title for a post that says Check This Out and place it in the Announcements category, its address will appear as this:

```
www.yoursite.com/announcements/check-this-out.html
```

Changing Your Nickname

Your CMS stores your username for login purposes. By default, your username is likely to be something like Admin. If you're posting blog entries on your site, you'll want to log in to your CMS and specify a more recognizable name for your byline.

In WordPress, you can't change your username, but you can add your real name and choose a nickname. Log in to the dashboard, scroll down to Users (lower left), and click **Your Profile**. (You may need to click **Users** first to expand the menu.) Add the desired entries in the **First Name**, **Last Name**, and **Nickname** boxes. Open the **Display name publicly as** list, and click the version of your name you want to appear in your byline. Scroll to the bottom of the page and click **Update Profile**.

Adding Users to Help Manage Your Site

To make your site a collaborative project, you can add users and assign each user a different role that determines what he or she is able to do on the site. In WordPress, the following four user roles are available:

- **Administrator** has unrestricted access and total power—even to the extent of deleting the entire blog or changing your username and password!

- **Editor** can publish, edit, and delete anyone's posts; moderate comments; add or delete categories; and upload images, but he or she cannot change settings or add or remove plug-ins.

- **Author** can publish, edit, and delete only his or her own posts.

- **Contributor** can create and edit posts but cannot publish posts. An administrator must review the post and approve it before it's published.

To add a user in WordPress, log in to the dashboard, scroll down to Users (lower left), and click **Add New**. Enter the requested information, including a username and password, choose the desired role for this user, and click **Add User**.

Adding Features and Tools with Plug-Ins

Plug-ins accessorize your browser with new features. To give you some idea of what plug-ins can do, here's a list of WordPress plug-ins I use on almost all the sites I manage:

- **Dragon Design Form Mailer** places an e-mail contact form on your site that keeps your e-mail address hidden from spammers. I strongly discourage you from placing your e-mail address on your site where everyone can see it.

- **Askimet** helps control comment spam.

- **Peter's Custom Anti-Spam** requires that anyone posting a comment type a specific word to verify they're human and not a spambot. This cuts down significantly on comment spam before it even reaches the Askimet filter.

- **Simple Trackback Validation** helps prevent trackback spam—a trick used to bypass comment spam blockers and get your site to link to someone else's site.

- **W3 Total Cache** serves up static versions of pages and posts so the CMS doesn't need to construct them on the fly. This significantly speeds up a WordPress site.

- **Google XML Sitemaps** creates and updates a map of the site to help search engines index the pages properly. It's great for SEO.

You can add, activate, deactivate, and remove plug-ins via the WordPress dashboard, as shown in Figure 3.9. Most plug-ins also add one or more options to the Settings menu, which you can click to adjust a plug-in's settings or learn more about its features.

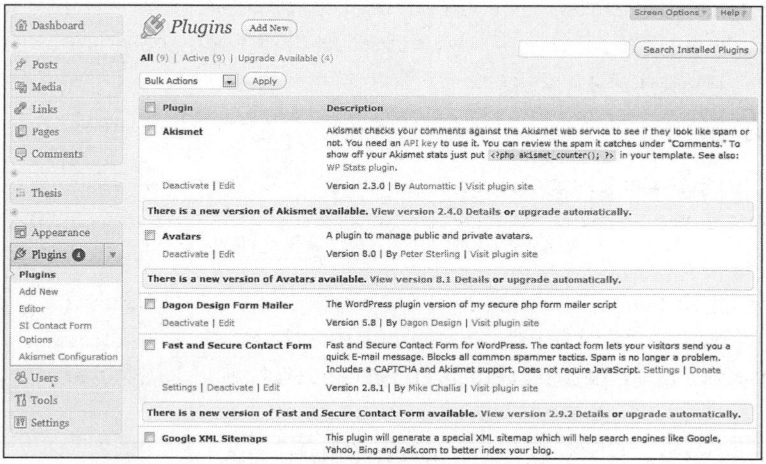

Figure 3.9: *Manage WordPress plug-ins from the dashboard.*

Accessorizing Your Site with Widgets

Widgets are components you can add to your site, typically in one of the sidebars. Widgets enable you to add all sorts of stuff, including a list of recent posts or comments, a list of your favorite blogs and websites, custom menus, search boxes, and links to pages on your site. The Text widget enables you to create a custom widget complete with text and images.

Adding widgets in WordPress is a snap. Log in to the dashboard and below Appearance, click **Widgets**. Drag the desired widget to the sidebar where you want it to appear, release the mouse button, and supply any information you're prompted to enter (see Figure 3.10). You can drag and drop widgets within a sidebar to rearrange them.

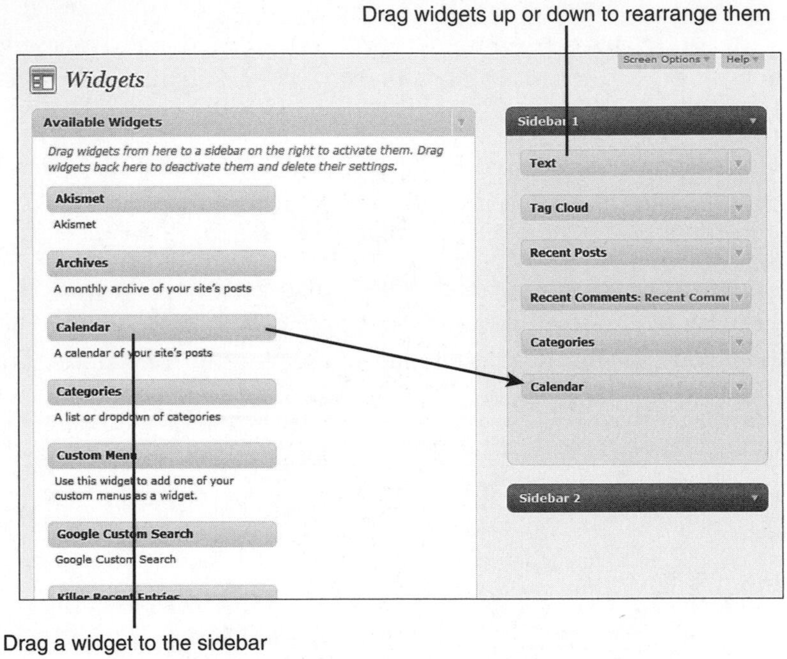

Drag widgets up or down to rearrange them

Drag a widget to the sidebar

Figure 3.10: *Add widgets to sidebars.*

The Least You Need to Know

- Use a CMS, such as WordPress, Joomla!, or concrete5, to create and manage your site.
- With most web hosting service providers, you can install your CMS via the provider's control panel.
- Logging in to your CMS enables you to configure it and add content.
- With a CMS, you can completely change your site's appearance and layout at any time, simply by choosing a different theme.

- After installing a CMS, log in to it and check out its many options and settings. Spend some time customizing your site so it looks and functions as you want it to.

- Even though a CMS significantly simplifies site creation and management, knowing HTML and CSS is essential for troubleshooting problems and tweaking the theme.

Authoring Pages and Posts with HTML

Hypertext markup language (HTML) consists of dozens of tags you use to label elements that comprise each web page, such as <article> for articles; <p> for paragraphs; <h1>, <h2>, and <h3> for headings; and <img> for digital photos and other image types. Using HTML, you build a framework for each web page and then stuff it full of content.

Part 2 begins by showing you how to build the framework—the container for all the other elements on the page. You also discover how to tag the most common text-based elements, including headings and paragraphs. In subsequent chapters, I show you how to create numbered and unnumbered (bulleted) lists and blockquotes that typically function as sidebars. You find out how to create clickable links, insert photos and other graphics, enhance your pages with audio and video, create tables, and gather feedback and other data with forms.

In the process, I show you how to make your job a whole lot easier by posting content via a content management system (CMS), which is sort of like a desktop publishing program for the web!

Creating a Bare-Bones Web Page

In This Chapter

- Building the framework for a web page
- Adding headings and paragraphs
- Enhancing text with boldface and italics
- Inserting horizontal lines and special characters
- Inserting comments, meta tags, and other invisible items
- Structuring your pages with new HTML5 structure tags

Although web pages can get pretty fancy, they all have modest beginnings—a few tags that identify the document as a web page and bracket its content, along with a couple headings and a few paragraphs.

This chapter takes you through the process of building a very basic web page and then viewing it in the browser of your choice.

Brushing Up on HTML and XHTML Fundamentals

Before you start building your web page, take some time to understand HTML *elements*, *attributes*, and *entities*, and the rules and regulations for writing well-structured HTML.

Recognizing Elements

HTML *elements* are the basic components of every web page, including paragraphs, ordered and unordered lists, images, links, headings, quotes, and so on. Each element contains one or two tags along with the content in those tags. Tags can be paired or unpaired:

- **Paired:** Paired tags consist of an opening tag that turns on the element and a closing tag that turns it off. For example, a paragraph begins with the <p> tag and ends with the </p> tag.

- **Unpaired:** Unpaired tags fly solo—one tag serves to open and close the element; for example, <img /> for inserting an image. The <hr /> tag, used to insert a horizontal rule (line), is also an unpaired tag.

Recognizing Attributes of Elements

HTML *attributes* provide additional information about an element that browsers use to determine what to display and how to display it. All attributes are specified in the opening tag and are structured as follows:

```
name="value"
```

Here's an example of a couple <img> attributes in action:

```
<img src="http://joekraynak.com/images/pighead.jpg" height="268"
   ➡ width="202" />
```

This tag tells the browser to fetch the image named pighead.jpg with a height of 268 pixels and a width of 202 pixels that's located at http://joekraynak.com in the images folder.

HTML includes three types of attributes:

- **Standard attributes** can be applied to nearly every HTML element. They include class, ID, and style for applying CSS styles; context menu; contented-itable; draggable; hidden; title; and spellcheck.

- **Element-specific attributes** apply only to certain elements; for example, HTML form elements have several attributes exclusively for forms.

- **Event attributes** trigger actions in a web browser when certain events occur; for example, you can add the onclick attribute to trigger an action when a user clicks an element. The action typically consists of running a script. See Part 4 for more about making your web pages interactive.

You'll encounter attributes throughout this book as they relate to specific HTML tags and CSS styles. See Appendix B for a list of common attributes.

Grasping the Nature of Entities

Entities are characters, punctuation marks, signs, and symbols you can't insert into a web page simply by typing them on your keyboard. Instead, you must type something like © to insert ©. Later in this chapter, you meet some common entities. Appendix D provides a comprehensive list.

Following XHTML Rules and Regulations

You can get pretty sloppy with HTML and still have a decent-looking web page when you pull it up in a browser, but XHTML has a few rules and regulations you should follow:

- Type tags and attributes in lowercase.

- All elements must be closed. If you use the <p> tag to mark the beginning of a paragraph, for example, you must use the closing tag </p> to mark the end. Unpaired tags must end in />.

- When nesting elements, place closing tags in the opposite order of the opening tags. For example, to mark a phrase as bold and italic, bold italic is correct, whereas bold italic is incorrect.

- Always include a value when specifying an attribute.

- Always enclose attribute values in quotes.

- All XHTML documents must have a DOCTYPE declaration, html, head, title, and body elements, as explained in the following section.

- All XHTML elements must be nested within the <html> root element, as explained in the following section.

Creating a Web Page Skeleton

A web page skeleton is the framework on which you build your web page. Think of it as the underlying structure of a house. It must be a plain text document (no using your word processing program to format the text!), and it must be saved in a file with the extension .html or .htm.

The following sections explain how to create your HTML document and add the tags that comprise the skeleton.

Creating a Plain Text Document

If you're using a web page authoring program to create pages, all new documents you create in the program will be plain text documents. When you save and name your file, the program should tack on the .html or .htm extension for you.

If you're creating web pages in a plain text editor, create a new blank document and save it as a text-only file. When naming and saving the file, adhere to the following guidelines:

- **Save as a text-only file.** When you're saving a file for the first time, open the Save as type list and click the option to save the file as an HTML or text document.

- **Use lowercase letters.** Technically, you can use uppercase letters, but keeping everything lowercase prevents confusion later when you or someone else tries to open the page. The only item that almost always appears in all uppercase is the DOCTYPE declaration.

- **Don't use spaces.** If you need to separate words, type an underscore or hyphen.

- **Avoid funky characters and symbols.** Stick with letters and numbers and don't use characters like *, %, #, /, >, or }.

- **Add the filename extension .htm or .html.** This designates the web page as an HTML document.

INSIDE TIP

If you're using a Windows PC, Windows may be set up to hide filename extensions. I suggest you bring those extensions out of hiding to be sure your web documents have the proper extensions. In recent versions of Windows, including Windows 7, click **Start**, **Control Panel**, **Folder Options**; click the **View** tab; remove the check mark next to **Hide extensions for known file types**; and click **OK**. In earlier versions of Windows, click **Start**, **My Computer**, **Tools**, **Folder Options**; click the **View** tab; remove the check mark next to the option for hiding extensions for known file types; and click **OK**.

Building the Framework

To adhere to strict XHTML guidelines, your web page skeleton must include the following elements:

- **Document type declaration (DTD):** The DTD designates the content of the document as a web page that adheres to a specific HTML or XHTML standard. This allows web browsers to identify the content of the document as a web page and display it accordingly.

- **<html> tag:** An opening and a closing <html> tag bracket the page, indicating where it begins and ends. The opening <html> tag should designate the language in which the content is written; for example <html lang="en"> for English.

- **Head:** An opening and a closing <head> tag mark the beginning and end of the head area, which functions as a container for several other elements, including the page's title. Items in the head are not displayed as part of the web page but may appear in the title bar of the web browser.

- **Title:** The title is the title of the document as it appears in the browser window's title bar. This is also the title users see when they mark the page as a favorite or when a link to the page is displayed in search results.

- **Character encoding declaration:** The character encoding declaration specifies the method of converting bytes into characters.

- **Body:** An opening and a closing <body> tag mark the beginning and end of all the page's content—everything that appears when the page is open in a browser.

After saving your new, blank document, type the following codes in the order shown to create your web page skeleton:

```
<!DOCTYPE html>
<html lang="en">
<head>
<meta charset="utf-8" />
<title>
</title>
</head>
<body>
</body>
</html>
```

> The DTD in this example is the new HTML5 DTD—<!DOCTYPE html>. Other DTDs are available depending on which HTML or XHTML standard you choose to follow when tagging your content, but I recommend sticking with the simpler HTML5 DTD.

Modifying a CMS Template for HTML5

If you're using a CMS or blogging platform to manage your site, it builds the framework for you, but it may be using a DOCTYPE other than HTML5 DTD. To check, access your site in a browser and then use the browser to view the page's source code. In Internet Explorer, for example, you open the **Page** menu and choose **View Source**. If you see something other than <!DOCTYPE html> at the top of the page, you need to modify the template.

In standard templates, you typically modify the header.php file. If you're using WordPress, log in, click **Appearance**, **Editor**, and then **Header** (header.php), as shown in Figure 4.1. You can then change the DTD to <!DOCTYPE html> and delete any references to other standards, such as xhtml.

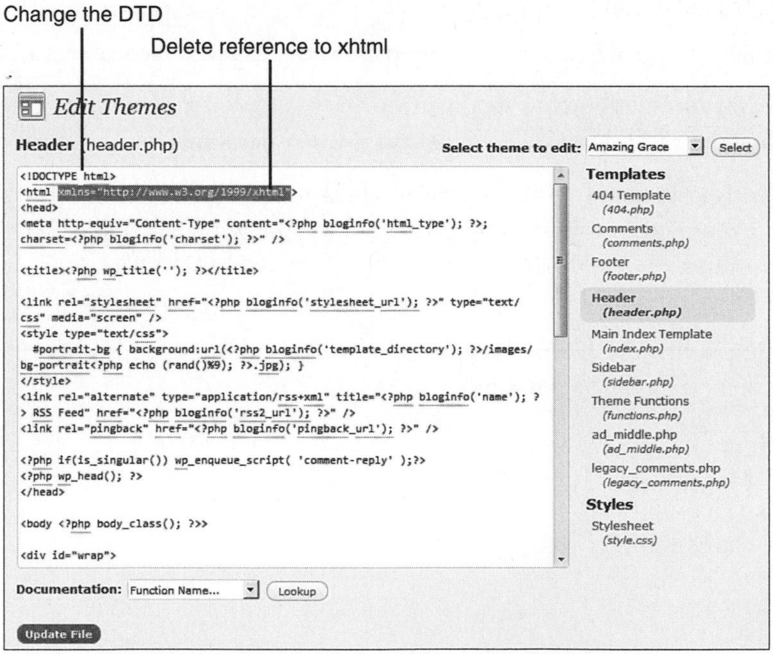

Figure 4.1: *Configure your CMS template for HTML5.*

WHOA!

Premium templates may have other methods for modifying the DTD. Consult the provider's help files or discussion forums for details.

Tossing In a Few Headings

Just as you can use headings in a word processor to break up and "label" text, you can and should use headings when creating lengthy HTML documents. To add a heading to a document, type the opening heading tag followed by the heading text, followed by the closing heading tag; for example:

```
<h1>Adding Headings</h1>
```

Specifying Your Heading Level of Choice

HTML supports up to six levels of headings:

```
<h1>Heading 1</h1>
<h2>Heading 2</h2>
<h3>Heading 3</h3>
<h4>Heading 4</h4>
<h5>Heading 5</h5>
<h6>Heading 6</h6>
```

Figure 4.2 shows how the different heading levels appear in Internet Explorer. Heading appearance varies depending on the browser. In addition, you can use CSS styles to control the appearance of headings, as explained in Part 3.

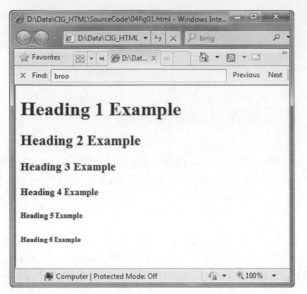

Figure 4.2: *HTML headings as they appear in Internet Explorer.*

Grouping Related Headings with <hgroup>

If you have a heading directly followed by a subheading (for example, to format headings you're using as a title and subtitle or title and tagline), group the headings with an opening and a closing <hgroup> tag, as shown here:

```
<hgroup>
<h1>Exploring Alternative Energy Solutions</h1>
<h2>Fueling 21st Century Growth</h2>
</hgroup>
```

This helps the browser identify the subtitle as a nonessential element in the outline so it can omit the subtitle from any table of contents it generates.

Inserting Paragraphs and Line Breaks

To break text into paragraphs, mark each paragraph with a beginning and ending <p> tag, as in the following example:

```
<p>I have four email accounts. In Outlook Express, all my email would
  pour into one Inbox. Very convenient. In Windows Live Mail,
  incoming mail for each account ends up in its own Inbox. Very
  inconvenient, at least for me.</p>
<p>If you're like me and you want all your email in one place, here's
  what you do:</p>
```

Technically speaking, you can divide text into paragraphs by pressing the **Enter** key twice and omitting the <p> tags. This inserts a blank line between the paragraphs. However, by using the <p> tags, you can apply special formatting to paragraphs later using CSS, as explained in Part 3.

To add a line break, use the unpaired tag <br />. I often use the <br /> tag in lists, as shown here:

```
<ul>
<li>Click <strong>Use the following DNS server addresses</strong> if
  ↪ this option is not already checked. If the option is checked,
  ↪ jot down the numbers in the Preferred and Alternate DNS server
  ↪ boxes, so you can change back to the original settings if this
  ↪ does not work.</li>
<li>Enter the following DNS server addresses:<br /> Preferred
  ↪ DNS server:<strong>208.67.222.222<br /> </strong>Alternate DNS
  ↪ server:<strong> 208.67.220.220</strong></li>
</ul>
```

The text that follows the <br /> tag simply moves down to the next line, as shown in Figure 4.3. (The trailing slash is optional; you may use <br /> or <br>.)

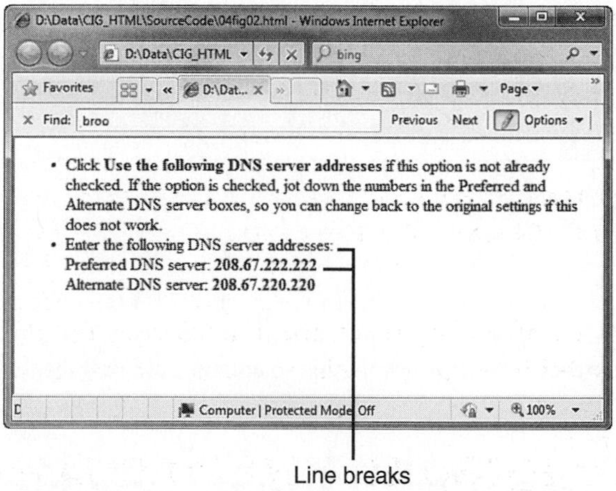

Line breaks

Figure 4.3: *Use the <br /> tag to create line breaks.*

Emphasizing Text with Phrase Tags: <em>, <strong>, and More

HTML contains several *phrase* tags for marking special text. The most commonly used phrase tags are <em> (for emphasis, italics) and <strong> (for stronger emphasis, bold). Simply bracket whatever you want to emphasize with opening and closing <em> or <strong> tags:

```
<em>This text will appear italic</em>
<strong>This text will appear bold</strong>
```

Table 4.1 lists HTML phrase tags and provides a brief description of each.

Table 4.1

HTML Phrase Tags

Tag	Description
<b>	Bold
<cite>	Creates a citation
<code>	Designates text as computer code
<dfn>	Designates text as a term being defined
<em>	Emphasizes text by displaying it in italics
<i>	Italics
<kbd>	Designates text as keyboard text
<samp>	Flags text as sample computer code
<strong>	Marks text as important by displaying it in bold
<var>	Defines a variable

NOTE

Use <cite> for citing books, articles, movies, and other resources. Use <em> and <strong> for emphasizing important words and phrases. Use <i> and <b> for all other instances in which you want text to appear bold or italic.

Inserting Horizontal Lines ... or Not

A horizontal line functions as a visual divider between somewhat unrelated content. It signals to readers a thematic shift in content rather than a smooth transition. To add a horizontal line to your web page, type the <hr /> tag. (*hr* stands for horizontal rule.) Figure 4.4 shows an <hr /> tag in action.

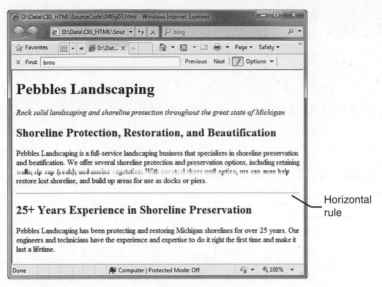

Figure 4.4: *Horizontal rule displayed in Internet Explorer.*

In most cases, you're better off not using the horizontal line. Using CSS, you can place items in boxes, and use borders to display any or all of the lines that define the box. See Chapter 16 for details.

©, ®, TM, and Other Unusual Characters

You can type most of the characters you need to create a web page directly on your keyboard, just as you do in a word processor. When you need to include special characters or symbols, such as a copyright ©, a registered trademark ® symbol, or even an em dash —, you must type a special character entity. Table 4.2 provides a list of common character entities.

Table 4.2
Common Special HTML Characters and Symbols

Tag	Character/Symbol	Tag	Character/Symbol
¢	¢	>	>
&cpy;	©	<	<
°	°	—	—
÷	÷	–	–
½	½	®	®
¼	¼	×	×
¾	¾	&tm;	™

Putting the Meta in HTML

Meta tags enable you to add information about a web document that users don't normally see. Search engines often use the information contained in meta tags to quickly identify the document and content type.

Your web page should already contain one meta tag—<meta charset="utf-8">—which tells browsers the character set to use. Consider adding two more meta tags to include a page description and a list of *keywords* the page contains (<meta> tags must be inserted between the opening and closing <head> tags):

```
<meta name="description" content="Basics of using meta tags in HTML
➥ documents." />
<meta name="keywords" contents="meta tags, meta tags, html, basics" />
```

When adding a meta description and keywords, don't go overboard. Any attempt to stuff your meta tags with keywords (to trick search engines into giving your page a higher ranking) could backfire. Some search engines penalize pages that contain too many keywords and/or keywords not used in the page's content. Adhere to the following guidelines:

- Limit your meta description to about 160 characters.

- Use only three to five keywords. The fewer the words, the more weight each word carries with the search engine.

- Be sure the keywords in your meta description and keywords tags match keywords included in the page contents (the headings and paragraphs).

> **DEFINITION**
>
> A **keyword** is an important word or phrase on a web page. Search engines use keywords to identify content and properly index a site.

If you're using a CMS, you may need to add the meta tags to the template's header.php file following the DTD. (See previous section "Modifying a CMS Template for HTML5" for details.) However, some templates include search engine optimization (SEO) features that enable you to add meta keywords and a description to the page by filling out a form. Or you can install a plug-in that adds SEO features.

Note to Self: Adding Hidden Comments

To help yourself or others who'll be managing the site, you can add comments to your HTML source code. Anything tagged as a comment does not appear when the page is displayed in a browser. It's visible only in the source code. To add a comment, type <!-- followed by your comment and then -->:

```
<!-- Do not change any of the following source code. -->
```

Adding Form and Function with HTML5 Structure Tags

HTML4 has some serious shortcomings, one of which is its inability to tag structural elements on a page. For example, HTML4 has no tag sets for headers, footers, or navigation bars. To work around this shortcoming, developers rolled their own makeshift tags by modifying the <div> (division) and <span> tags with class and ID attributes, as shown in Figure 4.5. (See Chapter 10 for more about using class and ID to coordinate HTML and CSS.)

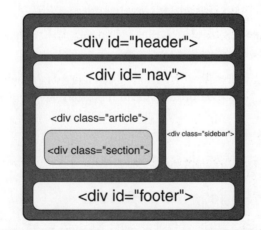

Figure 4.5: *Makeshift structure tags in HTML4.*

In terms of formatting, these customized <div> and <span> tags work quite well, and the technique is still widely used. They're a little convoluted, however, and because there's no standard for naming ID selectors for these structural elements, this technique leads to inconsistent source code, which makes it difficult for programs to identify the nature of specific structural elements.

HTML5 fills this gap by providing several structure tags for flagging content as a specific type: <header>, <nav> (navigation), <article>, <section>, <aside>, and <footer>. Figure 4.6 demonstrates how you can use the new structure tags to more clearly (and cleanly) designate the elements that comprise a web page.

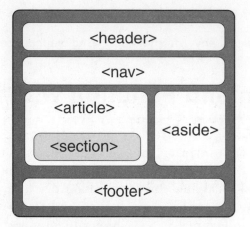

Figure 4.6: *HTML5 structure tags in action.*

These new structural tags deliver two key benefits:

- You can apply CSS styles to these elements rather than having to create your own custom <div> and <span> tags.

- Programs can identify the nature of each structural element by examining its tag, enabling assistive browsers and technologies to provide alternatives for viewing and navigating websites.

The following sections cover these new HTML5 structure tags in greater detail.

Topping Off Your Page with a Header

The header area appears at the top of a page, section, or article, and typically includes an <h1> heading. It may also include a subheading, byline, version information, and (if the header area introduces a page) the navigation area tagged as <nav>. The following sample code shows the <header> tag used at the top of a page:

```
<body>
<header>
<h1>Pebbles Landscaping</h1>
<p><em>Rock solid landscaping and shoreline protection throughout the
  ➥ great state of Michigan</em></p>
</header>
</body>
```

WHOA!

Don't confuse the <head> and <header> tags. Opening and closing <head> tags designate code that the browser sees but the user doesn't, including <meta> tags. <header> tags, which must appear somewhere between the opening and closing <body> tags, bracket readable elements on web pages.

Designating Your Main Navigation Area

Chapter 18 shows you how to add a navigation bar to your site. Until then, keep in mind that however you choose to create your navigation bar, bracket the code with an opening and a closing <nav> tag. The following code shows how to tag a simple navigation area that's set up as an unordered list:

```
<nav>
<ul>
<li><a href="home.html">Home</a></li>
<li><a href="products.html">Products</a></li>
<li><a href="services.html">Services</a></li>
<li><a href="about.html">About Us</a></li>
<li><a href="contact.html">Contact Us</a></li>
</ul>
</nav>
```

Tagging Content as an Article

In HTML5, any content that can stand on its own two feet is an *article*. It can be a single blog post, an article like you'd find in a newspaper or magazine, a product listing, or any other content that can be extracted for syndication and still make sense outside its original context.

An article is typically introduced by a header, but the article itself may contain its own headings and subheadings, as shown here:

```
<header>
<h1>Pebbles Landscaping</h1>
<p><em>Rock solid landscaping and shoreline protection throughout the
    great state of Michigan</em></p>
</header>
<article>
<h2>Shoreline Protection, Restoration, and Beautification</h2>
<p>Pebbles Landscaping is a full-service landscaping business that
    specializes in shoreline preservation and beatification. We
    offer several shoreline protection and preservation options,
    including retaining walls, rip-rap (rock), and marine vegetation.
    With our steel shore wall option, we can even help restore lost
    shoreline, and build up areas for use as docks or piers.</p>
<h2>25+ Years Experience in Shoreline Preservation</h2>
<p>Pebbles Landscaping has been protecting and restoring Michigan
    shorelines for over 25 years. Our engineers and technicians have
    the experience and expertise to do it right the first time and
    make it last a lifetime.</p>
</article>
```

Keep in mind that you can *nest* articles inside articles. For example, you may want to include the transcript of a video within an article that contains the video footage.

DEFINITION

Nesting consists of including one HTML element inside another. When nesting tags, arrange the closing tags in the reverse order of the opening tags:

```
<p><em>incredible</em></p>
```

Not:

```
<p><em>incredible</p></em>
```

Breaking an Article into Sections or Vice Versa

Sections group content thematically. You can use <section> tags to create a logical separation between sections within an article and/or between different articles on the same web page. The following example demonstrates the use of <section> tags within an article:

```
<article>
<h1>Beans, Rice, and Grains</h1>
<section>
<h2>Beans</h2>
<p>The term "bean" is a common name for plant seeds in the legume
  ➥ family that are consumed by humans as food or used in animal
  ➥ feed.</p>
</section>
<section>
<h2>Rice</h2>
<p>Technically speaking, rice is a cereal grain. It is also one of
  ➥ the most important staples for human consumption.</p>
</section>
<section>
<h2>Grains</h2>
<p>Grains are grasses grown and harvested for their fruit seeds,
  ➥ which are typically ground up to produce specific food items.
  ➥ Grains include corn (maize), rice, wheat, barley, oats, and
  ➥ rye.</p>
</section>
<p><strong>Remember:</strong> Combining beans and grains (including
  ➥ rice) during a meal helps ensure you consume all the essential
  ➥ amino acids to form complete proteins. </p>
</article>
```

If this same article were on a page with other articles, such as an article about the difference between nuts and seeds, you would bracket each article with an opening and closing <section> tag as well.

Setting Off Text as an Aside

An *aside* is sort of like a sidebar—it provides information that's tangential to the primary content on the page. Readers can skip the aside and still get the gist of the article. An aside may include its own header, paragraphs, lists, and other HTML elements, as shown here:

```
<aside>
<h3>Peanuts:Beans or Nuts?</h3>
<p>The peanut's identity issues are expressed in its name--it's part
  ➥ pea (bean family) and part nut. Botanically speaking, you can
  ➥ make a case for classifying the peanut as a bean (legume), but
  ➥ based on its use in cooking, it functions more like a nut.</p>
</aside>
```

Wrapping It Up with a Footer

Scroll down to the bottom of most websites, and you'll discover a footer, which usually contains a copyright statement, some sort of contact information, and perhaps links to the main areas on the site. Your footer may contain just about any available HTML element, but you should always bracket the footer with an opening and closing <footer> tag, as shown here, placing the footer just before the closing </body> tag:

```
<footer>
<a href="http://sample.com">Home</a> | <a href="http://
   ➥ sample.com/philosophy">Philosophy</a> | <a href="http://
   ➥ sample.com/treatment">Treatment</a> | <a href="http://
   ➥ sample.com/policies">Policies</a> | <a href="http://
   ➥ sample.com/contact">Contact</a> | <a href="http://sample.com/
   ➥ publications">Publications</a> | <a href="http://sample.com/
   ➥ blog">Blog</a> | <a href="http://sample.com/links">Links</a>
   ➥ <p>Pat Carlson, M.D. * 6834 Billback Circle * Trenton, New
   ➥ Jersey</p><p>&copy; 2011-Present, Pat Carlson, M. D.</p>
</footer>
```

If you're using a CMS or blogging platform to manage your site, a template may generate the footer. Standard templates typically include a footer.php file that has the code for generating the footer. Your CMS or blogging platform should have a way to open and edit the file; for example, in WordPress, you open the **Appearance** menu, click **Editor**, and click **Footer** (footer.php). If the file formats the footer with <div> tags, such as <div id="footer">, change the <div> tags to <footer> tags.

The Unveiling: Viewing Your Page in a Browser

Congratulations! You are the proud parent of a new web page. If you created the page online in a CMS platform, you can immediately open your creation in your web browser and see how it's shaping up. Simply click the **Preview** button or link, as shown in Figure 4.7.

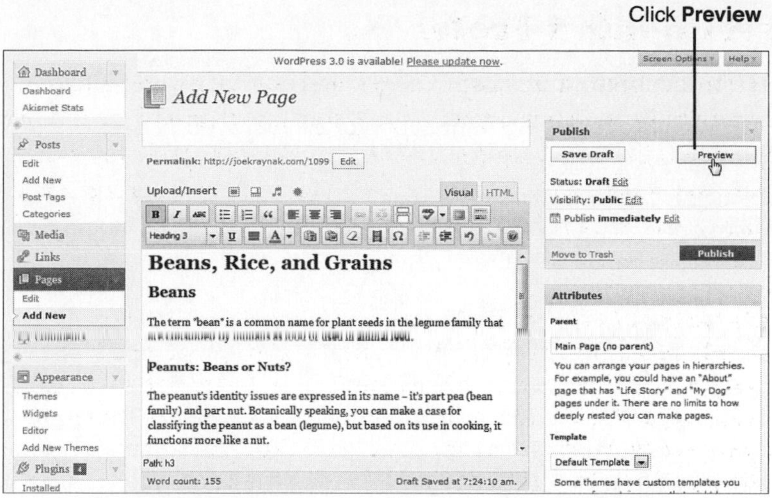

Click **Preview**

Figure 4.7: *Preview your page from an online CMS.*

If you created the page in a plain text editor or HTML authoring program, open the page in your browser. In most cases, all you need to do is find the HTML document you created and double-click it. Your operating system will use the default browser to open and display the document, as shown in Figure 4.8.

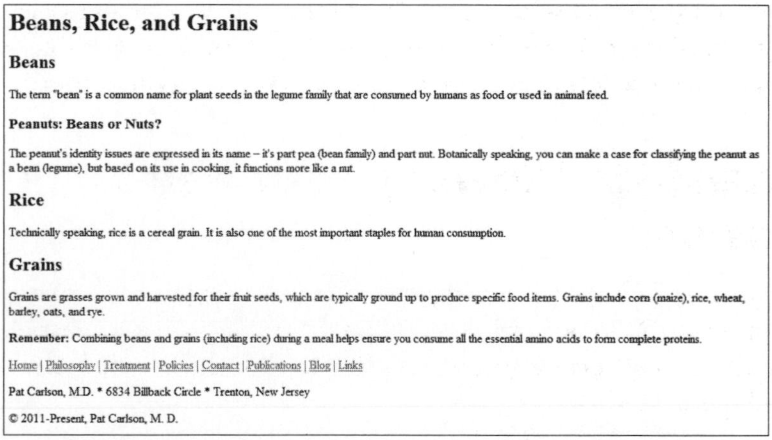

Figure 4.8: *A bare-bones web page as displayed in Internet Explorer.*

WHOA!

Most CMSs include a visual and HTML editor. If you're seeing HTML tags when viewing your web page in a browser, you probably typed tags in the visual editor. When you type tags directly into a page or post, always do so in the HTML editor, not the visual editor.

The Least You Need to Know

- HTML documents must be text-only files, not (for example) Word documents.
- Start with the following framework for all your web pages:

```
<!DOCTYPE html>
<html lang="en">
<head>
<meta charset="utf-8" />
<title>
</title>
</head>
<body>
</body>
</html>
```

- Use the tags <h1>, <h2>, <h3>, <h4>, <h5>, and <h6> to add headings to your document.
- Begin each paragraph with the <p> tag and end it with the </p> tag.
- Organize your document using HTML5 structure tags: <header>, <nav>, <article>, <section>, <aside>, and <footer>.

Breaking Up Text with Lists and Quotes

In This Chapter

- Creating bulleted and numbered lists and sublists
- Building a list of terms and definitions
- Indenting text in a blockquote
- Tossing in some cool HTML5 elements

In case you haven't noticed, I love lists. As a writer, lists enable you to …

- Write more efficiently and concisely.
- Avoid having to transition smoothly from one sentence to the next.
- Ensure that you cover all the main points.
- More easily spot and remove redundant material.

Most readers love lists, too, especially on the web. Here's why:

- Lists add white space, making text seem lighter and more inviting.
- Readers don't have to dig through dense paragraphs to discover a few gems.
- Readers can more easily skip what they find uninteresting or irrelevant to their current needs.

In the following sections, I show you how to create lists and sublists using HTML list elements. I also explain how to use other HTML elements to break up the text so your pages are more visually engaging and accessible to readers.

Building Lists

You can use lists in a number of ways—to present step-by-step instructions, an outline, key points or details, or even a collection of links. HTML enables you to create two types of lists: ordered (typically numbered) and unordered (typically bulleted).

The following sections introduce the tags required to create ordered and unordered lists.

Getting Unorderly with Unordered Lists

To create an unordered list, bracket the list with an opening and closing <ul> tag, and bracket each list item with an opening and closing <li> tag, like so:

```
<p>Most readers love lists, too, especially on the Web. Here's why:</p>
<ul>
<li>Lists add white space, making text seem lighter and more
➥ inviting.</li>
<li>Readers don't have to dig through dense paragraphs to discover a
➥ few gems.</li>
<li>Readers can more easily skip what they find uninteresting or
➥ irrelevant for their current needs.</li>
</ul>
```

Figure 5.1 shows what this list looks like when displayed in Internet Explorer.

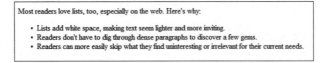

Most readers love lists, too, especially on the web. Here's why:

- Lists add white space, making text seem lighter and more inviting.
- Readers don't have to dig through dense paragraphs to discover a few gems.
- Readers can more easily skip what they find uninteresting or irrelevant for their current needs.

Figure 5.1: *Here's an unordered list displayed in Internet Explorer.*

INSIDE TIP

To further enhance an unnumbered list, consider leading off each list item with one or more words in bold, if appropriate, like this:

```
<ul>
<li><b>Sunlight:</b> Requires 8 hours of full sun.</li>
<li><b>Water:</b> Water only when soil is dry to the touch.
</li>
<li><b>Fertilizer:</b> Fertilize once every two weeks with
➥ general purpose fertilizer.</li>
</ul>
```

Getting Sequential with Ordered Lists

To create an ordered list, bracket the list with an opening and closing <ol> tag, and bracket each list item with an opening and closing <li> tag, like so:

```
<p>Take the following steps to prepare brown rice:</p>
<ol>
<li>Bring 4 cups water to a full boil.</li>
<li>Add 2 cups short grain brown rice.</li>
<li>When water boils, reduce heat to medium-low, and cook covered for
     10 minutes.</li>
</ol>
```

Figure 5.2 shows what this list looks like when displayed in Internet Explorer.

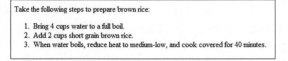

Figure 5.2: *An ordered list displayed in Internet Explorer.*

Creating Sublists—Lists Within Lists

HTML enables you to create sublists. To do so, you nest one list inside the other. Here's an example:

```
<ol>
<li>Bring 4 cups water to a full boil. </li>
<li>Add 2 cups rice:</li>
<ul>
<li>Short-grain brown rice</li>
<li>Medium grain brown rice</li>
<p>or</p>
<li>Long-grain brown rice</li>
</ul>
<li>When water boils, reduce heat to medium-low, and cook covered for
     40 minutes.</li>
</ol>
```

Figure 5.3 shows what the list and sublist look like when displayed in Internet Explorer.

Figure 5.3: *An ordered list with an unordered sublist.*

List Formatting No-No's

HTML is solely for creating a numbered or unnumbered list. How the list is formatted is a function of CSS styles. Figure 5.4 shows various ways numbered and unnumbered lists can be formatted using CSS. Unless you specify otherwise (using CSS), browsers typically display ordered lists as numbered lists (1, 2, 3, …) and use a circle for unordered list items.

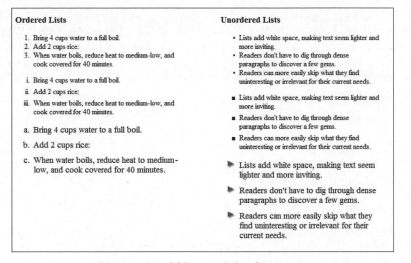

Figure 5.4: *CSS controls list formatting.*

Stick with CSS formatting, and avoid using deprecated list attributes, including type, which allowed you to specify the type of bullet to use for unordered lists—circle, disc (filled in circle), square, and so on. See Chapter 14 for details on how to change the formatting for list items.

Making a List of Terms and Definitions

When posting content that contains terminology or acronyms that may be unfamiliar to your audience, consider creating your own mini-glossary, complete with a list of terms and definitions. To create such a list, bracket the entire list with opening and closing <dl> (definition list) tags, each term with opening and closing <dt> (definition term) tags, and each definition with opening and closing <dd> (definition definition) tags. I like to give each term strong emphasis, so it typically appears bold, like so:

```
<dl>
<dt><strong>cache</strong></dt>
<dd>A temporary storage area in memory or on disk that computer
   components and various programs use to quickly access data.
   Pronounced cash.</dd>
<dt><strong>CD burner</strong></dt>
<dd>A disc drive that lets you copy CDs and record tracks from audio
   CDs to blank CDs.</dd>
<dt><strong>CD ripper</strong></dt>
<dd>A program that reads tracks from an audio CD and converts them
   into a digital file format that your computer can play. Using
   a CD ripper, you can create your own music mixes on your
   computer, transfer them to a portable MP3 player, and (with a
   CD burner) record your mixes to blank CDs. See also MP3 and CD
   burner.</dd>
</dl>
```

Figure 5.5 shows how this list appears when displayed in Internet Explorer.

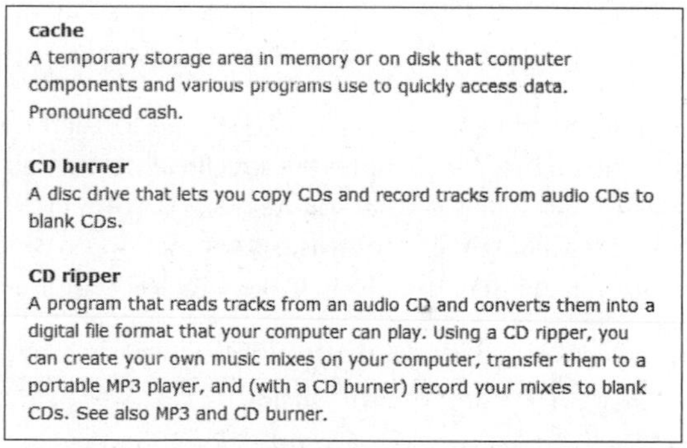

Figure 5.5: *A definition list in Internet Explorer.*

Setting Off Text as a Blockquote

When posting content that contains a long quotation from another source, set it off as a blockquote by bracketing it with an opening and closing <blockquote> tag, like so:

```
<blockquote>
<p>Can the content expert write a book on his or her own? Probably.
  ➥ But most of the content experts I team up with earn
  ➥ substantially more money per hour in their field than by writing
  ➥ books. They write books more for recognition and positioning
  ➥ than for royalties, so teaming up with a professional writer to
  ➥ complete the project as quickly and efficiently as possible is,
  ➥ for them, a sound financial decision.</p>
</blockquote>
```

To reference the source on the web, use the cite attribute in the opening blockquote tag; for example:

```
<blockquote cite="http://joekraynak.com/publishing/
  ➥ the-team-writing-advantage.html">
```

This doesn't link the quote to the source. It only provides information about the source in case a user wants or needs that information.

Unless you create a special style for it, your blockquote may look no different from a standard paragraph. I recommend indenting both sides of the blockquote using CSS padding and changing the font color and/or adding a shaded background so the quote really stands out.

WHOA!

Don't succumb to the temptation to use blockquotes for all the text you want to indent or put inside a box. Blockquotes are specifically intended for quoted material. Use CSS boxes without the <blockquote> tags for other text you want to set off in a "block." See Chapter 16 for details. Sometimes, the <aside> element is more suitable, but you still need to use CSS to make your asides appear as boxed text.

Tag brief quotes with an opening and closing <q> tag. You may add the cite attribute to the opening <q> tag as well.

Adding a Few Special HTML5 Elements

HTML5 features several additional elements for breaking up text and tagging unique content. The following sections describe and provide guidance on how to use each tag.

Highlighting Text

The HTML <m> tag (*m* stands for *markup*) enables you to indicate text that's marked up in some way—typically highlighted text. In the spirit of HTML's growing focus on tagging content without formatting, the <m> tag doesn't change the appearance of the text. You'll need to create a CSS style for the element if you want the text highlighted.

The good news is that with CSS, you can highlight the text however you wish; for example, you can specify a yellow background to have the text appear as though it's highlighted in yellow.

Flagging Dates and Times

When including a date and/or time in an HTML document, tag it with an opening and closing <time> tag. You can include the datetime attribute in the opening <time> tag to enter additional details about the date and/or time element. Following are examples:

```
Meeting is next <time>Tuesday at 2:30</time>
Come celebrate <time datetime="2011-02-22">George Washington's
   ➥ Birthday</time>
Meeting is next <time datetime="2011-11-01T14:30-15:30">Tuesday at
   ➥ 2:30</time>
```

Flagging a Value in a Range with the Meter Element

In browsers that support it, the meter element displays a graphic representation of a value in a particular range. Browsers that don't support the meter element simply display whatever values you enter between the opening and closing <meter> tags. Following is an example.

```
<p><label>Empty:</label></p>
<p><meter min="0" max="10" value="0">0</meter></p>
<p><label>Mid-range:</label></p>
<p><meter min="0" max="10" value="5"></meter></p>
<p><label>Optimum:</label></p>
<p><meter min="0" max="10" optimum="7" value="7"></meter></p>
<p><label>Too much:</label></p>
<p><meter min="0" max="10" low="3" high="8" value="9"></meter></p>
<p><label>Full:</label></p>
<p><meter min="0" max="10" value="10">10 out of 10</meter></p>
```

INSIDE TIP

During the writing of this book, very few browsers offered support for the <meter> and <progress> elements. If you're having trouble with these elements, try viewing your page in Google Chrome.

Figure 5.6 shows how this source code might appear in a browser that supports the meter element.

Figure 5.6: *The meter element in a browser that supports it.*

Table 5.1 lists and describes the attributes used with the <meter> tag. If you use attributes, always add them to the opening <meter> tag.

Table 5.1
Attributes for the <meter> Tag

Attribute	Value	Description
min	#	Lowest possible value, 0 is the default
max	#	Highest possible value, 1 is the default
high	#	Point at which the value is considered high
low	#	Point at which the value is considered low
optimum	#	If optimum is higher than the "high" value, the higher value is acceptable (typically green); if optimum is lower than the "low" value, the lower value is acceptable (typically green)
value	#	Specifies the actual value

Reflecting Ongoing Progress

HTML5's new progress element displays the progress of a function or process being performed. In its simplest form, you can use it to show a user's progress in performing a step-by-step process on your site. For example, if the user clicks **Next** to go to Step 2, you could include the following progress element on the Step 2 page:

```
<progress value="2" max="5">Step 2 of 5</progress>
```

Figure 5.7 shows what the progress bar would look like in a browser that supports it.

Figure 5.7: *The progress element shows progress toward completion.*

You can also use the progress element to show the progress of a file being downloaded or uploaded or a video or large graphic or script being loaded. Used in this way, the progress element helps you manage user expectations, so a user knows the wait time and will be less likely to bail out before the process is complete. Of course, if the progress is overly slow, the progress indicator may actually convince the person to bail out sooner.

The progress element has only two attributes: max and value. The max attribute indicates at what point the progress is complete; for example, the size of a file being downloaded in megabytes. The value attribute indicates the current point in the process; for example, the number of megabytes downloaded up to this point.

How does the tag "know" how close a process is to being complete? Well, that's the tough part. It has to do with writing a relatively complex script in JavaScript or Hypertext Preprocessor (PHP) and integrating it with the <progress> tag, which is beyond the scope of this book. Part 4 provides a glimpse of how you can make web pages more dynamic with jQuery, CSS, and forms.

The Least You Need to Know

- HTML for an unordered list looks like this:

```
<ul>
<li>Item</li>
<li>Another item</li>
<li>Another item</li>
</ul>
```

- HTML for an ordered list looks like this:

```
<ol>
<li>Step one</li>
<li>Step two</li>
<li>Step three</li>
</ol>
```

- HTML for a definition list looks like this:

```
<dl>
<dt>Term</dt>
<dd>Definition</dd>
<dt>Term</dt>
<dd>Definition</dd>
</dl>
```

- To create a blockquote (typically indented), start with HTML like this:

```
<blockquote>
Quotation goes here ....
</blockquote>
```

- To format marked-up text (highlighted), use <m> tags like this:

```
<m>This is marked-up text</m>
```

- Tag times and/or dates like so:

```
<time datetime="2011-11-01T14:30-15:30">Tuesday at 2:30</time>
```

- Use the <meter> tag, to display a meter:

```
<meter min="0" max="10" value="5"></meter>
```

Inserting Links and Interactive Elements

In This Chapter

- Saying hello to URLs
- Establishing a base URL
- Linking your pages to others on and off your site
- Linking to a specific location on a page
- Recognizing the risks of mailto: links

Links, also known as *hyperlinks*, take you from point A to point B at warp speed. In fact, they're what make the web a web by interconnecting sites, web pages, and a host of other media and resources. Links enable visitors to navigate your site, and they enable you to link your site to other sites around the world.

In this chapter, you discover how to add links to your pages so visitors can navigate your site and visit other sites you choose to link to.

Understanding URLs: Addresses in Cyberspace

You use web page addresses, also called *URLs* (uniform resource locators), all the time when you surf the web. For example, when you type www.whitehouse.gov in your browser's address bar, you're entering a URL that tells the browser where to go to access the White House website. Type www.whitehouse.gov/issues, and you're telling your browser to go to the WhiteHouse.gov website and open the default page in its "issues" folder.

A typical URL contains four distinct parts, as shown in Figure 6.1:

http://us.penguingroup.com/static/pages/publishers/adult/alpha.html

Protocol   Domain   Path   Filename

Figure 6.1: *A URL has four parts.*

To gain a better understanding of URLs and how they work, let's review the four parts of a typical URL:

- **Protocol:** A protocol is a set of rules that govern the transfer of data. On the web, the protocol is http, as in **http://** (*http* stands for hyper text transfer protocol). Other Internet protocols include *ftp* (file transfer protocol) and *mailto* (e-mail protocol).

- **Domain:** The site address or domain tells the browser where to go to access the site.

- **Path:** The path is the route to the folder that contains the web page or resource. If no path is specified, the file is stored in the site's *root directory* (root folder); for example, www.yoursite.com/index.html.

- **Filename:** The filename is at the very end of the URL. If no filename is specified, the browser will look for a file named index.html, default.html, index.php, or something similar.

NOTE

In a URL, the domain name is not case-sensitive, so you can use whatever you think is best when referring to your site. For example, I always display my site address as JoeKraynak.com, even though the official designation is joekraynak.com. Visitors can access the site using joekraynak.com, JoeKraynak.com, or even JoEkRAyNaK.com. However, path and filenames may be case-sensitive, so to avoid any confusion, stick with all lowercase. Some browsers may be able to locate a file named Index.html whether someone types Index.html or index.html, but some may not.

Using URLs on Your Site

You can use URLs to link to and reference files on your site and others. Combine a URL and an anchor tag, for example, and you can create a link to a website:

```
<a href="http://www.amazon.com">Amazon.com<a>
```

Combine a URL with an image tag to pull an image into a web page:

```
<img src="http://joekraynak.com/images/zorgandandyposter.jpg" />
```

 In previous versions of HTML, you had to include the protocol (http://), and the URL had to be enclosed in quotation marks, but this is optional in HTML5. In browsers that support HTML5, the following three links are treated the same:

```
<a href="http://www.whitehouse.gov">White House</a>
<a href=http://www.whitehouse.gov>White House</a>
<a href=www.whitehouse.gov>White House</a>
```

In this book, I maintain the traditional approach, including the http:// designation and enclosing the entire URL in double quotes.

When using URLs to reference pages and resources on your own site, you're usually better off using *relative* URLs. When linking to pages and files on other sites, you must use *absolute* URLs. The following sections reveal the differences between relative and absolute URLs.

> **INSIDE TIP**
>
> Consider creating separate folders on your web server for different types of files. You may want a separate folder for images and another for video clips. If your site has multiple areas, such as Products, Services, and Technical Support, create a separate folder for the HTML files you create for each area. This makes your site easier to manage as it grows.

Absolute URLs

An absolute URL links to a particular resource from anywhere on the Internet and consists of the entire URL, including the protocol and domain name; for example:

```
http://www.yoursite.com/business/images/logo.jpg
```

You use absolute URLs to link to external sites, pages, and resources, such as those stored on another computer, disk drive, or website. Absolute URLs work just fine in referencing pages and resources on your own web server, but relative URLs are better for this purpose. Let's look at why that is.

Relative URLs

Relative URLs indicate the location of a file relative to the current directory. So, for example, if a web page in the /business directory requires a file in the /business/images directory called logo.jpg, instead of using the following absolute URL …

```
http://www.yoursite.com/business/images/logo.jpg
```

… you can reference the file by using the following relative URL:

```
images/logo.jpg
```

Relative URLs offer two benefits:

- They're shorter (less to type).
- If you move your site to a different domain, you don't need to edit your relative URLs, assuming you keep all the files you move in their original directories.

Relative URLs typically come in the following three forms:

filename.html to reference a file that's in the same directory

directory/filename.html to reference a file that's in a subdirectory of the current directory

../filename.html to reference a file that's in the directory one level higher than the current subdirectory

Of course, relative URLs can become much more involved, depending on the directory structure on your site. If you have a very deep directory/subdirectory structure, you could end up with long paths in your relative URLs, such as …

```
business/store/automotive/images/logo.jpg
```

Likewise, if you need to reference a file several levels higher than the current directory, you could end up with something like this that tells the browser to look for the file three directories up from the current subdirectory:

```
../../../housewares.html
```

You may also encounter instances in which you want to back up one or more directories and then reference a subdirectory. For example, suppose you have all your images in the following directory:

```
www.yoursite.com/images
```

... and you have the following page, which requires the image logo.jpg:

```
www.yoursite.com/business/store/automotive/index.html
```

In the file index.html, the relative URL referencing that image would be as follows:

```
../../../images/logo.jpg
```

This tells the browser to go up one level (from automotive to store), up another level (from store to business), up another level (from business to the root directory), and then down one level (from the root directory to images), and access the file named logo.jpg.

Designating a Starting Point with a Base URL

A *base URL* enables you to specify a default directory for a specific page other than the directory where the page is stored. For example, you might store a page in the root directory of your site that references a bunch of files stored in the images/products directory. To avoid having to type "images/products" every time you reference a file, you can make that directory the default, so you can reference files in that directory by filename only.

To specify a base URL, insert a <base /> tag between the page's opening and closing <head> tags:

```
<base="http://www.site.com/directory/subdirectory/" />
```

Of course, if you're referencing a directory on your site, you can omit the http://www.site.com and simply use something like this:

```
<base="directory/subdirectory/" />
```

Now that you've changed the base URL for the page, its default directory is no longer the directory where the page is stored. So if you use a relative URL to reference a file in a different directory, remember that the directory is now relative to the base URL, not to the directory where the page is stored.

Suppose the web page is stored in the root directory, and the base URL is images/products. To use a relative URL to reference a file in the images directory (say, gadget.jpg), you wouldn't use "images/gadget.jpg". Instead, you would use "../gadget.jpg" because the images folder is up one level from the base URL products folder.

Transforming Text into Links

Creating links in HTML is a snap. You simply bracket anything you want to use as a link with an opening and closing anchor tag <a> that references the page you want to link to. The opening <a> tag must include the URL of the page. To link to the official site of the White House, for example, you might create the following link:

```
Visit the <a href="http://www.whitehouse.gov">White House</a>!
```

Figure 6.2 shows how this link appears in Internet Explorer.

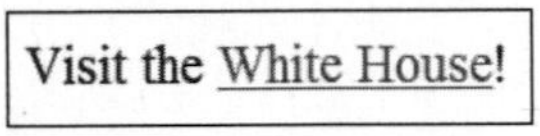

Visit the White House!

Figure 6.2: *Text becomes a link with the anchor tag.*

If you're creating links that will ultimately comprise a navigation bar for your site, be sure to bracket the entire group of links with an opening and closing <nav> tag (explained in Chapter 4).

One final word about hypertext links: they are *inline elements*, not *block elements*. A block element, such as <p> and <h1>, begins on a new line. Inline elements follow the normal content flow. What's most important is that you almost always include inline elements, such as <a>, inside block elements. You never include a block element inside an inline element.

INSIDE TIP

To avoid making a typo in the URL that renders your link inoperable, consider opening the page you want to link to in your browser and copying and pasting the URL into the opening <a> tag.

Linking to a Specific Location on a Page

You can use the ID attribute to link to a specific location on the same page or on a different page on your site. This is great for creating a clickable table of contents to navigate a long page or link to specific terms in a glossary.

First, add the ID attribute. Open the page that contains the destination point. At the beginning of the desired destination point, tag an element, such as <p> or <h1> or <dt>, so it includes an ID attribute with a unique name:

```
<h1 id="vegetables">Vegetables</h1>
```

Next, create your link as described in the previous section, and use the ID name as your href:

```
<a href="#vegetables">See Vegetables</a>
```

To link to the anchor from a different page on your site, include the page's URL followed by the ID name, like so:

```
<a href="/fruits-and-vegetables.html#vegetables">See Vegetables</a>
```

Clicking this link opens the designated page and then scrolls down to the <h1> element named "Vegetables."

Linking to Other Types of Files

Links aren't designed solely for web page (HTML) files. You can link to any file stored on your web or FTP server, including documents, spreadsheets, and compressed files. The easiest way to share files publicly is to upload the files to a separate folder on your web server and then create a link, something like this:

```
<a href="downloads/acme.zip">Click to download.</a>
```

What happens when someone clicks the link depends on the file type and browser. If the file is an image in the JPG, PNG, or GIF format or a PDF document, the browser will open and display it. If the browser can't open the file, it typically displays a dialog box prompting the user to save or open the file.

Opening a Link in a New Window

In most browsers, when you click a link, the linked page appears, replacing the previous page (which most people expect and prefer). Unfortunately, this takes a visitor from your site to someone else's site, which may not be your intent.

If you want to keep the visitor on your site, consider opening the linked page in its own browser window. Simply add the target=_blank attribute to your link, like so:

```
<a href="http://www.whitehouse.gov" target="blank">White House</a>!
```

WHOA!

Use the target=_blank attribute sparingly if at all. Most people find pop-up windows more annoying than helpful.

Contact Us: Inserting an E-Mail (mailto:) Link

You can quickly and easily place a link on your site that visitors can click to send you an e-mail message. Instead of including a web page address in the href attribute, use mailto: followed by your e-mail address, like so:

```
<a href="mailto:you@yoursitename.com">E-mail Me</a>
```

I don't use mailto, because it makes it too easy for spammers to snatch my e-mail address, even if I employ tricks to hide it. Some of these tricks include the following:

- Using a graphic image of your e-mail address instead of text.

- Hiding the @ symbol or period in your e-mail address; for example, you@email dot com.

- Using some sort of script to cloak your e-mail address.

Spammers are able to circumvent all these security measures. I prefer using a secure e-mail contact form plug-in for my CMS. Such a plug-in enables visitors to complete and submit a form that sends the information to me via e-mail without displaying or disclosing my e-mail address.

Not just any form will do. A standard form typically includes your e-mail address in the source code, making it readily accessible to spammers who know where to look for it. Search the web for a secure e-mail contact form plug-in for whichever CMS you're using.

The Least You Need to Know

- Use absolute URLs primarily to link to pages on other sites.
- Use relative URLs (omitting the domain name) primarily to link to pages and resources on your own site.
- To transform text into a link, bracket the text with an opening and closing <a> tag, like so:

  ```
  <a href="http://www.google.com">Google</a>
  ```

- To link to a specific location on a page, first add an ID attribute to an opening tag near the desired destination, like so:

  ```
  <h1 id="jokes">Jokes</h1>
  ```

  You can then link to this specific location by creating a link to the page that ends in #, followed by the ID name:

  ```
  <a href="fun/laughter/stories-jokes.html#jokes">Click here for
  ➥ jokes.</a>
  ```

- Avoid using mailto links, unless you really enjoy being spammed.

Adding Photos and Other Graphics

In This Chapter

- Making your photos look their best
- Uploading and managing images
- Adding images to web pages and blog posts
- Making images clickable links
- Using thumbnail and background images
- Drawing Scalable Vector Graphics (SVG)

The web is much more than text and hypertext. It also contains photos, illustrations, logos, maps, buttons, and all sorts of other images that are decorative, functional, or both. In this chapter, you discover how to add some eye candy to your web pages. Along the way, you also find out how to do some cool stuff, including how to transform an image into a link.

Keep in mind that this chapter doesn't include all there is to know about graphics. While HTML has some powerful graphics features, some of the coolest graphics features are available through CSS, including background images, borders, shading, and color. Part 3 provides information on these graphics features and more.

Prepping Photos: Adjusting Quality and Size

Digital cameras and online photo sharing services, including Flickr, Picasa, and even Facebook, have made the process of uploading photos brain-dead easy. It's so easy, in fact, that people often overlook the quality of the photos they're sharing.

Before inserting photos into your web pages, do a little prep work first, focusing both on quality and file size, so your photos look good without taking forever to appear. The following sections show you what to do and how.

Using a Suitable File Format

Photos can be stored in any of dozens of file formats, but for use on web pages, stick with the JPEG (JPG) format. JPEG, short for Joint Photographic Experts Group, is a standard for compressing images so they take up less storage space and travel faster over the Internet.

JPEG is a *lossy* compression standard, meaning images sacrifice some of their quality for the benefits of size and speed. Most digital cameras have quality settings, so you control the amount of compression. For best results, snap photos at the highest setting. You can always compress the file more later, but you can't improve the quality of a highly compressed original.

> **INSIDE TIP**
>
> Professional digital cameras may save photo files in the RAW or TIF format, which are nonlossy formats. These files can be huge, ranging from more than 1MB to upward of 50MB. You don't want to stick those on a web page. If you need to provide access to high-quality versions, however, you can link to those files, as explained in Chapter 6.

Airbrushing Photos with Common Enhancements

Before you even think about inserting a photo on a web page, open it in a photo editing program and try to make it look its best. Chances are good that your camera or printer came with a digital photo editing program. If not, you can find plenty of good, free programs on the web, including Photoscape, shown in Figure 7.1. Visit photoscape.org for links to the free download.

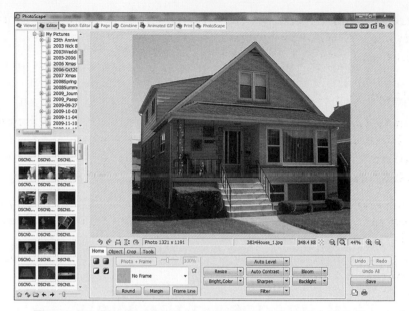

Figure 7.1: *Photoscape can help you make your photos look their best.*

Cropping and Resizing Your Photos

Your digital photo editor also contains tools for cropping and resizing your images. Use the tools in that order—first crop out anything you don't need and then shrink the image to the size you want. In most cases, you want the image no larger than 600×800 pixels, but you obviously want it to be large enough so people don't have to squint to see it. Note the dimensions of the image. You'll need them later.

WHOA!

Some digital photo editors create different versions of the photo as you edit it and save your changes, so the original remains untouched, but check your editor to be sure. If yours doesn't offer this feature, use **File**, **Save As** to save a copy under a different name and edit the copy.

Techniques for Shrinking File Sizes

Whether your photo's dimensions are large or small, you can make the file size smaller so it'll load faster in browsers. Following are a few techniques for reducing a photo's file size. Not all these options are available in all digital photo editors, but most are:

- Crop out what doesn't need to show.

- Reduce the photo's dimensions.

- Increase compression, reducing image quality.

- Reduce the number of colors—another reduction in quality.

Adjusting file size is a trade-off. Your goal is to create a reasonable balance between quality and the speed at which the image loads.

Putting Your Images on the Web

If you're using a CMS to create and manage your site, you may be able to insert images into pages and posts on the fly. The process usually consists of clicking a button to insert an image and then clicking **Browse** and selecting the image file on your computer. The CMS uploads the image to its media library and then inserts the source code required to pull the image into the page or post.

If you're not using a CMS, you need to upload your photos to the web manually. Two options are available:

- Create a separate folder on your web server, and upload your images to the folder.

- Upload your photos to an online photo sharing service, such as Flickr (flickr. com) or Photobucket (photobucket.com). Each photo will have a separate URL you can use to pull the photos into your pages and posts.

I prefer the first option because it gives me total control. I have an "images" folder on my web server that contains all the images I use on all my sites. Within this folder are subfolders to help me keep the images organized. When I need to insert a specific image, I use my browser to open the images folder and I pull up the image in my browser. I can then copy and paste its URL into my page or post.

Inserting an Image into a Page or Post

Inserting a photo or other image into a page or post is a snap. You either use your CMS to insert the image, just as you would insert an image into a document on your computer, or you add an <img> tag where you want the image to appear. The image tag must include the src attribute specifying the image location. Here's an example:

```
<img src="yoursite.com/images/roses.jpg" />
```

Unfortunately, all that tag does is plop the image on the page. To adjust its alignment, wrap text around it, add a border, or do other cool and useful stuff, you need CSS styles, as explained in Part 3. In the following sections, I cover a few attributes that provide some control over images with HTML.

NOTE

In HTML5, the quotation marks around attribute values and the forward slash near the end are optional. You can use <img src="yoursite.com/images/roses.jpg" /> or <img src=yoursite.com/images/roses.jpg>.

Specifying Image Dimensions

Always include the dimensions of the image in its <img> tag using the height and width attributes:

```
<img src=yoursite.com/images/roses.jpg height=250 width=300 >
```

This tells browsers how much space to reserve for the image as it loads—in this case, a rectangle 250 pixels tall by 300 pixels wide. (You can specify height and width in percentage, instead; for example, height=75% width=75%.) If you omit the image dimensions, the text loads and then must rewrap when the image arrives, which can be very distracting to visitors.

Adding Alternative Text ... When the Image Can't Be Seen

Visitors who have images turned off in their browsers or have a visual impairment may not see your images, so include alternate text that's displayed in lieu of the image.

```
<img src="yoursite.com/images/roses.jpg" height="250" width="300"
  ➥ alt="Roses" />
```

Figure 7.2 shows alt text displayed in place of an image.

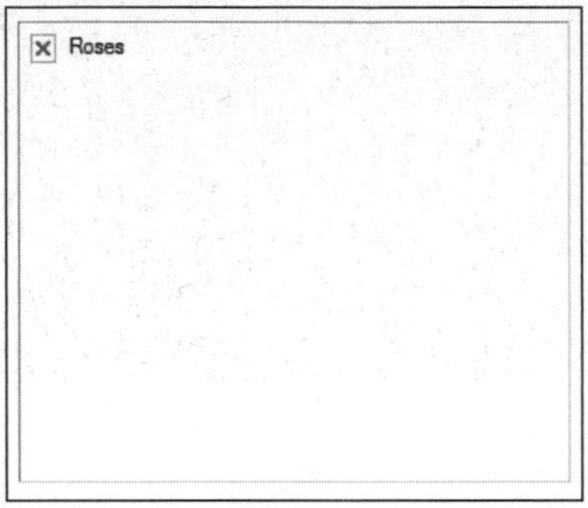

Figure 7.2: *Alt text appears in place of an image.*

You can also use the title attribute to describe an image, but alt is better because it's specifically for images. Using both is overkill.

Annotating Images and Adding Captions

HTML5 introduces two elements that enable you to annotate images, illustrations, and examples: <figure> and <figcaption>. Use <figcaption> to add a caption for your figure, and use <figure> to group everything that comprises the figure, including the caption. Here's an example:

```
<figure>
<img src="images/lake-holiday-home.jpg" height="344" width="614"
  ➥ alt="Home on Lake Holiday" />
<p><figcaption>Lake Holiday Home</figcaption></p>
</figure>
```

Figure 7.3 shows how this would appear in a browser.

Lake Holiday Home

Figure 7.3: *Add a caption to your images.*

You can pretty much tag any content that's not essential to an article but serves in a supporting role as a figure, including audio, video, charts, and tables. W3C's rule on what qualifies as a figure is fairly vague:

> … a unit of content … that is self-contained, that is typically referenced as a single unit from the main flow of the document, and that can be moved away from the main flow of the document without affecting the document's meaning.

You can use the figure element more creatively. Consider using it to group two or more images with a single caption below them. You may also want to use it to tag computer code used as an example or to group an image and a blockquote that describes the image.

Transforming an Image into a Clickable Link

Chapter 6 shows you how to convert text into hyperlinks, but you can also turn images into hyperlinks and create your own image maps. An image map is a graphic image that contains several hotspots that link to different resources. Image maps are useful for creating navigation bars and other creative, image-based navigation objects.

The following sections show you how to use an image as a link and create your own image map.

Using an Image as a Link

To transform an image into a hyperlink, enclose the <img> tag with opening and closing <a> tags, like so:

```
<a href="http://www.nimh.nih.gov/index.shtml"><img src="yoursite.com/
➥ images/health.jpg" height="250" width="300" alt="Home on Lake
➥ Holiday" /></a>
```

This doesn't change the appearance of the image at all. The only difference is that when you roll your mouse pointer over the image, the pointer turns into a hand icon, indicating that you can click the image to access whatever the image is linked to.

Building Your Own Art Gallery with Thumbnail Images

You've seen thumbnail images in action. They're often used on e-commerce sites to display the product and give shoppers the option to click to see a larger version. Thumbnails are often useful for image galleries, where you want visitors to browse a collection and then click to see an image in all its glory. This enables your gallery to load faster and lets visitors decide what they want to examine more closely.

Many CMSs include a feature that automatically generates thumbnail images for you when you choose to insert an image, as shown in Figure 7.4.

If you're a do-it-yourselfer, simply create and upload two versions of the image—one small one for the thumbnail and the larger, high-quality original. Then, link the thumbnail to the original, using the <a> tag, like so:

```
<a href="images/my-house-big.jpg"><img src=images/my-house-small.jpg"
➥ height="150" width="150" alt="Home on Lake Holiday" /></a>
```

Thumbnail

Figure 7.4: *WordPress can create thumbnail images on the fly.*

Creating an Image Map

To transform an image into an image map with multiple hotspots, you essentially define the coordinates, shape, and dimensions of each hotspot and then assign each hotspot a URL. Figure 7.5 shows a very basic image map with a few hotspots marked.

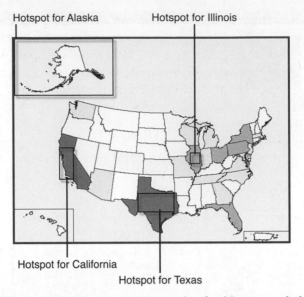

Figure 7.5: *A basic image map with a few hotspots marked.*
(U.S. Census Bureau, Population Estimates Program)

Following is the source code for that image map:

```
<img src="us-map.gif" width="575" height="425" alt="US Map"
➡ usemap="#us-map" />
<map name=us-map>
<area shape="rect" coords="264,320,331,365" href="texas.htm"
➡ alt="Texas" />
<area shape="rect" coords="367,238,387,265" href="illinois.htm"
➡ alt="Illinois" />
<area shape="rect" coords="100,245,119,288" href="california.htm"
➡ alt="California" />
<area shape="rect" coords="0,0,203,116" href="alaska.htm"
➡ alt="Alaska" />
</map>
```

Let's deconstruct the code to see how this works:

- The first tag, the <img> tag, contains the attribute usemap=#us-map, which matches the name of the map as specified in the tag below it—the <map> tag.

- The opening and closing <map> tags (second and last tags) define the map and give it the name "us-map."

- The <area> tags, between the opening and closing <map> tags, specify the coordinates for the hotspots. In this case, all the hotspots are rectangles, so the coordinates are defined by the location of the upper-left and lower-right corner of the rectangle. For example, upper-left corner of the hotspot for Alaska is located at X=0, Y=0, and the lower-right corner is at X=203, Y=116. See Figure 7.6.

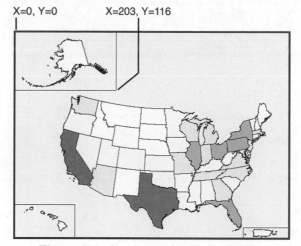

Figure 7.6: *Coordinates for Alaska's hotspot.*

To obtain the X,Y coordinates for any pixel in the image, here's what you do:

1. Open the image in your web browser and copy its address from the address bar.

2. Create an HTML skeleton, as explained in Chapter 4.

3. Between the two <body> tags, add the following <img> tag:

   ```
   <img src= ismap= />
   ```

4. Move the insertion point to just after src=, and paste the address you copied in step 1.

5. Save the file in the text-only format, giving it the .html filename extension.

6. Open the file in your browser.

7. Mouse over the image, and the X,Y coordinates indicating the mouse pointer's position will appear in your browser's status bar. See Figure 7.7.

8. Jot down the coordinates for the upper-left and lower-right corners of each hotspot.

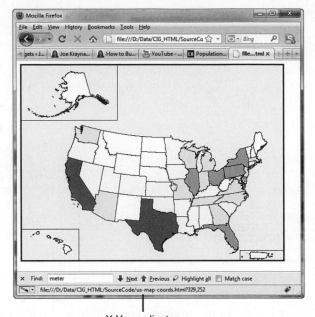

X,Y coordinates

Figure 7.7: *Identify the X,Y coordinates.*

Hotspots don't need to be rectangles. They can be circles, triangles, or polygons. For a circle, specify the X,Y coordinates of its center followed by the number of pixels for its desired radius. For example, the coordinates for a circular hotspot on my map of Texas might be 292,347,28—the center would be at X,Y 292,347, and the circle would have a radius of 28 pixels.

A polygon is a little more involved, but it would be better for a state like California. To define the hotspot, you would need X,Y coordinates for each vertex (the point at which two lines meet). Be sure to list the coordinates in the order in which you're "drawing" the imaginary line segments. If the coordinates are out of order, you may end up with a funky-shape hotspot.

Getting Creative with Scalable Vector Graphics

 Scalable Vector Graphics (SVG) is an image file format written in XML that instructs browsers on how to render images that scale smoothly to different sizes without any change in resolution. Here's a very simple example of SVG used to render a rectangle with a green 5-pixel-wide border and yellow shading (see Figure 7.8):

```
<?xml version="1.0" standalone="no"?>
  ➡ <!DOCTYPE svg PUBLIC "-//W3C//DTD SVG 1.1//EN"
  ➡ "http://www.w3.org/Graphics/SVG/1.1/DTD/svg11.dtd">
<svg viewBox = "0 0 400 400" version = "1.1">
<rect x = "50" y = "50" width = "200" height = "100" fill = "yellow"
  ➡ stroke = "green" stroke-width = "5"/>
</svg>
```

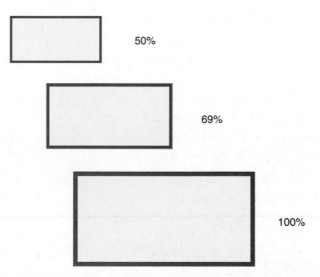

Figure 7.8: *SVG images scale to any size with no decrease in resolution.*

You can store the code in a plain text file, name the file using the .svg filename extension, and insert SVG images into your web pages using the <img> tag. You can also add the height and width attributes to scale the image size up or down with no change in resolution. The following codes, for example, render the same rectangle in three different sizes:

```
<p><img src="rectangle.svg" height="25%" width="25%" /></p>
<p><img src="rectangle.svg" height="50%" width="50%" /></p>
<p><img src="rectangle.svg" /></p>
```

Of course, you don't want to draw objects by writing a bunch of source code. Use a graphics program, instead. Inkscape, shown in Figure 7.9, is a free SVG graphics program that's powerful and fairly easy to use.

Figure 7.9: *Create SVG images in Inkscape.*

INSIDE TIP

You can download free, public domain SVG images from the Open Clipart Library at openclipart.org.

The Least You Need to Know

- Before you even think about uploading a photo, open it in a digital photo editor and make it look its best.

- You must upload a photo to a photo sharing service or to a folder on your web server before you can insert it into a web page.

- To bring an image into a web page, use the <img> tag, like so:

```
<img src="http://yoursite.com/images/imagename.jpg" />
```

- To transform an image into a hyperlink, sandwich the <img> tag between an opening and closing <a> tag, like so:

```
<a href="http://wherever.com/page.html">
➥ <img src="http://yoursite.com/images/imagename.jpg" /></a>
```

- SVG images scale to any size with no loss in resolution and can help you make your site more interactive.

Enhancing Your Page with Audio and Video

In This Chapter

- Playing video on your web pages
- Adding music and other audio to your site
- Managing how a browser plays audio and video

Early web browsers were ill-equipped to handle anything more than text and graphics. If you wanted to play audio or video, you needed a separate program, or you had to install a plug-in or ActiveX control. Fortunately, modern browsers are up to the task. HTML5 has made audio and video an integral part of the browsing experience, meaning the browser itself—not a plug-in—plays the media. This new approach offers three big advantages:

- Audio and video source code is less cumbersome.

- Styling the audio or video player inside the browser windows with CSS is much easier.

- You can manipulate the audio and video objects using CSS or jQuery just as you can manipulate other HTML elements.

This chapter shows you just how easy it is to add audio and video to your web pages in HTML5. You'll also find coverage of using the <object> and <embed> tags to accommodate older browsers.

Roll 'Em! Adding Video to a Web Page

You can add video to a web page in any number of ways—some easy and some not so easy. The following sections reveal your options, starting with the easiest.

> **INSIDE TIP**
>
> Keep in mind that if you're creating and managing your site with a CMS, it may provide built-in features for adding audio and video to your pages and posts. If it doesn't, a plug-in is probably available.

Embedding a YouTube Video

Embedding a YouTube video on a web page is a snap. Here's what you do:

1. Sign in to YouTube at youtube.com. (If you don't have a free YouTube account, you must register first.)

2. Click the **Upload** link (top center) and follow the on-screen instructions to upload your video, or record yourself using a webcam. When the upload is complete, YouTube displays an embed code, as shown in Figure 8.1.

Figure 8.1: *Copy the embed code.*

3. Right-click in the **Embed** box and click **Copy**.
4. Display the source code for the page where you want the video to appear, and paste the embed code where you want the player to appear, as shown in Figure 8.2. (If you're using a visual editor, be sure to change to HTML view, so you post the embed code into the source code; otherwise, when you open the page in a browser, the code will appear instead of the video.)

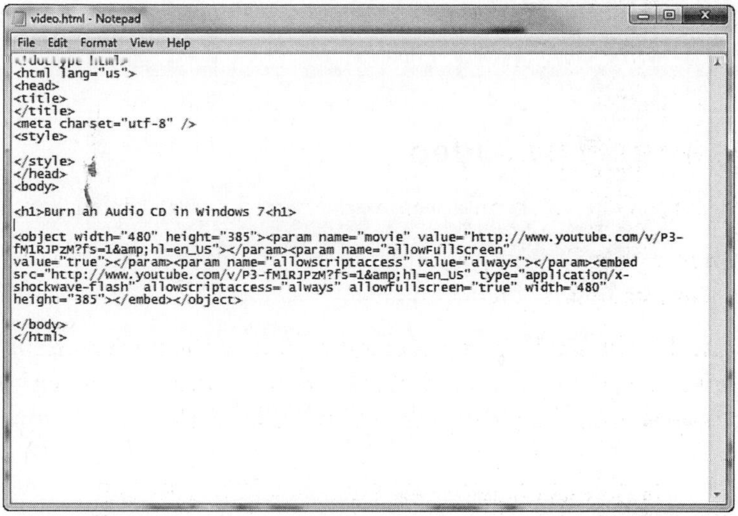

```
<!doctype html>
<html lang="us">
<head>
<title>
</title>
<meta charset="utf-8" />
<style>

</style>
</head>
<body>

<h1>Burn an Audio CD in Windows 7<h1>

<object width="480" height="385"><param name="movie" value="http://www.youtube.com/v/P3-fM1RJPzM?fs=1&amp;hl=en_US"></param><param name="allowFullScreen" value="true"></param><param name="allowscriptaccess" value="always"></param><embed src="http://www.youtube.com/v/P3-fM1RJPzM?fs=1&amp;hl=en_US" type="application/x-shockwave-flash" allowscriptaccess="always" allowfullscreen="true" width="480" height="385"></embed></object>

</body>
</html>
```

Figure 8.2: *Paste the embed code into the source code for your web page.*

5. Save the file.

When you open the page in a browser, the embed code displays the YouTube player with controls visitors can click to play the video, as shown in Figure 8.3.

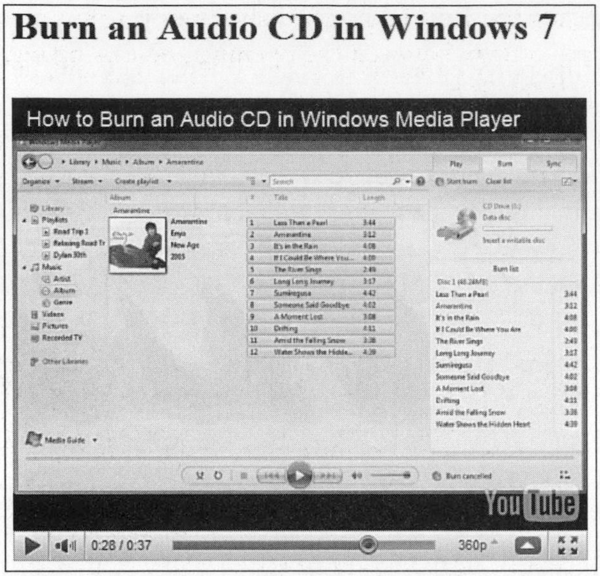

Figure 8.3: *Your YouTube video appears on your page.*

During the writing of this book, YouTube was gearing up for HTML5. By the time you read this, it may be using the HTML5 <video> tag described in the following section, rather than the <embed> and <object> tags, or the <video> tag method may at least be an option.

Using the HTML5 <video> Tag

The HTML5 <video> tag is designed to enable you to add video to your web pages as easily as you add images. The only problem (and it may not be a problem by the time you read this) is that developers are/were having a tough time agreeing on a video file format to use as the standard. During the writing of this book, WebM seemed to be in the lead for possible candidates, but Theora (Ogg) and H.264 (mov, mp4, and m4V) were running strong. I can't possibly predict the outcome, but I'd bet my money on WebM.

At any rate, here's the <video> tag in action with a sample WebM video file:

```
<video src="video/sample-video.webm" width="640px" height="480px"
  ➡ controls="controls" ></video>
```

Note that unlike the unpaired <img> tag, the <video> tag requires a closing tag. This enables you to place content between the opening and closing tag, which comes in very handy, as you'll see later.

The src attribute, the only required attribute, identifies the location of the video file. The height and width attributes define the dimensions of the box in which the video plays; to avoid distortion for most videos, retain an aspect ratio of 4:3 (for example, 640×480 or 500×375). The controls attribute tells the browser to display controls for playing and pausing the video. See Figure 8.4.

Figure 8.4: *With HTML5, the browser plays the video.*

The <video> tag includes some additional attributes that can come in handy:

- **autoplay** tells the browser to start playing the video immediately, so the user need not click the play button.

- **loop** keeps playing the video over and over until the user chooses to stop it or exits the page.

- **preload** loads the video as the page is loading, so it's ready to run. If the <video> tag contains the autoplay attribute, preload does nothing.

- **poster** shows an image until the first frame of the video is downloaded, replacing the poster. Follow this attribute with the URL of the image; for example:

    ```
    poster=images/poster.jpg
    ```

Most of the attributes have a value of true/false; for example, loop=loop. But because only one value is required to enable the attribute, you can drop the value. For example, loop without the =loop works just fine. So does control, autoplay, and preload.

> **INSIDE TIP**
>
> You can find free encoders on the web for WebM, Ogg, and other video codecs. Wildform (wildform.com), for example, offers a free copy of Flix WebM that enables you to create WebM video files. Encoding video is difficult and requires a lot of processing power, so be prepared to run into some glitches. You may need to try several encoding programs to find one that works for you.

Adding Flash Video

Adobe Flash has been the video standard on the web for several years. Chances are good that HTML5's efforts to make video an integral part of the browsing experience will eventually lead to the disappearance of Flash, but with gobs of Flash video already out there, it should remain an option for years to come.

As with any video file format, you must first encode your video and then upload the resulting file to your web server. (You can find video file converters on the web to convert existing video into Flash.) You can then embed the video using the <object> and <embed> tags, like so:

```
<object width="500" height="375">
<param name="movietitle" value="videos/sample-video.swf">
<embed src="videos/sample-video.flv" width="500" height="375">
</embed>
</object>
```

Using the <object> <param> tags and the <embed> tag to reference the same movie may seem redundant, but you do it so your movie can play in a variety of web browsers.

Catering to Different Browsers

Until the web settles on one video format (if that ever happens), you may need to offer browsers two or more file formats from which to choose—for example, MP4, WebM, and Ogg.

First, upload a video file in each of the formats you want to make available. Then, use something like the following source code to indicate to the browser which files are available and where they're located:

```
<video width="500" height="375" controls="controls">
<source src="videos/sample-video.mp4" type="video/mp4" />
<source src="videos/sample-video.webm" type="video/webm" />
<source src="videos/sample-video.ogv" type="video/ogg" />
Your browser does not support the available video formats. Click one
  ➥ of the following links to download the video:<a href="videos/
  ➥ sample-video.mp4">MP4</a><a href="videos/sample-video.webm">
  ➥ WebM</a> <a href="videos/sample-video.ogv">Ogg</a>
</video>
```

The browser proceeds through the code until it finds a format it can play and then plays the file in that format. If the browser doesn't support any of the available formats, a message appears giving users the option of downloading the video to play on their computers.

Making Your Site Sing with Audio Clips

Whether you want music to start playing when visitors land on your site or you want to provide users with links they can click to play music or download a podcast, HTML has you covered. In the following sections, you discover various ways to add audio to your site.

Adding Audio with the <audio> Tag

The new <audio> tag is the easiest way to add audio to your site. Like the new <video> tag, <audio> is a paired tag with the opening tag specifying the location of the file and other parameters. Here's an example for playing audio in the background whenever the page is opened in a browser:

```
<audio src="audio/sample-audio.ogg" autoplay="autoplay"></audio>
```

While the src attribute is required, the <audio> tag includes several optional attributes:

- **autoplay=autoplay** tells the browser to start playing the video immediately, so the user need not click a play button.

- **controls=controls** displays controls, including a play button. If you want audio that plays in the background when someone visits your site, omit the controls attribute and include autoplay.

- **loop=loop** keeps playing the audio over and over until the user chooses to stop it or exits the page. Go light on the looping—this can get really annoying really fast.

- **preload=preload** loads the audio as the page is loading, so it's ready to play. If the audio tag contains the autoplay attribute, preload does nothing.

> **NOTE**
>
> When an attribute name and value are the same, such as controls="controls", you can simply use the value: "controls" or controls (without the quotes).

Catering to Different Browsers

As with video, no single audio file format is the standard, but Ogg, MP3, and WAV files are the most common. To accommodate various formats, you can convert your audio files to different formats and make them available on your web server. You can then include the following source code on your web page to indicate the various formats available:

```
<audio controls="controls">
<source src="sample-audio.mp3" type="audio/mpeg" />
<source src="sample-audio.ogg" type="audio/ogg" />
Your browser does not support the available formats. Click one of
    ➥ the following links to download the video:<a href="audio/sample-
    ➥ audio.mp3">MP3</a> <a href="audio/sample-audio.ogg">Ogg</a>
</audio>
```

> **INSIDE TIP**
>
> You can find free tools on the web for converting your audio files to different formats. media.io, for example, enables you to convert numerous audio file formats to MP3, WAV, Ogg, or WMA and choose your audio quality preference.

The Least You Need to Know

- To add video to a page, use the new HTML5 <video> tag, like so:
  ```
  <video src="video/sample-video.webm" width="500px"
  ➥ height="375px" controls="controls"></video>
  ```

- To add background audio to a page, use the new HTML <audio> tag:
  ```
  <audio src="audio/sample-audio.ogg" autoplay="autoplay">
  ➥ </audio>
  ```

- To add audio that plays only when a user clicks the play button, remove the autoplay attribute and add the controls attribute.

Tabling Your Text in Rows and Columns

In This Chapter

- Organizing text in rows and columns
- Adjusting row height and column width
- Adding column and row headings
- Keeping your HTML format free
- Using tables to control web page layout

When you need to arrange text in rows and columns on a web page, you need HTML table tags. You can create a basic table with three simple tags: <table>, <tr> (table row), and <td> (table data). Add the <th> tag, and you have column and row headings. Add the <thead>, <tbody>, and <tfooter> tags, and you have a well-structured table divided into head, body, and footer. Add CSS, as explained in Part 3, and your tables really come to life with attractive borders and shading.

But first things first. In this chapter, you find out how to create tables with a handful of HTML table tags. Along the way, I point out a few things about tables you should never do and a couple things you can totally ignore.

Building a Table from the Top Down

The best way to start creating tables is to start small and keep adding stuff. Here's the source code for a very basic table with two rows and three columns (see Figure 9.1):

```
<table>

<tr>
<td>$100,000</td>
<td>$120,000</td>
<td>$116,050</td>
</tr>

<tr>
<td>$87,500</td>
<td>$89,350</td>
<td>$86,520</td>
</tr>

</table>
```

I grouped the tags to clarify how the tags function. The entire table is sandwiched between an opening and closing <table> tag. Each pair of <tr> tags defines a row, and each pair of <td> tags defines an entry in that row—in this case, three entries per row, creating a three-column table.

| $100,000 | $120,000 | $116,050 |
| $87,500 | $89,350 | $86,520 |

Figure 9.1: *A table with two rows and three columns.*

Adding Column Headings

You can add a row of column headings to your table to help visitors understand the entries in each row. By default, column headings appear bold and centered in most browsers. Using CSS styles, you can change their appearance, as explained in Chapter 19.

To add a row of headings to the top of the table, create a new row at the top of the table using a pair of <tr> tags. Use <th> instead of <td> to tag the items in that row. Finally, bracket the top row with an opening and closing <thead> tag and the rest of the table with an opening and closing <tbody> tag. The source code for our sample table now looks like this:

```
<table>

<thead>
<tr>
<th>January</th>
<th>February</th>
<th>March</th>
</tr>
<thead>

<tbody>

<tr>
<td>$100,000</td>
<td>$120,000</td>
<td>$116,050</td>
</tr>

<tr>
<td>$87,500</td>
<td>$89,350</td>
<td>$86,520</td>
</tr>

</tbody>

</table>
```

Figure 9.2 shows how the table is shaping up.

January	February	March
$100,000	$120,000	$116,050
$87,500	$89,350	$86,520

Figure 9.2: *The table with column headings in place.*

Adding a Footer

Most tables full of numbers have a row at the very bottom that essentially shows the bottom line—the sum total of the values in each column. In an HTML table, this row is the footer.

You can insert the footer before or after the header, or at the bottom of the table between the closing </tbody> tag and the closing </table> tag. It doesn't matter; browsers will display it at the very bottom of the table. Bracket the entire footer row with an opening and closing <tfoot> tab, and sandwich each entry in the row between opening and closing <td> tags. Here's the source code for the complete table with the footer row in place:

```
<table>

<thead>
<tr>
<th>January</th>
<th>February</th>
<th>March</th>
</tr>
</thead>

<tbody>

<tr>
<td>$100,000</td>
<td>$120,000</td>
<td>$116,050</td>
</tr>

<tr>
<td>$87,500</td>
<td>$89,350</td>
<td>$86,520</td>
</tr>

</tbody>

<tfoot>
<td>$12,500</td>
<td>$30,650</td>
<td>$29,530</td>
</tfoot>

</table>
```

Spanning Text Across Multiple Rows or Columns

Sometimes, you may need a table head or data entry to span two or more rows or columns, as shown in Figure 9.3. To accomplish this, use the rowspan or colspan attributes to specify the number of columns or rows the entry must span. Here's the source code used to create the table shown in Figure 9.3:

```
<table>

<thead>
<tr>
<th>January</th>
<th>February</th>
<th>March</th>
</tr>
</thead>

<tbody>

<tr>
<th colspan="3">Q1 Results</th>
</tr>

<tr>
<td>$100,000</td>
<td>$120,000</td>
<td>$116,050</td>
</tr>

<tr>
<td>$87,500</td>
<td>$89,350</td>
<td>$86,520</td>
</tr>

</tbody>

<tfoot>
<td>$12,500</td>
<td>$30,650</td>
<td>$29,530</td>
</tfoot>

</table>
```

Q1 Results		
January	February	March
$100,000	$120,000	$116,050
$87,500	$89,350	$86,520
$12,500	$30,650	$29,530

Figure 9.3: *A table head or data entry can span multiple rows or columns.*

Adding a Descriptive Caption

Adding a caption (such as "Table 3.1: Recent Sales Figures") is usually a good idea, to provide a context that helps users better understand the data they're looking at. To add a caption above the table, type your caption text above the table and between an opening and closing <caption> tag, like so:

```
<caption>Table 3.1:Recent Sales Figures</caption>
```

Saving Time with Column Tags

HTML has a couple more table tags most people never use, but these can save you some time when formatting your table:

- **<col>** enables you to apply attributes to entire columns rather than having to apply the attributes individually via <tr>, <td>, or <th> tags. Using the span attribute, you can apply attributes to more than one column; for example, you can make one or more columns bold and the other columns normal text.

- **<colgroup>** enables you to group related columns, and can save you additional time in applying attributes to groups of columns rather than applying the attributes to individual columns.

See Chapter 19 for more about using the <col> and <colgroup> tags with CSS to control the appearance and layout of columns in a table.

Nesting Tables

One final note about tables: you can nest tables one inside another. The reason I left this for last is because I have never in my life nested tables. But I figured I'd better cover it just in case.

All you do to nest tables is place one table inside another, sandwiching the nested table between an opening and closing <td> tag in the surrounding table. If you're nesting multiple tables, getting the source code just right can be tricky, but it's certainly possible.

Table and Cell Formatting No-No's

I have only one word about formatting tables in HTML: don't. The table tags are designed primarily to define the overall structure of the table and its columns, rows, header, footer, and so forth. In HTML5, all the table appearance attributes have been deprecated, meaning they're taboo.

To apply formatting, use CSS, as explained in Chapter 19. With CSS, you can add borders, shading, and padding (space between text and borders); adjust table width and height, column width, and row height; change text alignment in cells; and more. Figure 9.4 provides a taste of what you have to look forward to when you start applying CSS to your tables.

Q1 Results		
January	February	March
$100,000	$120,000	$116,050
$87,500	$89,350	$86,520
$12,500	$30,650	$29,530

Figure 9.4: *CSS brings a table to life.*

Structuring an Entire Web Page with a Table

A table is a grid. As such, you can use it to structure your web pages. You may, for example, create a table with four cells that define the four blocks that make up a typical web page:

- Header

- Left navigation bar

- Body

- Footer

Figure 9.5 shows how this application of the table feature might work.

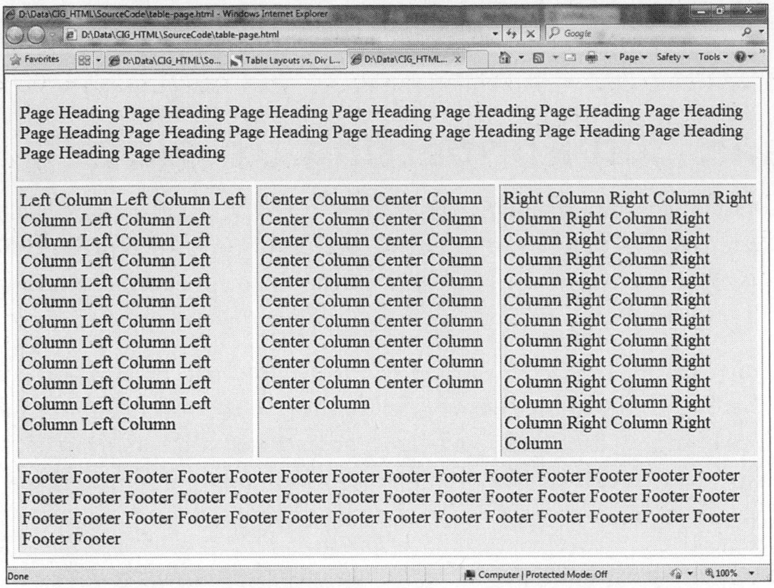

Figure 9.5: *Although you can structure web pages using tables, don't.*

However, I don't recommend using HTML tables to structure your web pages. It's primitive and cumbersome, and it restricts your creativity and ability to tweak your design later. See Chapter 18 for instructions on how to use CSS to structure pages more effectively and efficiently.

The Least You Need to Know

- Use the following source code to create a two-row, three-column table:

```
<table>
<tr>
<td></td>
<td></td>
<td></td>
</tr>
<tr>
<td></td>
<td></td>
<td></td>
</tr>
</table>
```

- To add column headings, add a row at the top, but tag individual entries in the row with <th> rather than <td>.

- Sandwich your table heading row between an opening and closing <thead> tag.

- Sandwich the rows containing the data in your table between an opening and closing <tbody> tag.

- To create a footer, add a row below the closing <tbody> tag, and sandwich it between an opening and closing <tfoot> tag.

- Don't even think about formatting your table with HTML attributes. Use CSS Instead.

Formatting and Layout with CSS Styles

CSS is like CPR for web pages. It transforms colorless, lifeless web pages into dazzling, dynamic media—giving you full control over fonts and colors, enabling you to structure pages in columns, and providing you with the option to place content in boxes complete with colorful backgrounds, borders, and even drop-shadows. You do all this by creating style rules that apply formatting to the various HTML elements.

The chapters in Part 3 show you how to create CSS style rules and use selectors to apply those rules to specific elements. Chapter 10 gets you up to speed on the basics, and Chapter 11 shows you how to take a shortcut by starting with a CSS theme. The remaining chapters cover specific CSS topics: formatting text, adding colors, customizing backgrounds, creating drop-shadows, and using CSS3 to create nifty animation effects without knowing anything about programming.

Best of all, by using cascading style sheets to format your pages, you significantly reduce the hassles and headaches of redesigning your site. Instead of formatting every element on every page, you simply modify a style in a CSS file, and that change is applied throughout your site!

Wrapping Your Brain Around CSS

Chapter 10

In This Chapter

- Understanding the cascading concept
- Applying styles to HTML elements
- Writing style rules to specify formatting preferences
- Sizing text, images, and other objects
- Adding comments to styles for future reference

At first glance, CSS can be overwhelming. Open a style sheet, and all you see is a bunch of cryptic code. When you wrap your brain around the concept of CSS and break it down into its essential components, however, it becomes much easier to understand and use.

This chapter takes you behind the scenes with CSS. Here, you get your first encounter with CSS style sheets, discover how to write your own CSS rules, find out how to use rules to specify the size of text and other objects, and use the cascading nature of CSS to your advantage.

With the knowledge you gain from this chapter, you're much better equipped to figure out what a particular style rule does and how to use CSS to take control of your web page's appearance and layout.

Starting with a Theme

You can save yourself a great deal of time and effort by starting with a CSS theme. A theme consists of one or more CSS style sheets that control the appearance and layout of a site. See Chapter 11 for details. Themes are available for almost all content management systems, including WordPress, Joomla!, Drupal, and concrete5. You can start with a theme that's pretty close to what you want and customize it by editing the theme's CSS rules.

Deconstructing Style Rules

In CSS, you specify formatting by creating *style rules*. A style rule consists of a *selector* followed by a *declaration*, as shown in Figure 10.1. The selector matches something in the tag, so whenever a browser reads the tag, it "knows" which style rule to apply to the element. The declaration contains at least one *property* set to a particular *value* in the form *{property:value; }*.

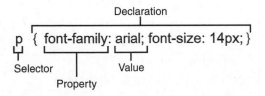

Figure 10.1: *With CSS, you use style rules to establish formatting.*

A style rule may have multiple *property:value* pairs enclosed within a single set of curly brackets. Here's an example that specifies the font family, color, and text alignment for a paragraph:

```
p {font-family:arial; color:red; text-align:center; }
```

Style rules may also include several selectors, separated by commas, to apply the same style to different elements, as in the following example:

```
h1, h2, h3 {font-family:arial; color:blue; margin-top:18px; }
```

Be sure each *property:value;* pair ends in a semicolon; otherwise, browsers may have trouble reading the style rule. Spaces don't make a difference, but they come in handy for making sure your styles don't get bunched up.

INSIDE TIP

Web designers often place each declaration on a separate line to make their style sheets easier to read and understand. Here's an example:

```
h1, h2, h3 {
font-family:arial;
color:blue;
margin-top:18px;
 }
```

Applying Styles: External, Internal, and Inline

Before you get into the nitty gritty of creating style rules to format your HTML elements, you need to know where you'll be creating these rules. You have three options:

- External style sheet
- Internal style sheet
- Inline styles

The following sections describe each option in detail.

External Style Sheets

An *external style sheet* is usually best because you can place all your style rules in one file. If you ever need to change the appearance of an element throughout your site, you change the style rule for that element in the external style sheet.

DEFINITION

An **external style sheet** is a separate text-only file that has the .css filename extension and contains CSS style rules to any HTML document that references the style sheet.

To create an external style sheet, create a text-only file with the .css filename extension. You can call it something like styles.css.

To have a browser apply to your web documents the style rules defined in an external style sheet, you must add a link near the top of each HTML document that specifies the location and name of the style sheet. To link to a style sheet, insert a <link />

tag between the opening and closing <head> tags near the top of the document. The resulting code will look something like this:

```
<head>
<link rel="style sheet" type="text/css" href="styles.css" />
</head>
```

If you store the style sheet file in the same directory as the web pages that link to it, you can set the href attribute equal to the style sheet's filename. Otherwise, you must specify its location, in addition to its filename; for example, href="styles/styles.css". For details on how to specify the location of files on your website, see Chapter 6.

Internal Style Sheets

An *internal style sheet* resides inside and at the top of an HTML document, and applies style rules only to elements in that document. The reason you may want to steer clear of internal style sheets (in most cases) is because they don't allow you to apply formatting to all pages on your site. If you want to change the appearance of an element, you need to make the change in every single web page on your site.

Internal style sheets are acceptable if you have a page on your site with a totally unique layout and appearance.

To add an internal style sheet to a web document, type an opening and closing <style> tag near the top of the HTML document, between the two <head> tags. Add the attribute type="text/css" to the opening <style> tag. Type your style rules between the two <style> tags, like so:

```
<head>
<style type="text/css">
p {font-family:arial; color:red; text-align:center; }
h1, h2, h3 {font-family:arial; color:blue; margin-top:18px; }
</style>
</head>
```

Inline Styles

Using *inline styles* is kind of pointless. I only mention it because it's an option, but it really defeats the purpose of having styles—to keep the formatting and content separate.

To apply an inline style, add the style attribute to an element's tag and set its value equal to one or more style declarations in the form *property:value*; for example:

```
<p style="text-align:center; font-size:large">.
```

Targeting Elements to Format with Selectors

The *property:value* pair is fairly easy to understand. All you're doing is naming a property (characteristic) of the element and then specifying its format. The trickier part is dealing with selectors because you can use four different types of selectors:

- Tag
- Class
- ID
- Attribute

The following sections explain each type of selector in greater detail.

Tag Selectors

The concept of *tag selectors* is the easiest to grasp. You simply use the tag without the angle brackets to specify the HTML element you want the style rule to target; for example *p* for paragraphs, *img* for images, *h1* for level 1 headings, and so on. Using tag selectors, you can apply identical formatting to *all* instances of a particular HTML element throughout your site.

DEFINITION

A **tag selector** is the name of an HTML element used to identify the HTML element to which a CSS style applies. Tag selectors appear without angle brackets.

Class Selectors

Class selectors enable you to create multiple styles for a single HTML element. For example, you can create three paragraph classes for aligning paragraphs left, right, or center:

```
p.left {text-align:left; }
p.center {text-align:center; }
p.right {text-align:right; }
```

You can then add the class attribute to a paragraph's opening tag to specify which class to apply; for example, <p class="center">.

You can also create a class that is not associated with any given HTML element by omitting the element designation from the selector. Here's an example:

```
.center {text-align:center; }
```

You can apply this type of class style to any text element—paragraphs, headings, addresses, and so on—by adding the class="center" attribute to the element's opening tag.

ID Selectors

The *ID selector* is similar to the class selector, but it uses a pound sign (#) instead of a period, and it applies formatting to only a single occurrence of a specific HTML element on a page.

For example, you could apply *#left-block {display:block; float:left; width:250px; }* to a division of a document to create a narrow block on the left of the page into which you can place other elements.

Pseudo Selectors

Use *pseudo selectors* to format elements in different states. The most common use of pseudo selectors is for <a> tags, because you may want links to change appearance when they're pointed to or clicked. Following are the available link states:

> **link** is the link as it normally appears before being clicked.

> **visited** is the link after the user clicks it to visit the page to which it is linked.

> **focus** is the link when it's highlighted, typically by tabbing to it.

> **hover** is the link with the mouse pointer over it.

> **active** is the link as the visitor clicks it.

To use a pseudo selector, type the element's name followed by a colon and the desired state. The following example shows a pseudo selector for the link <a> element in the hover state, along with a style declaration making the link green:

```
a:hover {color:green; }
```

Structural Pseudo Selectors

CSS3 introduces a host of structural pseudo selectors to target elements more precisely. Perhaps the most useful of the structural pseudo selectors is this:

> *element:nth-child()*

This selector targets any element that has the specified number of siblings before it. Inside the parentheses, you type an argument that controls how the selector functions. The argument can be a number, keyword, or formula. A number specifies which element in a series of children to target:

> *p:nth-child(4)*

This targets all p elements that are the fourth child of the parent element.

Keywords enable you to target all child elements that are odd or even, which comes in very handy if you want to add shading to alternate rows in a table:

> *tr:nth-child(odd)*

> *tr:nth-child(even)*

Formulas enable you to target child elements however you wish:

> *tr:nth-child(3n+3)*

This targets every third table row. The browser performs the calculations to determine which rows are targeted:

> $3 \times 0 + 3 = 3$
>
> $3 \times 1 + 3 = 6$
>
> $3 \times 2 + 3 = 9$
>
> $3 \times 3 + 3 = 12$
>
> $3 \times 4 + 3 = 15$

tr:nth-child(2n+1) is the same as *tr:nth-child(odd)* and *tr:nth-child(2n)* is the same as *tr:nth-child(even)*.

Table 10.1 lists and describes the structural pseudo selectors introduced in CSS3. All selectors that include parentheses at the end take arguments.

Table 10.1
CSS Structural Pseudo Selectors

Selector	Targets ...
element:root	The root element, which is the HTML element in a web document
element:nth-child()	Any element that has the specified number of siblings before it; for example; *p:nth-child (4)* targets p elements that are the fourth child of the parent element
element:nth-last-child()	Any element that has the specified number of siblings after it; works just like :nth-child() but counts back from the last child rather than forward from the first child
element:nth-of-type()	Any element that has the specified number of siblings of the same element type before it
element:nth-last-of-type()	Any element that has the specified number of siblings of the same element type after it
element:last-child	Any element that is the last child of its parent element; equivalent to *:nth-last-child(1)*
element:first-of-type	Any element that is the first sibling of its kind; equivalent to *:nth-of-type(1)*
element:last-of-type	Any element that is the last sibling of its kind; equivalent to *:nth-last-of-type(1)*
element:only-child	An element whose parent has no other children
element:only-of-type	An element whose parent has no other children of the same element type
element:empty	An element that has no children

UI Element States Pseudo Selectors

CSS3 introduces several user interface (UI) states pseudo selectors specifically for targeting form elements. Table 10.2 lists and describes these selectors.

Table 10.2
CSS Structural Pseudo Selectors

Selector	Targets Any Form Control That's ...
element:enabled	Enabled
element:disabled	Disabled
element:checked	Selected, as in the case of checkbox and radio button options

More CSS3 Pseudo Selectors

CSS3 has a couple more pseudo selectors you should know about:

Target matches any element that's a target of a referring URL. As explained in Chapter 6, you can link not only to a specific page but to any location on a page by inserting an anchor at that location. The target pseudo selector enables you to apply formatting to the selection marked as an anchor. For example:

```
dt:target {outline:2px solid black; }
```

This adds a 2px black border around any definition term that's marked as an anchor after the user clicks the link that accesses the anchor.

Negation targets any element that doesn't match the specified simple selector. For example:

```
:not(blockquote) {font-family:georgia; }
```

This specifies Georgia as the font family for all text elements except blockquotes.

Setting Style Properties with <div> and <span> Tags

The <div> and <span> tags enable you to apply styles when you don't have a convenient selector. Prior to HTML5, many web designers used the <div> tag, for example, to style headers, footers, navigation bars, articles, and asides. With the introduction of HTML5 structure tags, you no longer need to use <div> tags for those items, but <div> and <span> tags still come in very handy when you encounter similar situations in which you don't have a well-defined selector.

Here are the differences between the two tags:

- **<div>** is useful for styling sections of text typically containing two or more elements.

- **<span>** is best for styling *within* an element, such as a few words or a sentence within a paragraph. Consider it more like an inline style, such as <b> (bold) and <i> (italic).

You usually use the <div> and <span> tags with ID or class attributes. You add the ID or class attribute to the tag and then use an ID or class selector when creating the CSS style rule. Your HTML source code, for example, may include something like the following:

```
<div class="note">
<h2>Note</h2>
<p>Some domestic cats sleep up to 20 hours a day, so don't be
➥ concerned if your cat seems to be sleeping too much. </p>
</div>
```

You would then include a class selector style rule, such as the following, to format the division:

```
.note {background-color:yellow; padding:0px 10px; float:left;
➥ width:200px; border:2px solid #00cccc; }
```

Figure 10.2 shows the result.

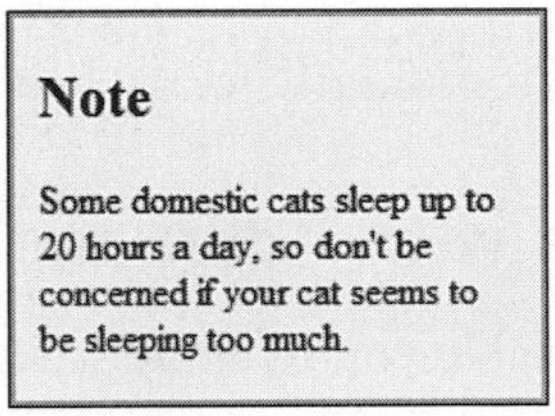

Note

Some domestic cats sleep up to 20 hours a day, so don't be concerned if your cat seems to be sleeping too much.

Figure 10.2: *The <div> tag is perfect for setting off text in boxes.*

Context Selectors: Combinators

You can select elements based on their relation to other elements, which is very useful in styling elements within larger elements, including <div>, <header>, <footer>, <section>, <article>, and <aside>. For example, you can have a paragraph's text look entirely different when the paragraph appears within a footer by using the footer selector as the context for the p selector:

```
footer p {font-size:.8em; color:#c0c0c0; }
```

Context selectors (officially known as *combinators*) can be very flexible, but can also be complicated in their contextual relationships (see Figure 10.3):

DEFINITION

A **combinator** consists of two simple selectors joined with a character that represents their relationship. Characters include a space, +, :, >, and ~.

Ancestor-descendant: In an ancestor-descendant relationship, the style is applied to all instances of the descendant element contained within its ancestor element. Here's an example of an ancestor-descendant selector:

```
article p {font-size:1.1em; }
```

Parent-child: The style is applied only to instances of descendant elements directly within the ancestor element, but not if the descendent appears inside another element within the ancestor. Here's an example of a parent-child selector:

```
article > p {font-size:1.1em; }
```

Parent-first child: The style is applied only to the first instance of a descendant element within the ancestor element. Here's an example of a parent-first child selector:

```
article p:first-child {font-size:1.1em; }
```

Adjacent siblings: An adjacent siblings selector consists of two simple selectors joined by a plus sign (+). The style is applied only to an instance of the second element directly following an instance of the first element when both elements have the same parent:

```
p+ul {font-size:1.1em; }
```

 General sibling: The style is applied to any instance of the second element following (but not necessarily directly following) the first element. Here's an example of an general sibling selector:

```
p~ul {font-size:1.1em; }
```

Both elements must have the same parent element, so they're siblings, but they need not be adjacent siblings.

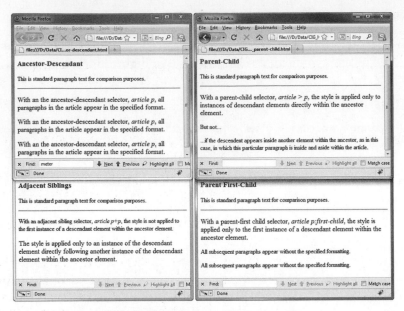

Figure 10.3: *Context selectors in action.*

Selecting Part of an Element

To select the first line or first letter of an element, type the tag's name followed by a colon and then *first-line* or *first-letter:*

```
p:first-letter {font-size:125%; }
```

Attribute Selectors

Almost all CSS style rules use tag, class, or ID selectors, so you can probably skip this section and blissfully ignore anything related to attribute selectors. In the off chance you can benefit from attribute selectors, however, Table 10.3 provides a list with a description of each. Keep in mind that attribute selectors use square brackets; for example, the selector for <img src="images/puppy.jpg" title="puppy" /> might be [puppy] or img[puppy].

Table 10.3
CSS Attribute Selectors

Selector	Matches Any ...
[attribute]	Element that contains the attribute; for example, [title]
a[attribute]	"a" element that contains the attribute; for example, a[title]
[attribute="value"]	Element that contains the attribute set to the specified value; for example, [title="Tip"]
[attribute~="value"]	Element that contains the attribute set to the specified value, even if the value contains spaces; for example, [title~=tip] would match elements with title="tip", title="quick tip", and title="tip for you", but not title="tips"
[attribute|="value"]	Element that contains the attribute set to the specified value, even if the value contains hyphens; for example, [title|=tip] would match elements with title="tip", title="quick-tip", and title="tip-for-you", but not title="quick tip" or title="tips"
[attribute^="valuebegins"]	Element that contains the attribute set to a value that begins with the specified text; for example, [lang^="en"] matches any element with the lang attribute's value beginning in "en"
[attribute$="valueends"]	Element that contains the attribute set to a value that ends with the specified text; for example, [src$=".jpg"] matches any element with the src attribute's value ending in .jpg
[attribute*="valuecontains"]	Element that contains the attribute set to a value that contains the specified text; for example, [title*="keep"] matches any element with the title attribute's value containing "keep," including title="keep", title="keepsake", and title="bookkeeper"

Attribute selectors are especially useful in applying CSS to form input fields because of the type of attribute used to specify the type of data for each field, including text, e-mail, date, time, password, submit, and button. Instead of creating several class selectors to format the various input types differently, you can use attribute selectors. For more about forms, check out Chapter 21.

Mix 'n' Match: Combining Selectors

If you need to get very specific about something you want to select, you can combine selectors. Just be sure to combine them in the proper order:

First: Context selector

Second: Element selector

Third: Class or ID selector

Fourth: Pseudo class selector

Fifth: Attribute selector

Grouping and Nesting Selectors

To streamline your CSS, you can group selectors, applying the same styles to two or more elements at a time. You can also nest selector to target elements more precisely. The following sections show you how.

Grouping Selectors

To apply the same formatting to two or more HTML elements or class or ID selectors, *group* the selectors. To group selectors, separate them with commas, as shown here:

```
h1, h2, h3, h4, h5, {color:#FF0000; }
```

This applies color #FF0000 (red) to h1, h2, h3, h4, and h5.

Keep in mind that you can still make these headings look different by using additional styles to adjust the size and/or enhancements for the different headings, such as underlining, boldface, and italics.

Nesting Selectors

To style an element one way most of the time and another way when it appears within a specific element, use a *nested selector*—a selector inside a selector.

Suppose you want most unordered lists to be bulleted lists, but when the unordered list appears in a sidebar, you want a list without bullets. You don't have to do anything to have bullets appear, because they appear by default. To remove the bullets in the sidebar, you'd use a nested selector, like this:

```
#sidebar ul {list-style-type:none; }
```

This tells the browser that whenever an unordered list appears within an element that has the id="sidebar" attribute, the list items should appear without bullets.

Specifying Dimensions: Pixels, Percentages, and More

Much of the formatting you're likely to do includes specifying the size, dimensions, and positions of elements, including text, margins, boxes, borders, padding, columns, and rows. With CSS, you can specify your preferred measurement units, but most web designers stick with px (pixels), em, and % (percentage).

Here are the units from which you can choose:

- **px** (pixel) is a dot on the computer screen and is the unit of measure for when you want to be precise and have more control over size and dimensions.

- **em** (em unit) is equivalent to the current font size. 1cm is the font size, 2em is double the font size, and so on. In other words, size varies depending on the default font style and size. This makes the em unit very useful in CSS because if the user chooses to change the font style or size in the browser, everything on the page automatically scales up or down to accommodate the change.

- **ex** (ex unit) is equivalent to the height of the font, which is typically about half the font size.

- **%** (percentage) is sort of like em in that it's relative. This comes in handy for sizing columns, for example, because you can make column widths a percentage of the window width. If the user resizes the window, the column widths adjust accordingly.

- **in** (inch) is an absolute unit in inches.

- **cm** (centimeter) is an absolute unit in centimeters.

- **mm** (millimeter) is an absolute unit in millimeters.

- **pt** (point) is an absolute unit in points—an inch is approximately 72 points. Points are useful in specifying font size, if you're accustomed to working with point sizes in a word processing program, for example.

- **pc** (pica) is an absolute unit equivalent to 12 points.

Adding Comments: FYI Only

Whenever you're working with styles, consider adding comments to describe what each style does. This makes it much easier for you or someone else to find and modify styles later. To add a comment, simply type your comment, enclosing it between /* and */. Here's an example:

```
/* Center footer */
footer {text-align:center; }
```

Understanding How This Cascading Thing Works

Styles from various sources can influence the appearance of a web page. Browsers have their own internal style sheets that control the default appearance of elements on a page. You can apply three different levels of styles (external, internal, or inline) that enhance or override browser styles. And in most browsers, users can adjust settings or even apply their own CSS style sheets to enhance or override your styles.

The *cascading* part of this is that styles can enhance one another, sort of like layering transparencies on an overhead projector. Suppose you create a style like h1 {font-color:blue; } and the browser's built-in styles are already set to display h1 headings in 32px serif bold. When your style is applied, the text remains in 32px serif bold and your style adds the blue.

In cases in which styles conflict (for example, if the browser style for the h1 element specifies a 32px font size and your style calls for a 24px font), specific criteria govern which style declaration takes precedence:

Inheritance: With certain properties, an element inside another element inherits its properties, so if you bold some text in a paragraph, the bold text appears just like the rest of the text in the paragraph, except it's bold. Some properties, such as border, are not inherited.

Specificity: The more specific selector takes precedence; for example, styles applied via a class selector take precedence over styles applied via a tag selector. The ID selector is the most specific.

Location: If style conflicts can't be determined by inheritance and specificity, the location criterion kicks in. Styles that come later in the cascade sequence take precedence. For example, if you create an external style sheet and then apply a conflicting style via an internal style sheet, the declarations in the internal style sheet take precedence.

You can force specific properties in a style to take precedence over others regardless of the criteria. To force an element to inherit a property, add the property to the element's style rule and setting its value to inherit, like so:

```
p.border {border:inherit; }
```

To give a property precedence regardless of its location, add *!important* to the end of the rule, as shown here:

```
p {text-indent:1.5em !important }
```

WHOA!

Browser support for styles introduced in CSS3 varies. Some browsers do not support certain features, while others may require a prefix, such as –moz- for the Mozilla Firefox browser or –webkit- for WebKit-enabled browsers including Safari and Google Chrome. Throughout this book, we point out properties that may require prefixes. See Chapter 24 for additional details on making your web pages compatible with different browsers.

The Least You Need to Know

- Follow this model when creating style rules:

  ```
  selector {property:value; property:value; property:value; }
  ```

- To create an external style sheet, create a text-only file with the filename extension .css.

- To link to an external style sheet, type a link tag between the opening and closing <head> tags in the HTML document, like so:

  ```
  <link rel="style sheet" type="text/css" href="styles.css" />
  ```

- A tag selector consists of the HTML element's tag without the brackets; for example, the *p* is the <p> tag selector.

- Use class selectors with a tag selector to apply different styles to the same element; for example, *p.center*.

Saving Time with a CSS Theme

In This Chapter

- Understanding what a CSS theme is
- Digging up attractive, functional themes
- Customizing a theme to suit your tastes
- Using Firebug to identify and troubleshoot styles

You can certainly build your own custom style sheets from the ground up, but you can save time by choosing a theme that's pretty close to what you want and then customizing it. In the process, you tend to learn a great deal about CSS simply by seeing how other designers use it.

This chapter introduces you to CSS themes, shows you where to find free and premier (not free) themes, and illustrates how you edit styles to customize a theme. In addition, you find out how to use a nifty Mozilla Firefox plug-in called Firebug that enables you to explore styles at work on web pages and experiment with them so you can mimic styles on other web pages.

What Is a CSS Theme?

A CSS theme (template) consists of one or more style sheets that control the appearance and layout of a site, as shown in Figure 11.1.

Most themes also contain scripts that add functionality to the site, especially if the theme is designed for a content management system (CMS), such as WordPress.

```
style.css - Notepad
File  Edit  Format  View  Help
/*
Theme Name: Twenty Ten
Theme URI: http://wordpress.org/
Description: The 2010 theme for WordPress is stylish, customizable, simple, and readable -- make it yours with a custom
menu, header image, and background. Twenty Ten supports six widgetized areas (two in the sidebar, four in the footer)
and featured images (thumbnails for gallery posts and custom header images for posts and pages). It includes stylesheets
for print and the admin visual Editor, special styles for posts in the "Asides" and "Gallery" categories, and has an
optional one-column page template that removes the sidebar.
Author: the WordPress team
Version: 1.1
Tags: black, blue, white, two-columns, fixed-width, custom-header, custom-background, threaded-comments, sticky-post,
translation-ready, microformats, rtl-language-support, editor-style
*/


/* =Reset default browser CSS. Based on work by Eric Meyer: http://meyerweb.com/eric/tools/css/reset/index.html
-------------------------------------------------------------- */

html, body, div, span, applet, object, iframe,
h1, h2, h3, h4, h5, h6, p, blockquote, pre,
a, abbr, acronym, address, big, cite, code,
del, dfn, em, font, img, ins, kbd, q, s, samp,
small, strike, strong, sub, sup, tt, var,
b, u, i, center,
dl, dt, dd, ol, ul, li,
fieldset, form, label, legend,
table, caption, tbody, tfoot, thead, tr, th, td {
        background: transparent;
        border: 0;
        margin: 0;
        padding: 0;
        vertical-align: baseline;
}
body {
        line-height: 1;
}
h1, h2, h3, h4, h5, h6 {
        clear: both;
        font-weight: normal;
}
ol, ul {
        list-style: none;
}
blockquote {
        quotes: none;
}
blockquote:before, blockquote:after {
        content: '';
        content: none;
}
del {
        text-decoration: line-through;
}
```

Figure 11.1: *A CSS theme controls the site's appearance and layout.*

WHOA!

Learning from someone else's design and taking the design are entirely different. If the designer is not specifically offering a template as free and customizable, either pay the requested licensing fee to use it or ask for permission. Using or adapting someone else's design without permission is unethical and might land you in legal trouble.

Finding and Trying on Different Themes

Trying different themes on your site is about as easy as trying on different suits. Themes have absolutely no effect on the content of your site, but a theme can completely change the appearance and layout of elements on each and every page. The following sections show you how to track down themes and try them out to find one that suits your tastes.

Qualities of a Good CSS Theme

Don't judge a theme solely by its appearance. A great-looking theme can be very buggy. When browsing theme collections, consider the following qualities of a good theme:

Good looking: Appearance is key, but layout is more important than colors because colors are easier to change. Pay special attention to the number of columns. Do you want pages divided into 1, 2, 3, or 4 columns?

CSS based: Not all themes are built with CSS. Some are Flash based, so be sure you're getting a CSS theme.

Positive rankings and reviews: Many theme libraries include rankings and reviews of themes in the collection. Steer clear of any themes with negative or even lukewarm reviews or ratings. These themes are usually buggy or difficult to customize.

Support for your CMS's features: Some themes don't support features built into the CMS they're designed for, including widgets and the ability to upload custom header images. You can usually tell by reading reviews if a theme doesn't support a popular feature of the CMS.

Well-commented style sheets: Open style.css and any other .css files included with the theme, and be sure it contains comments describing what each style or group of styles does. Comments help immensely in customizing the template.

Minimal images: Some themes look great only because they use lots of images. Numerous images can slow down your site and make customizing the theme difficult.

Feature-rich: Many themes add functionality to the CMS. Some themes, for example, provide options for changing the layout to use 1, 2, or 3 columns. They may also include the ability to change the color scheme with a single click, additional fields you can fill out when publishing a page or post to help with search engine optimization (SEO), and more.

Checking Out Free Themes

Regardless of which CMS you use, it comes with one or two standard themes to get you started. In addition, designers often create their own themes and make them available for free. You may be able to access these free themes via your CMS's dashboard or control panel. In WordPress, for example, you log in to the dashboard, click **Themes**, and click the **Install Themes** tab to view a page that enables you to search for themes (see Figure 11.2).

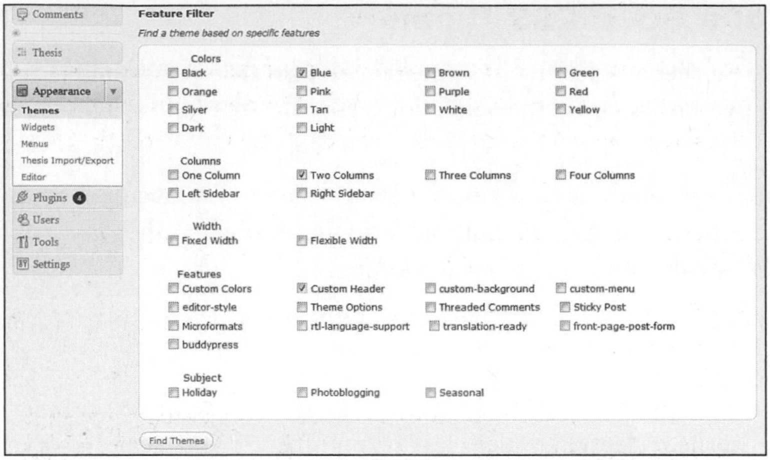

Figure 11.2: *You can search for themes from the WordPress dashboard.*

You can also go to the CMS's home page and search from there: Joomla! (joomla.org), WordPress (wordpress.org), concrete5 (concrete5.org), and Drupal (drupal.org).

> **INSIDE TIP**
>
> You can find plenty of free CSS template galleries on the web. Use your favorite search engine to search for "free css themes" or "free css templates". To find themes designed for a specific CMS, add the CMS name to your search; for example, "free wordpress themes" or "free joomla themes".

Purchasing a Premium Theme

Premium themes are professional grade with a price tag attached, typically in the range of $25 to $75. In addition to a professional design, premium themes often include additional features. The Thesis theme for WordPress, for example, includes its own control panel that enables you to quickly and easily customize your site without having to edit style rules. (Knowing CSS is still very helpful in making changes you can't make through the control panel.)

To find premium themes on the web, replace "free" in your search phrase with "premium"; for example, "premium wordpress themes" or "premium drupal themes". If you're using WordPress, check out premiumwp.com, where you can find links to several of the top premium WordPress template developers, including Solostream, Thesis, and WooThemes.

Installing and Activating a Theme

The procedure for installing a theme varies depending on your CMS. In WordPress, for example, you log in to the dashboard, click **Themes**, and click the **Install Themes** tab, where you can search for and install themes directly from the dashboard, as shown in Figure 11.3.

Figure 11.3: *You can find and install themes from the WordPress dashboard.*

If you can't download and install themes from your CMS, you can typically download the theme you want to use and unzip the theme files into a separate folder on your computer. You then use your FTP program to upload the folder containing the theme files to the themes directory on your web server. Upon completion of the upload, you must then log in to your CMS and activate the theme.

Premium themes may have additional setup options, typically explained on the theme developer's site, in a readme.txt file included with the theme's files, or both. Be sure to check for specific instructions.

Personalizing the Theme

A theme is rarely everything you want it to be right out of the box. You may not like the color scheme, the space between paragraphs or list items, the font style, the size or appearance of the heading, and so on. Fortunately, you can make adjustments. The following sections show you how.

Editing Styles Directly

Every theme contains one or more style sheets you can open from your CMS or in any text editor. You can then edit style rules, delete rules, and add your own rules to fully customize the appearance and layout of your web pages, as shown in Figure 11.4.

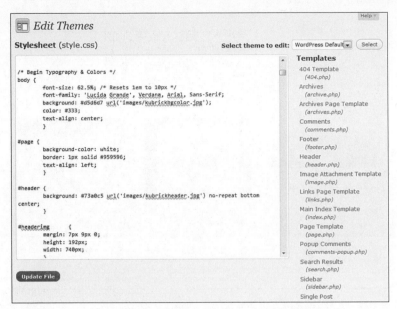

Figure 11.4: *Edit styles in .css files.*

WHOA!

Keep a written record of all the changes you make. If the change is relatively minor, you can add a comment enclosed between /* and */. Instead of deleting a style rule, comment it out by typing /* before it and */ after it. If you need to make a major change to a style, copy and paste the style, comment out the original, and edit the copy. A minor mistake can have major repercussions on your site; by keeping a written record of your changes, troubleshooting problems later is much easier.

Tweaking Settings in a Premium Theme

In premium themes, you may be able to customize the appearance and layout of your site—at least to some degree—without ever touching the style rules. In Thesis, for example, you can change to a 1-, 2-, or 3-column layout; change the background color; choose different fonts; and style various elements, including the navigation menu, header, footer, and content area all by selecting options rather than editing styles, as shown in Figure 11.5.

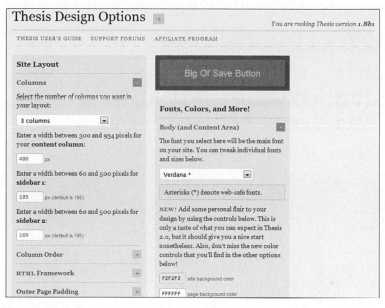

Figure 11.5: *Some premium themes, such as Thesis, simplify customization.*

Making More Changes in Premium Themes

Premium themes may simplify the process of making the most common changes to a site, such as the number of columns and the color scheme, but you may need to go behind the scenes and edit the CSS style rules yourself to make less-common adjustments.

In the Thesis theme, for example, you can make changes by editing two files: custom.css and custom_functions.php. To modify a style rule, you add the class selector *.custom* to the beginning of the existing selector for the element you want to format and then add your declaration. For example, to add 10 pixels of space after list items in the content area, you would add the following to the custom.css file:

```
.custom #content li {padding-bottom:10px; }
```

Making adjustments using the custom_functions.php file is more difficult and risky, but it enables you to make more fundamental changes to the theme, such as moving the navigation bar. To make changes, you use *hooks* to indicate where elements need to be positioned or to replace existing functions with your own custom functions. Using hooks to customize a theme is beyond the scope of this book, but realize that this may be an option in some premium themes. (For details on how to use hooks in WordPress, check out codex.wordpress.org/Plugin_API.)

Identifying Styles at Work: Behind the Scenes

You face two major challenges when working with CSS:

- Figuring out which selector is being used to apply formatting to an element.

- Identifying the formatting that's responsible for making an element appear as it does.

These challenges are especially difficult when you're trying to learn how another designer made an element appear a certain way. Fortunately, a plug-in called Firebug is available for the Mozilla Firefox web browser. Firebug reveals the HTML and CSS working behind the scenes. This valuable tool even enables you to experiment with the CSS to change the appearance of elements.

The following sections show you how to get Firebug up and running and use it to inspect and experiment with CSS style rules on your site and others.

Downloading and Installing Firefox and Firebug

If you use a web browser other than Mozilla Firefox, the first order of business is to download and install Firefox. Use your current browser to go to mozilla.com/firefox, click the **Free Download** button, and follow the on-screen instructions to download and install Firefox.

To install Firebug, run Firefox, click **Tools, Addons, Get Addons**, search for "firebug", and follow the on-screen cues to install Firebug. You must then restart Firefox to enable the new add-on.

Inspecting Elements and Styles with Firebug

You can't always tell what an element on a web page is or how it's styled just by look-ing at it, but you can tell by looking at it through Firebug's eyes. Here's how:

1. Run Firefox, and open the page that contains the HTML element you want to inspect.

2. In the lower-right corner of the window, click the Firebug icon. This displays two panes at the bottom of the window: one shows the page's HTML and the other shows the CSS style rules (see Figure 11.6).

3. Click the **Inspect Element** icon in Firebug's toolbar (just to the right of the bug).

4. Mouseover the element you want to inspect. Firebug displays a box around the element. Remember that many elements are embedded in other elements, so be sure the box is around the correct element. (You can also select ele-ments by clicking them in the HTML pane.)

5. When the box is around the correct element, click the mouse button to select it. Firefox displays the style rule for the selected element in the right pane.

6. To verify whether a style declaration is doing what you think it's doing, rest the mouse pointer on the style declaration and then click the circle with the line through it that appears to the left of it. This disables the style declara-tion, so you can see whether the element changed as you expected it would.

7. To change a style declaration, click it and type your change. Firebug immedi-ately applies the new style declaration to the element.

8. To add a style declaration, double-click inside the curly brackets for the element's selector and then type your declaration in the form *property:value*. Firebug applies the new declaration.

9. Make note of your style changes, so you can make the changes to your style sheets.

None of the style changes you make in Firebug are permanent. They simply affect the appearance of the page as displayed in Firefox at this moment.

Selected HTML element   Selection box

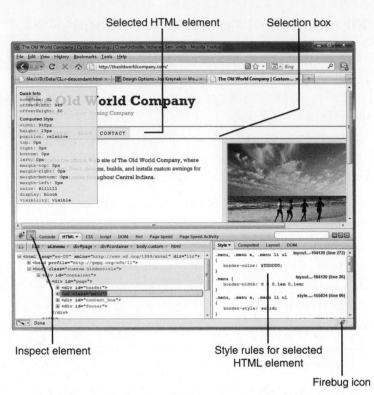

Inspect element   Style rules for selected
                                        HTML element

                                              Firebug icon

Figure 11.6: *Inspect HTML elements with Firebug.*

INSIDE TIP

Numerous Firefox add-ons are available for designing, testing, and fine-tuning websites. Visit addons.mozilla.org to check out what's available.

The Least You Need to Know

- When choosing a CSS theme, consider more than looks, including ratings, reviews, and support for the CMS you use.
- Search for themes on your CMS's website and via your favorite web search engine.
- You may be able to customize a theme by adjusting settings using its control panel.

- To customize most themes, you must edit the CSS style rules in the theme's .css files.

- Get Firebug and use it to inspect HTML elements and the CSS style rules responsible for the way they're formatted.

Giving Your Text a Makeover

Chapter 12

In This Chapter

- Tips for picking a font and font size
- Making text bold or italic
- Giving your text color
- Adding drop-shadows for a 3D effect
- Exploring other text and font formatting options

Chapter 4 shows you how to make text appear bold or italic through the use of HTML tags, but HTML is not geared for any heavy-duty text formatting. Text formatting is CSS's job. Using a variety of CSS font and text properties and their numerous values, you can take complete control over the appearance of all text elements, including body text, headings, lists, and blockquotes.

This chapter shows you how to format text using the CSS font and text properties and their associated values.

Applying Font Formatting

The *font* property enables you to choose a *font family* (such as Arial or Times New Roman), font weight (bold or not), type size, and style (italic or not). The following sections show you how to use the *font* property to control the appearance of text.

DEFINITION

The term **font family** refers to the appearance of text regardless of size, weight, color, or style.

Choosing a Font Family

Unless you specify your preference, the font family is determined by the web browser's default font-family setting. Unless you specify the font family, each user's browser has total control over which font to use when displaying your site's text.

Several font families are considered web-safe because they reside on both Windows and Mac OS computers. These fonts are Arial, Arial Black, Comic Sans MS, Courier New, Georgia, Lucida Console, Tahoma, Times New Roman, Trebuchet MS, and Verdana. See Figure 12.1.

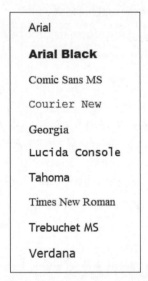

Figure 12.1: *Web-safe font families.*

To declare a font family, include the *font-family* property along with the name of the desired font family in the style rule. Better yet, declare your top two or three font families, in order of preference, followed by a generic font family: serif, sans-serif, or monospace. If a font-family name is two or more words, enclose the words in quotation marks. Here's an example:

```
body {font-family:Verdana, Georgia, "Times New Roman", serif; }
```

The generic font family declaration at the end instructs the browser to choose a font in that font family if none of the specified font families is present.

Here's a breakdown of the different types of font families:

- Serif fonts have small lines on the ends of many characters. Times New Roman and Georgia are examples of serif fonts.

- Sans-serif fonts have no small lines on the ends of characters, such as Comic Sans and Tahoma.

- Monospace fonts have characters all the same width, such as Lucida Console.

Making a Font Bigger or Smaller

HTML isn't meant to control font size. You can choose an element with a larger font size (for example, an <h1> compared to a <p>), but that doesn't allow for very precise sizing. Fortunately, CSS provides a *font-size* property that gives you more control. To specify a font size, create a style rule that includes the *font-size* property followed by the desired size, like so:

```
ul li {font-size:10px; }
```

You can specify font size using an absolute or relative unit. Absolute units are:

- px (pixel)
- in (inch)
- cm (centimeter)
- mm (millimeter)
- pt (point)
- pc (pica)

If you specify a size in an absolute unit, that's the size it appears.

Relative units are:

- em (width of one character)
- ex (height of one character)
- % (percentage)

If you specify a size in a relative unit, the size depends on the size of something else; for example, .75em is three quarters of the default font size.

> **NOTE**
>
> In the past, the difference between absolute and relative font sizes was significant because browsers did not scale absolute units. Now, most browsers scale regardless of unit as the user zooms in or out.

Specifying a Font Weight: How Bold Should You Go?

You can use the HTML <b> and <strong> tags to make small selections of text appear bold on a page, but if you want to make an element appear bold throughout your site, use a CSS style rule to apply the *font-weight* property to the element, like so:

```
p.important {font-weight:bold; }
```

The *font-weight* property has several values in addition to bold:

- **normal** is the default.
- **bold** makes characters appear darker and thicker.
- **bolder** makes characters appear even darker and even thicker.
- **lighter** makes characters appear lighter/thinner than normal.
- **100, 200, 300, 400, 500, 600, 700, 800,** or **900** specifies the relative thickness, with *400* equal to normal and *700* the same as bold.

Choosing a Font Style (Italics)

HTML provides the <i> and <em> tags to italicize selections of text on a web page. To italicize an element throughout your site, add the *font-style* property to the element's style rule. Here's an example:

```
footer {font-style:italic; }
```

The *font-style* property has three different values: normal, italic, and oblique (but oblique is so obscure, it's best to ignore it).

Specifying Web Fonts with @*font-face*

Web-safe fonts can be rather restrictive, especially for the most creative minds. To unshackle yourself from this limitation, consider embedding the special font you want to use with the @*font-face* property. Simply upload the font you want to use to a directory on your web server, and use the @*font-face* property to refer to the font. Here's an example:

```
@font-face {font-family:AwesomeFont;
   ➡ src:url('fonts/AwesomeFont.ttf'); }
```

I bet you're wondering where to go to get cool fonts. One place is the Google Font Directory at code.google.com/webfonts. You don't even need to upload the font file to a directory on your web server. All you do is choose the desired font, click **Get the code**, and copy and paste the required <link> tag between the opening and closing <head> tags on your web pages. When someone opens your page, the <link> tag lets the browser know where the font-family files are located.

You can find plenty of free web fonts online. Use your favorite web search tool to search for "free web fonts". For professional web fonts, search for "purchase web fonts".

Applying the Small Caps Variant

You probably don't want to present huge blocks of text in all uppercase characters, but formatting small blocks of text, such as headings, in small caps can add a nice touch. To format text in small caps, add *font-variant:small-caps* to the element's style rule, as shown below:

```
h2 {font-variant:small-caps; }
```

Figure 12.2 shows a sample <h1> without and with small caps.

Without Small Caps Variant

With Small Caps Variant

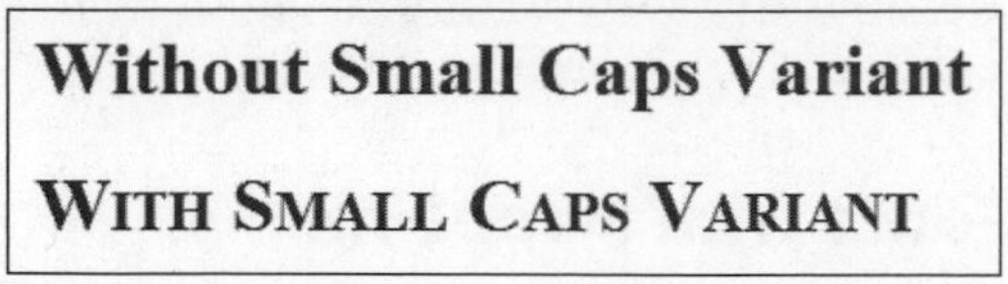

Figure 12.2: *Heading without and with small caps.*

Like the *font-style* property, *font-variant* has a couple other values you can safely ignore: normal and inherit.

Applying All Font Formatting in a Single Declaration

Use the *font* property to apply all font formatting within a single declaration. Your font declaration must include the font-style and font-family values but may include other font properties as well. Start with *font* and then specify the values in the following order, replacing the property names with the desired value for each property:

```
body p {font:font-style font-variant font-weight
    ➡ font-size/line-height font-family; }
```

Here's an example:

```
body p {font:italic small-caps bolder 12px/18px "comic sans ms",
    ➡ sans; }
```

NOTE

When using this shorthand method of applying font formatting, you need not include the font property names, only the values. The browser can determine the property based on the value and its relative position in the declaration.

Applying Text Formatting

Text formatting controls various characteristics of text, including color, line height, letter spacing, horizontal and vertical alignment, indents, word spacing, and text shadow. The following sections show you how to apply text formatting.

Coloring Your Text

Changing text color is easy. Add the *color* property to the element's style rule followed by the desired *color value*. Here's an example:

```
h1 {color:red; }
```

Color values can take several forms:

Color name: You can specify some colors by name; for example, *color:purple*. Check out the color insert for a complete list of named colors.

Hex code: This six-character code consisting of numbers 0 through 9 and letters A through F represents one of more than 16 million colors; for example, *color:#ADFF2F* for *greenishyellow*.

RGB value: A combination of three values, each 0 to 255, this represents a specific mixture of red, green, and blue; for example, *color:rgb(173,255,47)* for *greenishyellow*.

For more about colors, see Chapter 13 and the color insert.

Aligning and Indenting Text

By default, text is aligned left. You can center, right-align, or justify text using the *text-align* property. Here's an example:

```
p.news {text-align:justify; }
```

To indent the first line of an element, such as the first line in a paragraph, use the *text-indent* property, like so:

```
p {text-indent:.5in; }
```

Adjusting Line Height

You can adjust the line height to have more or less space between lines of text in an element such as a paragraph. To do so, add the *line-height* property to the element's style declaration. The following example double-spaces the text:

```
p.double {line-height:2; }
```

You can use any of the following values with the *line-height* property:

- **number** multiplies the number by the current font size to determine line spacing.

- **length** specifies a fixed line height in px, pt, pc, and so on.

- **%** makes the line height a percentage of the current font size.

Adjusting Letter and Word Spacing

To increase or decrease the space between characters, add the *letter-spacing* property to the element's style declaration, and set its value to the desired amount of space. Here's an example:

```
h3 {letter-spacing:3px; }
```

The *word-spacing* property works in much the same way. Add the *word-spacing* property to the element's style declaration, and set its value to the desired amount of space; for example:

```
h1 {word-spacing:10px; }
```

Decorating Your Text

Don't get too excited when you see the term "decorating." In CSS, the *text-decoration* property has four humdrum values:

- **underline**
- **overline** (a line above the text)
- **line-through** (another name for strikethrough)
- **blink** (which is too annoying to use)

To "decorate" your text, add a *text-decoration* property to the element's style rule, like so:

```
h4 {text-decoration:underline; }
```

Uppercasing and Lowercasing Text

You usually uppercase or lowercase text when typing it, but the *text-transform* property enables you to control case via a style rule. Simply add the *text-transform* property to a text element's style rule, specifying your capitalization preference:

- **capitalize** capitalizes the first character of each word.

- **uppercase** capitalizes all of the text.

- **lowercase** lowercases all of the text.

Here's an example:

```
h1 {text-transform:capitalize; }
```

Going 3D with Text Shadowing

To make text appear as though it's floating above the page and casting a shadow on the page, use the *text-shadow* property with the following four values in this order:

- color

- *x*-coordinate

- *y*-coordinate

- blur radius

Here's an example:

```
h1 {text-shadow:gray -2px 2px 5px; }
```

The negative *x*-coordinate value positions the shadow slightly left. The positive *y*-coordinate value positions the shadow slightly lower than the text. The blur radius makes the shadow more or less blurry. Figure 12.3 shows several variations of text shadowing in action.

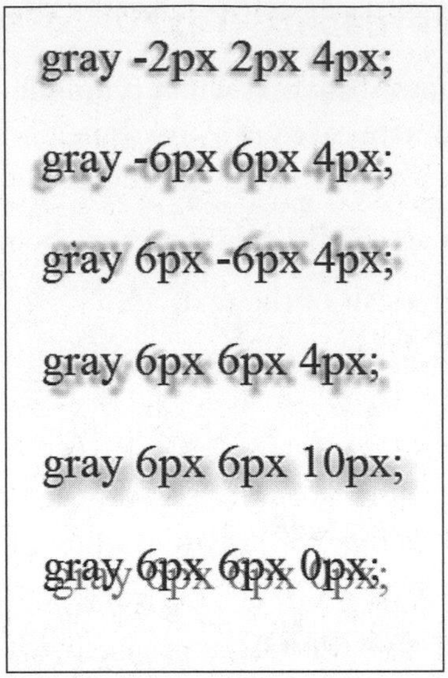

Figure 12.3: *Add drop-shadows to give your text an added dimension.*

Aligning Text Vertically

You can move an inline element up or down in relation to surrounding text, which is especially handy for formatting subscripts and superscripts. By default, the bottom of an inline element is positioned on the baseline—the imaginary line on which text sits. To adjust the vertical position of an inline element, add the *vertical-align* property to the element's style rule, like so:

```
.sup {vertical-align:super; }
```

You can specify your vertical alignment preference using any of the following values:

- A measurement, such as px or em; use a negative value to drop the element below the baseline.

- **baseline** is the default setting.

- **sub** creates a subscript.

- **super** creates a superscript.

- **top** aligns the top of the element with the top of the tallest element in the line.

- **text-top** aligns the element with the top of the parent element's font.

- **middle** centers the element vertically.

- **bottom** aligns the bottom of the element with the lowest element in the line.

- **text-bottom** aligns the element with the bottom of the parent element's font.

Managing Text Overflow

When you try to stuff text into boxes, you may end up with some unexpected and undesirable effects. If a word is too long to fit in the box, it may flow right out of the box. Also, if you try to stuff too much text into a box with a fixed height, the text at the end may not fit and is simply not shown.

Fortunately, CSS has solutions for these problems. To prevent a long word from running out over the side of a box, add the *word-wrap:break-word* declaration to the text's style rule. This enables long words to be broken and placed on two or more lines, as shown in Figure 12.4.

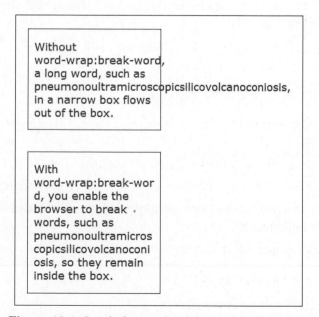

Figure 12.4: *Let the browser break long words, if necessary.*

To overcome the problem of having more text in a box than fits, add the *overflow* property to the style rule for the element that contains the text. You can set the *overflow* property to any of the following values:

- **visible** to have excess text appear outside the box
- **hidden** to clip the excess content so it's not visible
- **scroll** to display one or more scroll bars when necessary
- **auto** to let the browser choose

 If you set overflow to hidden, consider adding the *text-overflow:ellipsis* declaration to the element that contains the text. If the element is too small to contain all the text you add, excess text is hidden, but an ellipsis (…) appears, indicating that some of the text is not displayed.

> **NOTE**
>
> You can specify the type of scrollbar to display by using *overflow-x* to display a horizontal scroll bar or *overflow-y* to display a vertical scroll bar, instead of using just *overflow*.

The Least You Need to Know

- Use the *font-family* property to specify your font preference(s) for a text element.
- Use *font-size* to specify the font size for a text element.
- To make a text element a certain color, add the *color* property to its style rule.
- To align text, use the *text-align* property along with the desired alignment value: left, center, right, or justify.
- To double-space a text element, add line-height:2 to the element's style rule.

Adding a Splash of Color

In This Chapter

- Designing a color-coordinated site
- Simplifying your job with a color scheme generator
- Converting colors to codes and vice versa
- Making colors see-through

Even without adding any eye-popping graphics, you can significantly enhance your site's appearance by colorizing it. Using CSS, you can colorize all sorts of elements—text, borders, backgrounds, navigation bars, sidebars … you name it. The process of applying colors is a snap. The more challenging aspect is figuring out which colors to use.

In this chapter, I introduce you to the color wheel, which can help in choosing colors that look attractive together, provide guidance on choosing a color scheme that's attractive and functional, and hook you up with a few free tools that'll make your life a whole lot easier.

Of course, discussing colors while showing examples in gray scale is a little odd, so please reference the color insert as you read through this chapter.

Taking a Spin on the Color Wheel

If you've never met the color wheel, or you can't recall what you learned in fourth-grade art class, you're in for a treat. This wheel will completely revolutionize the way you see the world and perhaps even make your home or apartment look a little nicer. The color wheel can do all this by unlocking the secret of which colors look best together.

As shown in Figure 13.1 and in the first few images of the color insert, the color wheel doesn't look like much, but that's not the point. Its value is in how you use it.

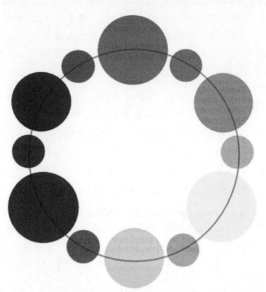

Figure 13.1: *The color wheel.*

The following sections show you how to use the color wheel to gain a clearer understanding of how colors work together and to begin thinking in terms of color schemes. I also show you how to create neutral colors and adjust color saturation and value to modify "pure" colors.

Checking Out the Primary Colors

Primary colors are those you mix to get all the other colors in the rainbow. Which colors are primary depends on the color model you're looking at.

Additive: The additive color model, or RGB (red, green, blue) color model, uses light to display colors. Hence, it's commonly used for computer displays. Adding red, green, and blue in equal proportions results in white.

Subtractive: The subtractive color model, or CMYK (cyan, magenta, yellow, black), uses ink to display colors. Hence, it's commonly used for printing. Subtracting all the colors leaves the paper white—assuming, of course, you're printing on white paper.

Keeping It Simple

The most basic color scheme is *achromatic*—no color, just black, white, and shades of gray. An achromatic scheme may sound boring, but it can be used very effectively. Many sites associated with weddings, for example, use a black-and-white scheme to convey a sense of formal elegance. In addition, just because your color scheme is black and white doesn't mean your site needs a complete absence of color. You can use photos and other graphics to add touches of color to the scheme.

Another very basic color scheme is *monochromatic*—one color along with black, white, and shades of gray. The color insert contains examples of both achromatic and monochromatic designs.

INSIDE TIP

Although monochromatic schemes are very basic, they can be very powerful and elegant. That one splash of color can really draw attention to the one thing on your page you don't want visitors to miss.

Nuancing Your Scheme with Analogous Colors

Analogous colors are those adjacent to each other on the color wheel, as shown in Figure 13.2 and the color insert. You usually use one color as dominant and the analogous colors on either side of it to enrich the scheme without adding much contrast.

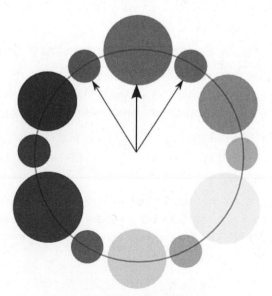

Figure 13.2: *Analogous colors.*

Pairing Up Complementary Colors

Complementary colors are those directly across from one another on the color wheel, as shown in Figure 13.3 and the color insert. They always look good together and provide plenty of contrast. Common complementary color pairs are red-green, blue-orange, and purple-yellow.

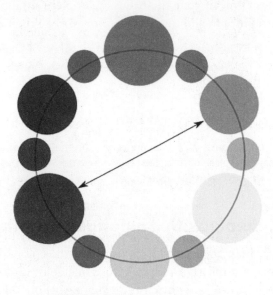

Figure 13.3: *Complementary colors.*

Adding Variety with a Split Complementary Scheme

A split complementary color scheme consists of a color and the two colors adjacent to its complementary color, as shown in Figure 13.4 and the color insert. This scheme provides almost as much contrast as a complementary scheme but with more variation.

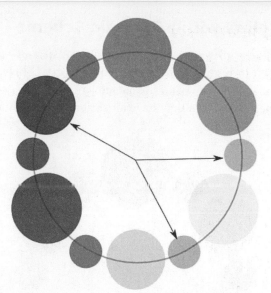

Figure 13.4: *A split complementary color scheme.*

Achieving Rich Contrast and Balance with a Triadic Scheme

A triadic color scheme consists of any three colors equidistant on the color wheel, as shown in Figure 13.5 and the color insert. This scheme provides less contrast than a complementary scheme but more variation and balance.

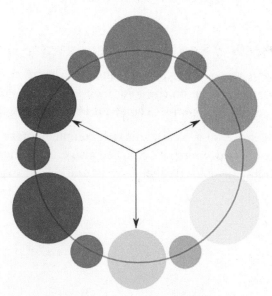

Figure 13.5: *A triadic color scheme.*

Juggling Four Colors with a Tetradic Scheme

A tetradic or double complementary color scheme consists of two sets of complementary colors, as shown in Figure 13.6 and the color insert. This scheme provides the most variation, but keeping the colors balanced can be quite a challenge. By using one color more than the others, you may have an easier time maintaining balance.

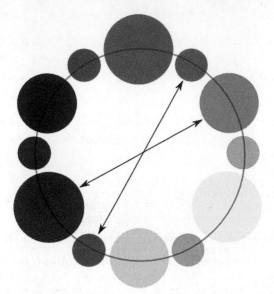

Figure 13.6: *A tetradic color scheme.*

Creating Neutral Colors

Neutral colors—beige, brown, gray, cream, and other earth tones—are bland. Although not the most exciting on the color block, neutral colors look good with other colors and are often the perfect choice for backgrounds.

To create neutral colors, you typically mix two complementary colors or the three primary colors in various proportions. You can also create neutrals by sucking the color out of just about any color (reducing its saturation), as explained in the following section.

Adjusting Hue, Saturation, and Value

As you work with colors and color schemes, you're likely to encounter not only the RGB and CMYK color models, but also the three color dimensions. In many graphics programs and some website templates, you choose colors by specifying dimensions of *hue*, *saturation*, and *value* (see Figure 13.7):

- **Hue:** The color itself—blue, green, yellow, or whatever.

- **Saturation:** Color intensity. Crank up a color's saturation setting to make it more intense. Dial it down for a more muted effect. When you dial down saturation, it's like adding black to it; at the highest possible saturation setting, a color appears black.

- **Value:** Color lightness or how washed out a color appears. When you crank up the color value, it's like adding white; at the highest possible value, a color appears white.

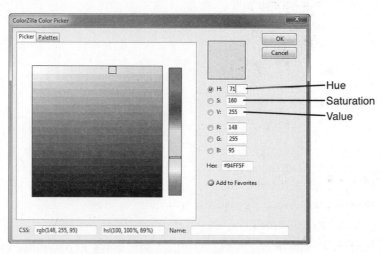

Figure 13.7: *Specify a color's dimensions.*

DEFINITION

Hue is the characteristic that categorizes a specific color blue, red, green, or whatever color it happens to be. **Saturation** refers to the intensity of a color—its purity and strength in the absence of white or black. **Value** refers to how light or dark a color appears.

Coming Up with an Attractive Color Scheme

Now that you have a fundamental understanding of colors, you can begin to choose an attractive color scheme for your site. You can go about developing a color scheme in any number of ways. In the following sections, I offer suggestions.

Considering Color Associations

Colors may make your site look pretty, but colors have emotional values that tend to have deep cultural roots. In the United States, when most people see pink, they think pretty or baby girl. See red, and they think passion and love, or the flip side—rage and evil. Green signifies affluence, rebirth, and freshness. Blue represents corporate professionalism and evokes trust.

Some colors are considered warm while others are cool. Warm colors such as purple, red, and orange heat things up. Cool colors like blue, green, and yellow tend to cool things down and calm the nerves.

As you develop a color scheme for your site, consider these color associations carefully. Your color scheme communicates, in a very subtle way, and helps evoke the desired response.

Checking Out Other Sites

To gather some ideas, visit other sites and check out their color combinations. I like to search the web for "web design gallery." That usually turns up links to several galleries of stunning designs. One such gallery (at styletheweb.com/gallery/color-schemes) is shown in Figure 13.8. In most galleries, you can click a thumbnail of the design to see a larger version of it, or actually visit the site.

If you're designing a site for business purposes, check out your competitors' sites, too. In some industries, certain colors are standard fare, and you may want to follow suit. Or maybe you want to break rank and make a statement with a totally different color combination.

INSIDE TIP

If you see a color you like, grab the color code for it. See "Converting Colors into Codes," later in this chapter, for details.

Figure 13.8: *Visit design galleries for inspiration.*

Starting with a Central Image

Sometimes, you can build a color scheme around an image, especially if you have a logo or existing color scheme for your business and want your site to match. This strategy also works well if your central image is a nature photo, because nature's colors always look good together.

Using a Color Scheme Generator

If interior decorating isn't your thing or you simply want confirmation that the colors you want to use will look good together, consider using a color scheme generator to build a scheme for you. You can find a free color scheme generator online at colorschemedesigner.com (see Figure 13.9).

Choose a color scheme type   Export the color scheme

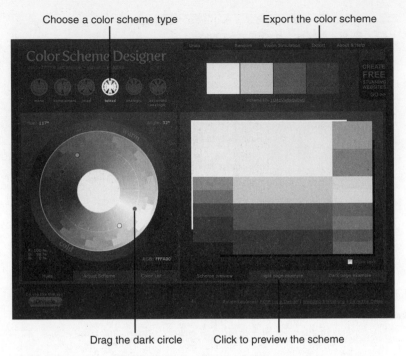

Drag the dark circle   Click to preview the scheme

Figure 13.9: *Color Scheme Designer.*

All you do is choose the desired type of color scheme (for example, analogic) and then drag the dark circle on the color wheel to the desired dominant color. As you drag the dark circle, the circles for all colors in the scheme move with it. You can then drag the other circles to make minor adjustments.

When the scheme is as you want it, move the mouse pointer to the upper right, over **Export**, and click **HTML + CSS....** Color Scheme Designer displays a color palette for the theme along with the hex code for each color, as shown in Figure 13.10. (For more about hex codes, see the next section.)

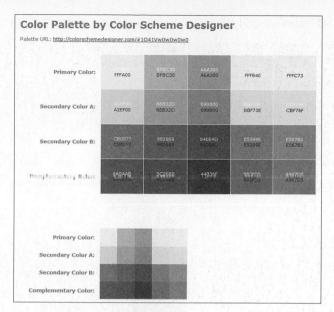

Figure 13.10: *Color scheme with hex codes.*

Converting Colors into Codes

Every color on a website can be traced back to the color's *hex code*, typically located in one of the site's cascading style sheets. Before you can specify a color for an element on your site, you must first identify the color's hex code (or its name, if it's a common color).

DEFINITION

A **hex code** (short for *hexadecimal code*) is a series of six letters and/or numbers that represent a color. The code includes a combination of the letters A through F and numbers 0 to 9. Each of the three sets of two characters represents a value for R, G, and B (red, green, and blue).

The Mozilla Firefox browser has a nifty add-on called ColorZilla that enables you to identify and copy a color's hex code from a web page or image so you don't have to guess what a color's code is. If you don't have Firefox, I recommend you download and install it (mozilla.com/firefox). Numerous Firefox add-ons are available for simplifying web design chores like this. After installing Firefox, perform the following steps to install Color Picker:

1. Run Mozilla Firefox.

2. Click **Tools, Add-ons**.

3. Click **Get Add-ons**.

4. Search for **ColorZilla**.

5. Click **Add to Firefox**.

6. Click **ColorZilla**.

7. Click **Install Now**.

8. When prompted, restart Firefox.

INSIDE TIP

You can use ColorZilla to convert hex codes into RGB or HSL values or vice versa. Open the ColorZilla menu, click **Color Picker**, and enter the color value you have—the hex code or RGB color value. ColorZilla presents the other values; for example, if you enter a hex code, ColorZilla provides the color's RGB and HSL values. You can find plenty of hex-RGB-HSL converters on the web. Just search for the conversion you want to do; for example, "hex rgb converter".

You can now use ColorZilla to pick up the color's hex code from the page. You can then paste the hex code into your CSS style rule, as explained later in this chapter. Here's how to pick up a color from a web page:

1. In Firefox, open the web page that has the desired color scheme.

2. Click the ColorZilla eyedropper icon, as shown in Figure 13.11.

3. Click the desired color.

4. Open the ColorZilla menu and copy the hex code.

Hold on to the hex code until you're ready to paste it into your CSS rule.

Click the color

ColorZilla eyedropper

Copy the hex code

Figure 13.11: *Pick up a color from a web page.*

Applying Color in CSS

The process of actually applying color in CSS is easy. You add whatever color property is required followed by the color's name, hex code, RGB, or HSL color value to the element's style. For example, say you want all of your h1 elements to appear red. You add the *color* property followed by color value for red to the *h1* style declaration. Because a color value can be a name, hex, RGB, or HSL value, the following three style declarations all result in making h1 elements red:

```
h1 {color:red; }
```

```
h1 {color:#FF0000; }
```

```
h1 {color:rgb(255,0,0); }
```

```
h1 {color:hsl(0,100%,50%); }
```

Admittedly, it's a little more complicated than that because you need to know some variations in color properties and values. The following sections bring you up to speed.

Recognizing Different Color Properties

In CSS, you can add colors to text (foreground), borders, and backgrounds. (You find out more about borders and backgrounds in Chapter 16.) You just need to use the right property for the item you want to colorize. Table 13.1 can help you out.

Table 13.1
CSS Color Properties

Property	Example
color	p {color:#00FF00; }
border-color	blockquote {border-color:#00FF00; }
background-color	blockquote {background-color:#00FF00; }
outline-color	aside {outline-color:#00FF00; }

If a style includes two or more properties for a border, background, or outline, you don't need the "-color" part of the property. You can simply add the color name or hex code, like this:

```
article {border:2px solid #00FF00;}
```

Specifying Color Values

CSS provides various ways to specify color values:

Hex code: In most cases, you see colors referenced by hex code, such as #FF0000 for red, #00FF00 for green, and #0000FF for blue.

Name: You can reference some colors by name: red, green, blue, yellow, pink, and purple, to name a few. Check out the color insert for a complete list.

RGB value: RGB values are similar to hex codes in that they mix the primary colors to specify any given color. The RGB value for blue is rgb(0,0,255), meaning it's 0 red, 0 green, and all blue. Numbers range from 0 to 255, so 255 is essentially 100 percent.

HSL value: An HSL value specifies a color in terms of its hue, saturation, and lightness. Hue ranges from 0 to 360 on the color wheel, with 0 and 360 in red territory, around 120 for greens, and around 240 for blues. Saturation and lightness are both specified in percentages. For saturation, 0% is gray scale, and 100% is full intensity. For lightness, 0% is dark, and 100% is lightest. The HSL color value for a shade of pink is hsl(320, 100%, 75%).

Making Colors More or Less Transparent

In CSS3, you can make colors more or less opaque (visible) or transparent by specifying an alpha value. The alpha value ranges from 1.0 (fully opaque, not at all transparent) to 0 (transparent to the point of being invisible). You can specify an alpha (A) value by adding it to the end of either an RGB or an HSL value. Following are some HSLA color values to specify different degrees of opacity:

```
{background:hsla(240, 35%, 50%, 0.08); }
{background:hsla(240, 35%, 50%, 0.2); }
{background:hsla(240, 35%, 50%, 0.4); }
{background:hsla(240, 35%, 50%, 0.6); }
{background:hsla(240, 35%, 50%, 0.8); }
```

I used these color codes to lay five horizontal bands of blue over the color wheel, as shown in Figure 13.12. Each band has the same hue, saturation, and value but a different alpha value, making the top band transparent almost to the point of invisibility, while the bottom band almost completely obscures the image behind it.

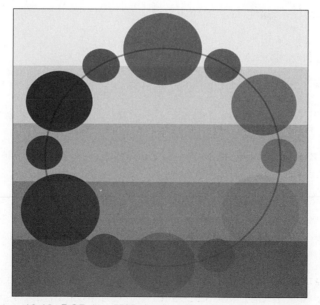

Figure 13.12: *RGBA or HSLA values let you make colors transparent.*

The Least You Need to Know

- Hue is the color, saturation is the intensity, and value is the brightness.
- Use Color Scheme Designer (colorschemedesigner.com) to identify harmonious colors.
- Use ColorZilla, an add-on for the Firefox browser, to pick up colors from web pages or images.
- Be sure the colors you choose set the right tone or evoke the desired emotion.
- You can specify a color, such as blue, by its name, hex code, RGB value, or HSL value. Add the A value to make the color transparent.

Formatting Margins and Lists

In This Chapter

- Setting paragraph margins
- Taking control of ordered and unordered lists
- Manipulating list items
- Giving your bullets a major overhaul

Unless you're a photographer, visual artist, or game developer, a good chunk of the content on your site will consist of text—primarily headings, paragraphs, and lists. To make this content attractive, you need to be able to control the space in and around these elements along with the appearance of bullets for unordered lists and numbers for ordered lists. This chapter shows you how to do all this and more.

Taking Control of Paragraphs and Other Text-Based Elements

CSS features several properties that enable you to control the appearance of text-based elements, including headings, paragraphs, and lists. Using CSS styles, you can align elements left, right, or center; justify text; and even create a first-line indent, as explained in Chapter 12. You can also control the left and right margins and the space between paragraphs, as explained in the following sections.

Setting Margins

To control the space around a block element, such as a paragraph, heading, or division, use the CSS *margin* property to specify the margin and amount of space. Following are some examples:

```
p {margin-left:10px; }
h2 {margin-top:.5em; }
p {margin-right:.5em; }
h3 {margin-bottom:12px; }
```

To save time and write tighter CSS, consider using one style declaration to set one to four margin properties for an element. For example, you can specify all four margins by using a single declaration such as the following:

```
{margin:10px; }
```

Table 14.1 lists the different shorthand entries for margin declarations.

Table 14.1
Margin-Setting Shorthand Entries

Format	Example
{margin:top right bottom left; }	{margin:10px 20px 30px 40px; }
{margin:top right&left bottom; }	{margin:10px 20px 30px; }
{margin:top&bottom right&left; }	{margin:10px 20px; }
{margin:all; }	{margin:10px; }

Setting Margins for Lists and List Items

If you need to set margins for lists, you must decide which element gets the margin settings—the list or the items in the list. Set the margins for a list—a <ul> or <ol> element—to control the space between the list and the element before or after it or to either side of it. Change margins for list items—tagged <li>—to control the space between items; for example:

```
li {margin-bottom:10px; }
```

Figure 14.1 shows list items with and without a bottom margin of 10px. As you can see, a little extra space can greatly help to keep list items from running together.

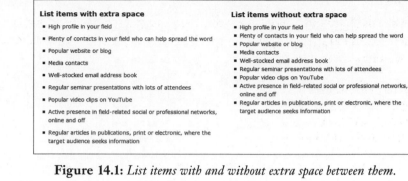

Figure 14.1: *List items with and without extra space between them.*

WHOA!

List items in the content area and sidebars may be styled differently. If you use the *li* selector alone, you change the style for *all* list items. Check the selectors in your style sheets carefully to be sure you're modifying the style for the right elements. For more about selectors, see Chapter 10.

Choosing a Bullet Style for Unordered Lists

Unless you specify otherwise, browsers typically display unordered list items as bulleted items with a small solid circle as the bullet. You can change the appearance of the bullet by applying the *list-style-type* property to the *ul* selector. Following are some examples; Figure 14.2 shows these styles in action:

```
ul {list-style-type:circle; }
ul {list-style-type:square; }
ul {list-style-type:disc; }
ul {list-style-type:none; }
```

Circle	Disc
○ Sample list item	• Sample list item
○ Sample list item	• Sample list item
○ Sample list item	• Sample list item
○ Sample list item	• Sample list item

Square	None
■ Sample list item	Sample list item
■ Sample list item	Sample list item
■ Sample list item	Sample list item
■ Sample list item	Sample list item

Figure 14.2: *Unordered list types.*

In most cases, you won't run into problems with bullets, but if you insert them in tables, you're likely to see something like what's shown in Figure 14.3. The bullets are hanging outside the cell borders. To fix this, add the *list-style-position:inside;* declaration to the ul style; for example:

```
ul {list-style-type:square; list-style-position:inside; }
```

Position Outside
- ■ Sample list item
- ■ Sample list item
- ■ Sample list item
- ■ Sample list item

Position Inside
- ■ Sample list item
- ■ Sample list item
- ■ Sample list item
- ■ Sample list item

Figure 14.3: *Position the bullet inside the content flow.*

Using an Image as the List Item Marker

If you don't like any of the unordered list styles, consider using a small image for your bullets. You can find gobs of free bullet art on the web at places like WebsiteBullets. com. Search for "free website bullets" to find plenty more.

Upload the bullet image to a folder on your site, as explained in Chapter 1, and use the *list-style-image* property in place of *list-style-type* to specify the bullet you want to use. Here's an example:

```
ul {list-style-image:url('images/bullet.gif'); }
```

Unfortunately, not all browsers display the list image in the same position relative to the text. To position the image more precisely, try the following CSS:

```
ul {list-style-type:none; padding:0px; margin-left:10px; }
li {background-image:url('images/bullet.gif');
  ➡ background-repeat:no-repeat; background-position:10px 5px;
  ➡ padding-left:50px; }
```

The first line disables the list-style-type bullet, removes any padding from around the list, and adds 10px margin space to the left of the list to indent it. The second line adds the bullet as a background image, tells the browser to display it only once, positions the image left 10px and down 5px, and adds 50px between the bullet and the text. Figure 14.4 shows the result.

Figure 14.4: *Use an image as your bullet.*

Choosing a Value for Ordered Lists

By default, ordered list items appear with Arabic numerals—1, 2, 3, and so on—next to them. You can change that through the *list-style-type* property. For example, to use Roman numerals instead, you would use the *upper-roman* value, like so:

```
ol {list-style-type:upper-roman; }
```

Table 14.2 describes commonly used ordered list types, which are used primarily for creating outlines. To create an outline, create lists inside of lists to produce indented sublists. Chapter 5 shows you how to nest lists.

Table 14.2
Ordered List Values

Format	Example
lower-latin	a, b, c, d, e
lower-roman	i, ii, iii, iv, v
upper-alpha	A, B, C, D, E
upper-latin	A, B, C, D, E
upper-roman	I, II, III, IV, V

The Least You Need to Know

- Add the *margin* property to an element's style declaration to add space above, below, or to the left or right of the element:

  ```
  h1 {margin-top:.5em; }
  ```

- To set margins for a list, use the *ul* selector. To set margins for items in the list, use the *li* selector.

- To use an image as a bullet, upload the image to your site and use the following CSS to display the image next to unordered list items (you may need to tweak the values):

  ```
  ul {list-style-type:none; padding:0px; margin:0px; }
  li {background-image:url('images/bullet.gif');
  ➥ background-repeat:no-repeat; background-position:10px 5px;
  ➥ padding-left:40px; }
  ```

- Ordered lists are great for step-by-step instructions, but they can also be used for outlines.

Chapter 15

Jazzing Up Hyperlinks

In This Chapter

- Modifying the look of visited and unvisited links
- Making a link change appearance on a mouseover
- Adding a background color to a link

Browsers traditionally display links as blue, underlined text. That was fine in the old days when users surfing the web needed a clear indication of what to click. Now, the web is more sophisticated, and so are its users. As long as links look a little different from the surrounding text, users can easily identify them on a page. This allows you to be more creative with your links. In this chapter, I show you options for styling links and how to use CSS to customize their appearance.

Using Pseudo Classes to Apply Styles Dynamically

You've probably noticed that, on most sites, links change appearance as you interact with them. They may appear blue before you click them, for example, and purple after you click the link to visit the site it links to. Links perform this magic through the use of pseudo selectors, as explained in Chapter 10. Using pseudo selectors, you can specify different styles for each of the link's *states:*

- **link** is the link as it normally appears before being clicked.
- **visited** is the link after the user clicks it.

- **focus** is the link when it's highlighted, typically by tabbing to it.

- **hover** is the link with the mouse pointer over it.

- **active** is the link as the visitor clicks it.

To use a pseudo selector, type the element's name followed by a colon and the desired state. The following example shows pseudo selectors that remove the underlining and display a link as red before it's clicked, gray after it's clicked, with a light gray background when highlighted, white text on a red background when the mouse pointer is over it, and bold red as the user clicks it (see Figure 15.1):

```
a:link {color:black; font-weight:bold; text-decoration:none; }
a:visited {color:gray; font-weight:bold; text-decoration:none; }
a:focus {color:black; border:1px dotted; text-decoration:none; }
a:hover {color:white; background:gray; text-decoration:none; }
a:active {font-weight:bold; background:lightgray;
   ➡ text-decoration:none; }
```

Figure 15.1: *Different looks for different states.*

Choosing Link Properties to Modify

You can change the appearance of link text in all sorts of ways, including changing the font family, size, color, style (for example, italic), weight, and variant. See Chapter 12 for details on formatting text with CSS.

Here are some common properties used to modify the appearance of links:

color: Specify a color for the link text.

text-decoration: This is most often used to remove the underline that appears by default under linked text.

background: Add a colorful background to a link. This comes in very handy for building navigation bars. You may use one background color for the link in its default state and another color for the currently selected link.

border: Adding a border around a link is particularly useful for indicating focus—a link that's highlighted but not yet activated.

cursor: For a:hover, consider adding the style declaration *cursor:crosshair* to have the cursor appear as a crosshair pointer or *cursor:help* to have it appear as a question mark.

display: You can use *display:block;* and add width and height properties to create a rectangle that functions as a link, as shown in Figure 15.2. The style to create this block is as follows:

```
a:link {display:block; height:100px; width:100px;
   ➥ background:.whitesmoke; border:1px solid gainsboro;
   ➥ text-decoration:none; text-align:center; }

p {vertical-align:middle; }
```

Figure 15.2: *Make a clickable box.*

Note that the entire block is clickable, not just the text inside it.

WHOA!

If your link text does not appear as you expect it to after applying the style, check whether your tags are properly nested. For example, if you're trying to change the appearance of a heading you're using as a link and you have it tagged something like this:

```
<a href="http://yoursite.com"><h1>Click Me!</h1></a>
```

Try moving the opening and closing <h1> tags to the outside, so the <a> tags are next to the text, like so:

```
<h1><a href="http://yoursite.com">Click Me!</a></h1>
```

Styling Images Used as Hyperlinks

When using an image as a hyperlink, the biggest problem most people run into is removing the blue border that appears around the image to indicate it's a hyperlink. To remove the border, create a style for image links that includes the *border:none* declaration, like so:

```
a img {border:none; }
```

If you simply use the *img* selector without the *a* selector, you remove borders applied to all images on your site. If your other images don't use CSS borders, this isn't a problem; otherwise, it is, because your borders won't appear.

You may also encounter situations in which you want to use a background image as a link. Neither CSS nor HTML is equipped to handle situations like this, but it is possible. Here's what you do:

1. Create a text link where you want the image to appear in your HTML document, and assign it a unique ID like so:

   ```
   <a href="http://www.site.com" id="img-link">Link Text</a>
   ```

2. Create a style declaration for the ID selector that inserts the image, transforms the link into a block element that's the same size as the image, and moves the text off the page:

   ```
   img-link {background-image:url(/wp-content/images/img-link.jpg);
     ➥ display:block; height:50px; width:75px;
     ➥ text-indent:-9999px; }
   ```

The last declaration is crucial. The huge negative left indent moves the text nearly 10,000 pixels to the left, so it is not superimposed on the background image, as shown in Figure 15.3.

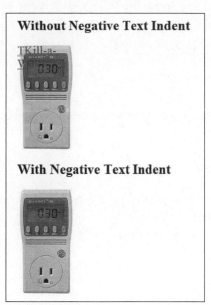

Figure 15.3: *Add a large negative text indent to hide the text link.*

The Least You Need to Know

- Use the following link pseudo classes to make links appear differently for each link state:

  ```
  a:link
  a:visited
  a:focus
  a:hover
  a:active
  ```

- You can apply numerous declarations to pseudo classes to change the appearance of a link's color; font family, size, color, style, and weight; border; background; and more.

- To remove the blue border that appears around images used as links, add the *border:none* style declaration to the *a img* selector, like so:

  ```
  a img {border:none; }
  ```

Packing Stuff in Boxes

In This Chapter

- Modularizing your pages by sticking stuff in boxes
- Adding backgrounds, borders, margins, and padding
- Creating cool background effects with gradients and background images
- Dealing with overflow when stuff doesn't fit

Although not initially noticeable, HTML places every element in a box. This is most obvious with block elements. Unless you specify otherwise, the box is pretty much the size of whatever is in it, and it doesn't contain anything flashy, such as a background or border. In addition, HTML is clumsy when it comes to arranging boxes on a page.

CSS to the rescue! With CSS, you have complete control over the appearance and dimensions of these boxes. You can add space between the box and what's inside it and outside it. You can add borders, background shading, and background images. With CSS3, you can even add a drop-shadow. This chapter shows you how.

Comprehending the CSS Box Model

Before you start stuffing content into boxes, take a bird's-eye view of the CSS box model to see how boxes are constructed. As shown in Figure 16.1, boxes consist of the following six components:

- **Content:** Whatever's inside the box: headings, articles, sections, paragraphs, lists, graphics, video, you name it.
- **Border:** Any line you choose to display around the box.

- **Background:** The color or image (or lack thereof) behind the content.

- **Padding:** Space between the content and border.

- **Margin:** Space outside the box.

- **Outline:** A border around the actual border used primarily to highlight an element.

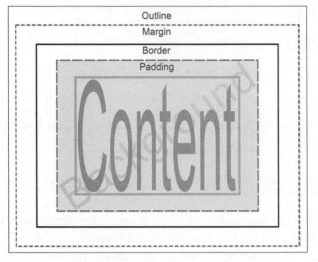

Figure 16.1: *The CSS box model.*

Displaying a Box as a Block or Inline Element

HTML has two types of elements:

- **Block:** A block element has a line break before and after it. Headings, paragraphs, lists, and divisions <div> are all block elements.

- **Inline:** An inline element goes with the flow, appearing "in line" with surrounding elements. <i>, <b>, <strong>, <em>, and <span>, to name a few, are inline elements.

CSS enables you to transform a block element into an inline element, and vice versa. You can even choose to hide an element if you don't want it to appear on a page. You do this with the display declaration, as explained in Table 16.1.

Table 16.1
CSS Display Properties

Declaration	Description
display:block	Converts an inline element into a block element
display:inline	Converts a block element into an inline element
display:inline-block	Keeps an inline element in line but creates space above and below it so it doesn't lie on top of surrounding content
display:none	Hides the item

WHOA!

Many people use *display:none* to hide their site's title and tagline when using a header image, but this is likely to negatively affect your site's search engine ranking. Consider using a huge negative margin instead, such as the following:

```
title {margin-left:-9999px; }
```

Specifying a Box's Dimensions

You can set the most basic properties of a box with height and width declarations. In many cases, you assign only a box width, so the height can automatically adjust to accommodate the content inside the box. Here's an example:

```
aside {width:150px; }
```

INSIDE TIP

If a box contains more content than fits inside it, the content overflows the box's bottom border. You can deal with this in a couple different ways, including adding a scroll bar to the box. See "Dealing with Text Overflow and Wrapping," later in this chapter, for details.

In CSS 2.1, the size of a box includes its dimensions + padding + border + margin, so if you want to include a box that occupies an area exactly 100px×100px, for example, you must account for padding, margin, and border space.

CSS3 includes a *box-sizing* property that enables you to specify how web browsers calculate box size. By default, *box-sizing* is set to *content-box*, which tells the browser to use the traditional method of sizing boxes. You can set it to *border-box* instead to have browsers include borders and padding when determining box sizes:

```
aside {box-sizing:border-box; width:150px; }
```

CSS3 also includes a *resize* property that enables users to resize boxes by dragging the lower-right corner of the box, as shown in Figure 16.2. Here's an example:

```
.tip {width:100px; height:100px; border:solid 1px; resize:both;
  ➥ overflow:auto; }
```

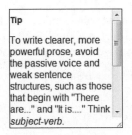

Tip

To write clearer, more powerful prose, avoid the passive voice and weak sentence structures, such as those that begin with "There are..." and "It is...." Think *subject-verb*.

Figure 16.2: *The* resize *property enables users to resize a box.*

Instead of *resize:both*, you can specify *resize:horizontal* or *resize:vertical* to make only one dimension of the box resizable. You may also want to include a max-width and/or max-height attribute to prevent users from making the box so big it makes the rest of the page look horrendous.

NOTE

During the writing of this book, few browsers supported the *resize* property without some additional tweaks.

Wrapping a Border Around Your Box

With CSS, you can add a border to any or all edges of a box and specify the border style, width, and color. In CSS3, you can even add a drop-shadow to make the box appear to be floating above the page and use the *border-radius* property to round the corners.

Border Style

CSS offers numerous border style types, including solid, dotted, dashed, and grooved, the latter of which is shown in Figure 16.3. To specify a border style, use the *border-style* property with the desired type; for example:

```
.tip {border-style:groove; border-width:8px;}
```

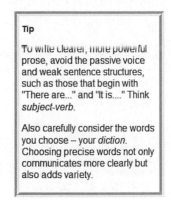

Figure 16.3: *Groove is one of the many CSS3 border styles available.*

Border Width

To specify a border width, include the *border-width* property, followed by the desired width. See Chapter 10 for details on the various measurement values you can use, including *px* and *em*.

Border Radius

Prior to CSS3, if you wanted a box to have rounded corners, you needed to employ graphics or some other savvy workarounds. The *border-radius* property has changed all that. To round all four corners uniformly, use the *border-radius* property followed by the desired measurement. You may need to adjust the *border-radius* property for different browsers, like so (see Figure 16.4):

```
aside {border:solid 2px ; border-radius:1.5em;
-moz-border-radius:1.5em; }
```

The smaller the value, the more angular the curve. To round corners individually, use the following properties:

```
border-top-right-radius
border-bottom-right-radius
border-top-left-radius
border-bottom-left-radius
```

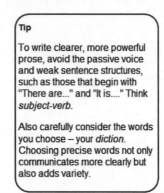

Tip

To write clearer, more powerful prose, avoid the passive voice and weak sentence structures, such as those that begin with "There are..." and "It is...." Think *subject-verb*.

Also carefully consider the words you choose – your *diction*. Choosing precise words not only communicates more clearly but also adds variety.

Figure 16.4: *Use* border-radius *to round box corners.*

Border Color

To specify a border color, use the *border-color* property:

```
aside {border-style:solid; border-color:#5F9EA0; }
```

With CSS3, you can set multiple border colors with the *border-colors* property. For example, if you have an 8px border, you can specify eight different colors and the browser will display eight border lines, each the color specified in the order specified from outside to inside. Because the different colors butt up to one another, you can use subtle changes in color to create a gradient that produces a 3D effect.

During the writing of this book, Firefox was the only browser supporting this feature. If you want to try it, here's an example (see Figure 16.5):

```
aside {width:200px; height:200px; border:8px solid;
-moz-border-bottom-colors:#002DFF #4F6EFF #7F95FF #AFBDFF #CFD7FF
  ➥ #CFD7FF #EFF2FF #FFFFFF ;
-moz-border-top-colors:#002DFF #4F6EFF #7F95FF #AFBDFF #CFD7FF #CFD7FF
  ➥ #EFF2FF #FFFFFF ;
-moz-border-left-colors:#002DFF #4F6EFF #7F95FF #AFBDFF #CFD7FF
  ➥ #CFD7FF #EFF2FF #FFFFFF ;
-moz-border-right-colors:#002DFF #4F6EFF #7F95FF #AFBDFF #CFD7FF
  ➥ #CFD7FF #EFF2FF #FFFFFF ;}
```

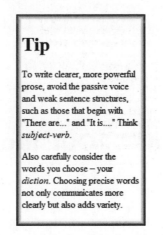

Figure 16.5: *A multi-colored border.*

Box Shadow

One of the coolest features CSS3 has introduced is the ability to add a drop-shadow to boxes. To create a drop-shadow, use the *box-shadow* property to specify the horizontal and vertical offset, a shadow color, and a blur radius. The offset values control the direction and distance the shadow sticks out from around the box. The blur radius controls how fuzzy the shadow looks.

During the writing of this book, not all browsers supported the *box-shadow* property. Here's an example that works in Firefox and WebKit (see Figure 16.6):

```
aside {-moz-box-shadow:10px 10px 10px #888;
-webkit-box-shadow:10px 10px 10px #888;}
```

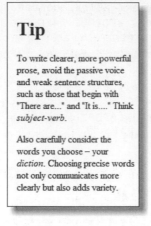

Tip

To write clearer, more powerful prose, avoid the passive voice and weak sentence structures, such as those that begin with "There are..." and "It is...." Think *subject-verb*.

Also carefully consider the words you choose — your *diction*. Choosing precise words not only communicates more clearly but also adds variety.

Figure 16.6: *Add a drop-shadow.*

Adding an Outline ... Outside the Border

If you like to think outside the box, CSS outlines are here to help. An outline enables you to place a box around a box to call attention to it ... as if the box wasn't enough. You won't bump into many outlines on the web, but you should know that the option is available. To add an outline, use the *outline* property and add all its values (color, type, and width) in one declaration, like so:

```
section {outline:red solid thin; }
```

To specify values individually, use the *outline-color*, *outline-style*, and *outline-width* properties. For color values, see Chapter 13. Outline styles are the same as border styles presented earlier in this chapter. You can enter a specific measurement value for width or use the value *thin*, *medium*, or *thick*.

Adding Space Around Stuff Inside and Outside Your Box

A box without padding and margins gets a little cramped. You need to give everything room to breathe. You do this by adjusting the margins and padding.

Setting Margins (Outside the Border)

To add space between a box and anything around the box, specify the desired margins using the *margin-left*, *margin-right*, *margin-top*, and *margin-bottom* properties followed by the desired measurement value:

```
#sidebar {margin-top:1em; margin-right:.5em; }
```

You may also use any of the margin shorthand entries presented in Chapter 14.

Adding Padding Between Border and Content

To add padding between a box's border and contents, use the *padding* property just like you use the *margin* property. In most cases, you use the same amount of padding on all four sides, and your style declaration looks something like this:

```
article {padding:4px; }
```

For more control, set the padding separately for each side, using the *padding-left*, *padding-right*, *padding-top*, and *padding-bottom* properties. You may also use any of the padding shorthand entries, shown in Table 16.2, to adjust various combinations of padding settings.

Table 16.2
Padding-Setting Shorthand Entries

Format	Example
{padding:top right bottom left; }	{padding:10px 20px 30px 40px; }
{padding:top right&left bottom; }	{padding:10px 20px 30px; }
{padding:top&bottom right&left; }	{padding:10px 20px; }
{padding:all; }	{padding:10px; }

Coloring the Box's Background

A color background helps define a box, especially if the box has no border. Adding color is a snap—just add the *background-color* property, like so:

```
.tip {background-color:#F5F5F5; }
```

Apply a CSS3 *linear-gradient* property to have one color fade into another across the box, as shown in Figure 16.7. Following are the style declarations to display linear gradients in Mozilla Firefox– and WebKit-compatible browsers:

```
.tip {width:200px; background:-moz-linear-gradient(top, #808080 0%,
    #F5F5F5 100%);
background:-webkit-gradient(linear, 0% 0%, 0% 100%, from(#808080),
    to(#FFFFFF)); }
```

Here's a rundown of the first declaration:

- The two color codes (#808080 and #F5F5F5) represent the beginning and ending colors.

- The *top* property is the starting point. It can be *top*, *center*, or *bottom* for a vertical fade; *left*, *center*, or *right* for a horizontal fade; or a specific percentage or measurement value. To start in a corner, add a degree measurement: *top 315deg* (top left), *top 45deg* (top right), *bottom 135deg* (lower right), and *bottom 225deg* (lower left).

- The percentages represent the relative position where the two colors start to blend; in this example, the first color starts to fade into the second at the very top, and the second color starts to fade into the first from the very bottom. If you were to change the first percentage to 50%, the first color would be solid halfway across the box and then start to fade into the second color. This value can be a percentage (0% to 100%) or a length (0 to 1.0).

The second declaration contains a gradient type property (*linear*) followed by the starting and ending point of the fade (the *x* and *y* coordinates in percentages), and ending with the start and end colors.

INSIDE TIP

Until the *linear-gradient* property is standardized, include a *background-color* property as a fallback for browsers that don't support it. You can also use *background-image* as a fallback, as explained in the next section.

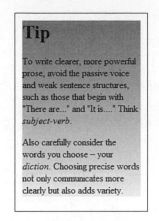

Figure 16.7: *The CSS3* linear-gradient *property in action.*

Following are a few additional examples to give you a better feel for how to create fades (see Figure 16.8 for the result of each fade):

- **3D fade:**

  ```
  .tip {width:200px; height:200px; border:solid, 1px;

  background:-moz-linear-gradient(center top, #0000FF,
    ➥ #9B9CFF 25%, #E6E6FF 50%, #9B9CFF 75%, #0000FF);

  background:-webkit-gradient(linear, center top, center bottom,
    ➥ from(#0000FF), color-stop(25%, #9B9CFF), color-stop(50%,
    ➥ #E6E6FF), color-stop(75%, #9B9CFF), to(#0000FF));}
  ```

- **Partial fade:**

  ```
  .tip {width:200px; height:200px;

  background:-moz-linear-gradient(left, #0000FF 0%, #FFFFFF 35%);

  background:-webkit-gradient(linear, left center, right center,
    ➥ from(#0000FF), color-stop(35%, #E6E6FF));}
  ```

- **Corner fade:**

  ```
  .tip {width:200px; height:200px; border:solid 1px;

  background:-moz-linear-gradient(left top 315deg, #0000FF,
    ➥ #E6E6FF 20%, #FFFFFF 50%);

  background:-webkit-gradient(linear, left top, right bottom,
    ➥ from(#0000FF), color-stop(20%, #E6E6FF), color-stop(50%,
    ➥ #FFFFFF)); }
  ```

- **Three-color fade:**

  ```
  .tip {height:200px; width:200px;

  background:-moz-linear-gradient(top left 315deg, yellow,
    ↪ green, blue);

  background:-webkit-gradient(linear, left top, right bottom,
    ↪ from(yellow), color-stop(50%, green), to(blue)); }
  ```

- **Radial fade:**

  ```
  .tip {width:200px; height:200px; border:solid 1px;

  background:-moz-radial-gradient(50% 50%, circle farthest-side,
    ↪ yellow, black 100%);

  background:-webkit-gradient(radial, 50% 50%, 0, 75% 75%, 350,
    ↪ from(yellow), to(black)); }
  ```

- **Radial fade #2:**

  ```
  .tip {width:200px; height:200px; border:solid 1px;

  background:-moz-radial-gradient(25% 25%,
    ↪ circle farthest-corner, yellow, black);

  background:-webkit-gradient(radial, 25% 25%, 20, 75% 75%, 40,
    ↪ from(yellow), to(black)); }
  ```

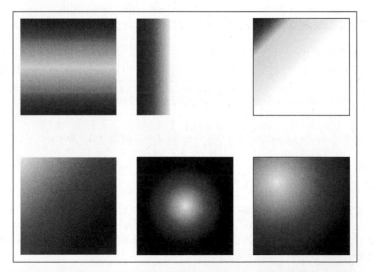

Figure 16.8: *Different types of fades: (top row, left to right) 3D, partial, corner; (bottom row, left to right) three-color, radial, and radial #2.*

The syntax for radial gradients is tricky, especially because it's different for different browsers. For Mozilla Firefox, the first two numbers establish the center of the circle; *circle* or *ellipse* specifies the shape; *farthest-side, closest-side, farthest-corner,* or *closest-corner* indicates the direction of the gradient; and *color1, color2* represent the colors involved.

The WebKit version is more complex and flexible. You specify the type of gradient (*radial*) first. The first set of three numbers specifies the location of the center of the first circle and its radius. The second set of three numbers specifies the location of the center of the second circle and its radius. And *from (color1), to (color2)* represent the colors involved.

Think of the difference between Mozilla and WebKit like this: WebKit has the gradient run between two circles, whereas Mozilla runs the gradient from a circle to an edge of the box.

Adding an Artistic Touch with a Background Image

When you're looking for something a little more sophisticated than color to place in the background, CSS provides the solution—one or more background images. In the following sections you discover how to add background images to your boxes.

Using an Image as the Background

To use an image as a box's background, first upload the image to your web server. Then add a *background-image* property to the element's style declaration, specifying the location and name of the file. Web designers often use a background image for the entire page by targeting the body element, like so:

```
body {background-image:url('images/background.png');}
```

INSIDE TIP

Specify a background color in case the image isn't available or the user chooses not to view images. Try to use a color that's consistent with the image, so content in the foreground is as clear or clearer as it is when the image is in the background.

Setting the Background Position

Unless you specify otherwise, browsers display the background image in the upper-left corner of whichever element it's associated with. You can specify a different position by adding the *background-position* property along with details on where to position the image: *left top*, *left center*, *left bottom*, *right top*, *right center*, *right bottom*, *center top*, *center center*, or *center bottom*. Another option is to specify the location by entering a distance from the upper-left corner of the box the image is in, like so:

```
body {background-image:url('images/background.png');
  ➡ background-position:25px 30px; }
```

This moves the image 25 pixels to the right on the *x* axis and 30 pixels down on the *y* axis.

{ } The border image position is measured from the upper-left corner of the border. You may choose to use the upper-left corner of the content box or the padding box instead. To do so, add the *background-origin* property and set it to *padding-box* or *content-box*. The default setting is *border-box*. Here's an example:

```
body {background-image:url('images/background.png');
  ➡ background-origin:content-box; }
```

{ } By default, an image positioned in the upper-left corner of the border box extends into the border area. To prevent this, you may be able to use the *background-clip* property and set it to *padding-box*.

During the writing of this book, the *background-clip* property was removed from the CSS3 specification, but it may find its way back in.

Repeating the Background Image

If the background image doesn't fill the box, it's repeated horizontally and vertically. To prevent or control how the image is repeated, add the *background-repeat* property with the desired value:

- *repeat-x* to repeat horizontally

- *repeat-y* to repeat vertically

- *no-repeat* to display only a single instance of the image

Colorizing Web Pages

Color Wheels

Traditional (Red Yellow Blue)

Red Green Blue (RGB)

Cyan Magenta Yellow Black (CMYK)

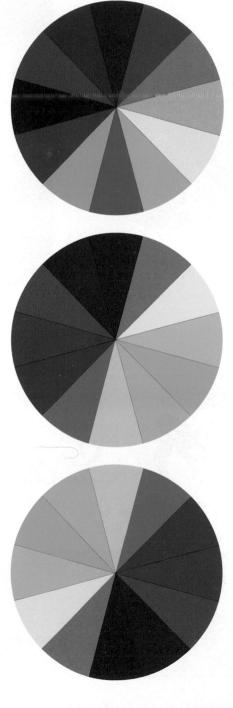

Color Schemes

Achromatic

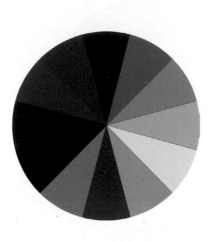

Monochromatic

Complementary

Split Complementary (Triadic)

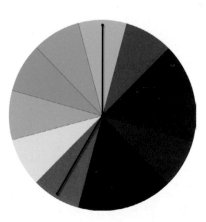

Analogic

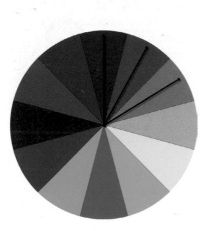

Color Tools

Color Scheme Designer

Access Color Scheme Designer at colorschemedesigner.com.

1. Choose a color scheme type.

2. Drag the dark circle to the desired primary color.

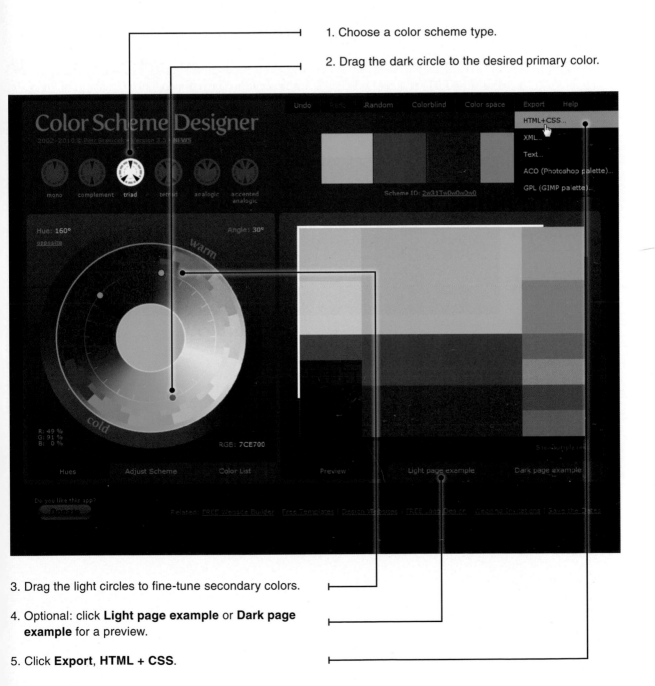

3. Drag the light circles to fine-tune secondary colors.

4. Optional: click **Light page example** or **Dark page example** for a preview.

5. Click **Export, HTML + CSS**.

6. Color Scheme Designer presents your color palette.

Color Palette by Color Scheme Designer

Palette URL: http://colorschemedesigner.com/#2w31Tw0w0w0w0
Color Space: RGB;

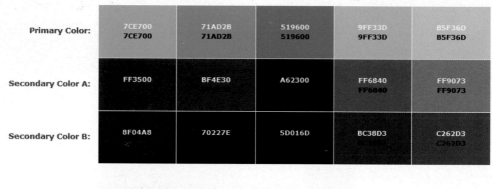

Primary Color:	7CE700 **7CE700**	71AD2B **71AD2B**	519600 **519600**	9FF33D **9FF33D**	B5F36D **B5F36D**
Secondary Color A:	FF3500	BF4E30	A62300	FF6840 **FF6840**	FF9073 **FF9073**
Secondary Color B:	8F04A8	70227E	5D016D	BC38D3	C262D3 **C262D3**

Primary Color:

Secondary Color A:

Secondary Color B:

See the HTML source for more details.
Use the *Save / Save As...* command in your browser to store the HTML for latter use.

Generated by Color Scheme Designer © Petr Stanicek 2002-2010

Color Schemer

Access Color Scheme Designer at colorschemer.com/online.html.

Click the main color you want to use.

You can specify the main color by RGB value or hex code.

Click to lighten the scheme.

Click to darken the scheme.

Color Schemer displays harmonious colors here.

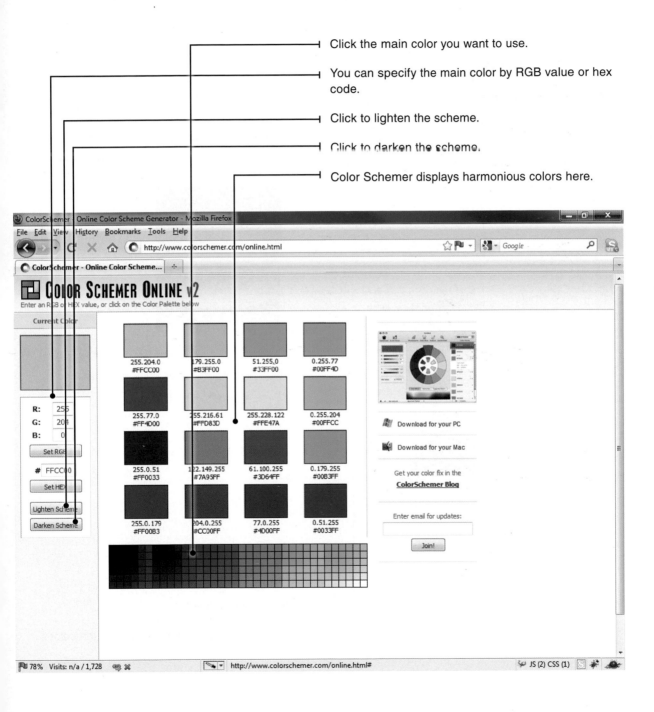

ColorZilla

ColorZilla is an add-on for the Mozilla Firefox web browser. To learn more about it, including how to download and install it, see Chapter 13.

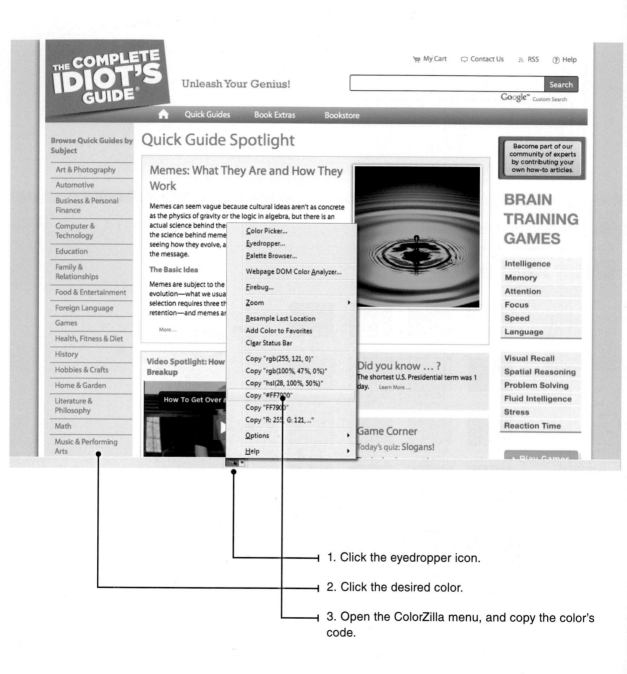

1. Click the eyedropper icon.

2. Click the desired color.

3. Open the ColorZilla menu, and copy the color's code.

CSS3 Gradient Generator

Access Ultimate CSS Gradient Generator at colorzilla.com/gradient-editor.

Click a preset gradient.

Double-click a color stop to change its color.

Choose the desired color for the color stop.

Drag a color stop off the bar to remove it.

Double-click just below the bar to add a color stop.

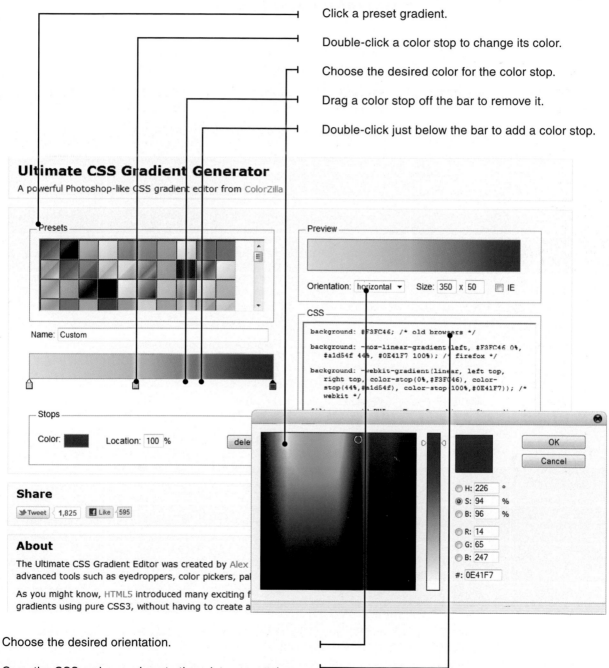

Choose the desired orientation.

Copy the CSS codes, and paste them into your style sheet.

Color Values and Names

Hex/RGB Color Chart

#FFFFFF 255, 255, 255	#FFFFEB 255, 255, 235	#FFFFD7 255, 255, 115	#FFFFC3 255, 255, 195	#FFFFAF 255, 255, 175	#FFFF9B 255, 255, 155
#FFFF87 255, 255, 135	#FFFF73 255, 255, 115	#FFFF5F 255, 255, 95	#FFFF4B 255, 255, 75	#FFFF37 255, 255, 55	#FFFF00 255, 255, 0
#FFEB00 255, 235, 0	#FFD700 255, 215, 0	#FF3C00 255, 195, 0	#FFAF00 255, 175, 0	#FF9B00 255, 155, 0	#FF8700 255, 135, 0
#FF7300 255, 115, 0	#FF5F00 255, 95, 0	#FF4B00 255, 75, 0	#FF3700 255, 55, 0	#FF1900 255, 25, 0	#FF0000 255, 0, 0
#EB0000 235, 0, 0	#D70000 215, 0, 0	#C30000 195, 0, 0	#AF0000 175, 0, 0	#9B0000 155, 0, 0	#870000 135, 0, 0
#9b000F 155, 0, 15	#9b0023 155, 0, 35	#9b0037 155, 0, 55	#9b004B 155, 0, 75	#9b005F 155, 0, 95	#9b0073 155, 0, 115
#9b0087 155, 0, 135	#9b009B 155, 0, 155	#9b00AF 155, 0, 175	#9b00C3 155, 0, 195	#9b00D7 155, 0, 215	#9b00EB 155, 0, 235
#9B00FF 155, 0, 255	#AF00FF 175, 0, 255	#C300FF 195, 0, 255	#D700FF 215, 0, 255	#EB00FF 235, 0, 255	#FF00FF 255, 0, 255
#FF0FFF 255, 15, 255	#FF23FF 255, 35, 255	#FF37FF 255, 55, 255	#FF4BFF 255, 75, 255	#FF5FFF 255, 95, 255	#FF73FF 255, 115, 255
#FF87FF 255, 135, 255	#FF9BFF 255, 155, 255	#FFAFFF 255, 175, 255	#FFC3FF 255, 195, 255	#FFD7FF 255, 215, 255	#FFEBFF 255, 235, 255
#EBEBFF 235, 235, 255	#D7D7FF 215, 215, 255	#C3C3FF 195, 195, 255	#AFAFFF 175, 175, 255	#9B9BFF 155, 155, 255	#8787FF 135, 135, 255
#7373FF 115, 115, 255	#5F5FFF 95, 95, 255	#4B4BFF 75, 75, 255	#3737FF 55, 55, 255	#2323FF 35, 35, 255	#0000FF 0, 0, 255
#0000EB 0, 0, 235	#0000D7 0, 0, 215	#0000C3 0, 0, 195	#0000AF 0, 0, 175	#00009B 0, 0, 155	#000087 0, 0, 135
#0023FF 0, 35, 255	#0037FF 0, 55, 255	#004BFF 0, 75, 255	#005FFF 0, 95, 255	#0073FF 0, 115, 255	#0087FF 0, 135, 255
#009BFF 0, 155, 255	#00AFFF 0, 175, 255	#00C3FF 0, 195, 255	#00D7FF 0, 215, 255	#00EBFF 0, 235, 255	#00FFFF 0, 255, 255
#00FFEB 0, 255, 235	#00FFD7 0, 255, 215	#00FFC3 0, 255, 195	#00FFAF 0, 255, 175	#00FF9B 0, 255, 155	#00FF87 0, 255, 135
#00FF73 0, 255, 115	#00FF5F 0, 255, 95	#00FF4B 0, 255, 75	#00FF37 0, 255, 55	#00FF23 0, 255, 35	#00FF00 0, 255, 0

#00EB00 0, 235, 0	#00D700 0, 215, 0	#00C300 0, 195, 0	#00AF00 0, 175, 0	#009B00 0, 155, 0	#008700 0, 135, 0
#007300 0, 115, 0	#005F00 0, 95, 0	#004B00 0, 75, 0	#003700 0, 55, 0	#002300 0, 35, 0	#000000 0, 0, 0
#23FF00 35, 255, 0	#37FF00 55, 255, 0	#4BFF00 75, 255, 0	#5FFF00 95, 255, 0	#73FF00 115, 255, 0	#87FF00 135, 255, 0
#9BFF00 155, 255, 0	#AFFF00 175, 255, 0	#C3FF00 195, 255, 0	#D7FF00 215, 255, 0	#EBFF00 235, 255, 0	#FFFF00 255, 255, 0

HSLA Colors

0°, 50%, 90%	0°, 75%, 90%	0°, 100%, 90%	60°, 50%, 90%	60°, 75%, 90%	60°, 100%, 90%
0°, 50%, 75%	0°, 75%, 75%	0°, 100%, 75%	60°, 50%, 75%	60°, 75%, 75%	60°, 100%, 75%
0°, 50%, 65%	0°, 75%, 65%	0°, 100%, 65%	60°, 50%, 65%	60°, 75%, 65%	60°, 100%, 65%
			60°, 50%, 50%	60°, 75%, 50%	60°, 100%, 50%
0°, 50%, 35%	0°, 75%, 35%	0°, 100%, 35%	60°, 50%, 35%	60°, 75%, 35%	60°, 100%, 35%
0°, 50%, 25%	0°, 75%, 25%	0°, 100%, 25%	60°, 50%, 25%	60°, 75%, 25%	60°, 100%, 25%
30°, 50%, 90%	30°, 75%, 90%	30°, 100%, 90%	90°, 50%, 90%	90°, 75%, 90%	90°, 100%, 90%
30°, 50%, 75%	30°, 75%, 75%	30°, 100%, 75%	90°, 50%, 75%	90°, 75%, 75%	90°, 100%, 75%
30°, 50%, 65%	30°, 75%, 65%	30°, 100%, 65%	90°, 50%, 65%	90°, 75%, 65%	90°, 100%, 65%
30°, 50%, 50%	30°, 75%, 50%	30°, 100%, 50%	90°, 50%, 50%	90°, 75%, 50%	90°, 100%, 50%
30°, 50%, 35%	30°, 75%, 35%	30°, 100%, 35%	90°, 50%, 35%	90°, 75%, 35%	90°, 100%, 35%
30°, 50%, 25%	30°, 75%, 25%	30°, 100%, 25%	90°, 50%, 25%	90°, 75%, 25%	90°, 100%, 25%
120°, 50%, 90%	120°, 75%, 90%	120°, 100%, 90%	180°, 50%, 90%	180°, 75%, 90%	180°, 100%, 90%
120°, 50%, 75%	120°, 75%, 75%	120°, 100%, 75%	180°, 50%, 75%	180°, 75%, 75%	180°, 100%, 75%

150°, 50%, 75%	150°, 75%, 75%	150°, 100%, 75%	210°, 50%, 75%	210°, 75%, 75%	210°, 100%, 75%
150°, 50%, 65%	150°, 75%, 65%	150°, 100%, 65%	210°, 50%, 65%	210°, 75%, 65%	210°, 100%, 65%
150°, 50%, 50%	150°, 75%, 50%	150°, 100%, 50%	210°, 50%, 50%	210°, 75%, 50%	210°, 100%, 50%
150°, 50%, 35%	150°, 75%, 35%	150°, 100%, 35%	210°, 50%, 35%	210°, 75%, 35%	210°, 100%, 35%
150°, 50%, 25%	150°, 75%, 25%	150°, 100%, 25%	210°, 50%, 25%	210°, 75%, 25%	210°, 100%, 25%
240°, 50%, 90%	240°, 75%, 90%	240°, 100%, 90%	300°, 50%, 90%	300°, 75%, 90%	300°, 100%, 90%
240°, 50%, 75%	240°, 75%, 75%	240°, 100%, 75%	300°, 50%, 75%	300°, 75%, 75%	300°, 100%, 75%
240°, 50%, 65%	240°, 75%, 65%	240°, 100%, 65%	300°, 50%, 65%	300°, 75%, 65%	300°, 100%, 65%
240°, 50%, 50%	240°, 75%, 50%	240°, 100%, 50%	300°, 50%, 50%	300°, 75%, 50%	300°, 100%, 50%
240°, 50%, 35%	240°, 75%, 35%	240°, 100%, 35%	300°, 50%, 35%	300°, 75%, 35%	300°, 100%, 35%
240°, 50%, 25%	240°, 75%, 25%	240°, 100%, 25%	300°, 50%, 25%	300°, 75%, 25%	300°, 100%, 25%
270°, 50%, 90%	270°, 75%, 90%	270°, 100%, 90%	330°, 50%, 90%	330°, 75%, 90%	330°, 100%, 90%
270°, 50%, 75%	270°, 75%, 75%	270°, 100%, 75%	330°, 50%, 75%	330°, 75%, 75%	330°, 100%, 75%
270°, 50%, 65%	270°, 75%, 65%	270°, 100%, 65%	330°, 50%, 65%	330°, 75%, 65%	330°, 100%, 65%
270°, 50%, 50%	270°, 75%, 50%	270°, 100%, 50%	330°, 50%, 50%		
270°, 50%, 35%	270°, 75%, 35%	270°, 100%, 35%	330°, 50%, 35%	330°, 75%, 35%	330°, 100%, 35%
270°, 50%, 25%	270°, 75%, 25%	270°, 100%, 25%	330°, 50%, 25%	330°, 75%, 25%	330°, 100%, 25%

Shades of Gray

#FFFFFF 255, 255, 255	#F7F7F7 247, 247, 247	#EFEFEF 239, 239, 239	#E7E7E7 231, 231, 231	#DFDFDF 223, 223, 223	#D7D7D7 215, 215, 215
#CFCFCF 207, 207, 207	#C7C7C7 199, 199, 199	#BFBFBF 191, 191, 191	#B7B7B7 183, 183, 183	#AFAFAF 175, 175, 175	#A7A7A7 167, 167, 167
#A0A0A0 160, 160, 160	#999999 153, 153, 153	#959595 149, 149, 149	#8E8E8E 142, 142, 142	#898989 137, 137, 137	#828282 130, 130, 130
#7B7B7B 123, 123, 123	#747474 116, 116, 116	#6D6D6D 109, 109 109	#666666 102,102,102	#5D5D5D 93, 93, 93	#565656 86, 86, 86
#4F4F4F 79, 79, 79	#484848 72, 72, 72	#414141 65, 65, 65	#3A3A3A 58, 58, 58	#333333 51, 51, 51	#2A2A2A 42, 42, 42
#232323 35, 35, 35	#1C1C1C 28, 28, 28	#151515 21, 21, 21	#0E0E0E 14, 14, 14	#070707 7, 7, 7	#000000 0, 0, 0

CSS Named Colors

Color	Color name	Hex Value	RGB Value		Color	Color name	Hex Value	RGB Value
	aliceblue	#F0F8FF	240,248,255			darkturquoise	#00CED1	0,206,209
	antiquewhite	#FAEBD7	250,235,215			darkviolet	#9400D3	148,0,211
	aqua	#00FFFF	0,255,255			deeppink	#FF1493	255,20,147
	aquamarine	#7FFFD4	127,255,212			deepskyblue	#00BFFF	0,191,255
	azure	#F0FFFF	240,255,255			dimgray	#696969	105,105,105
	beige	#F5F5DC	245,245,220			dimgrey	#696969	105,105,105
	bisque	#FFE4C4	255,228,196			dodgerblue	#1E90FF	30,144,255
	black	#000000	0,0,0			firebrick	#B22222	178,34,34
	blanchedalmond	#FFEBCD	255,235,205			floralwhite	#FFFAF0	255,250,240
	blue	#0000FF	0,0,255			forestgreen	#228B22	34,139,34
	blueviolet	#8A2BE2	138,43,226			fuchsia	#FF00FF	255,0,255
	brown	#A52A2A	165,42,42			gainsboro	#DCDCDC	220,220,220
	burlywood	#DEB887	222,184,135			ghostwhite	#F8F8FF	248,248,255
	cadetblue	#5F9EA0	95,158,160			gold	#FFD700	255,215,0
	chartreuse	#7FFF00	127,255,0			goldenrod	#DAA520	218,165,32
	chocolate	#D2691E	210,105,30			gray	#808080	128,128,128
	coral	#FF7F50	255,127,80			green	#008000	0,128,0
	cornflowerblue	#6495ED	100,149,237			greenyellow	#ADFF2F	173,255,47
	cornsilk	#FFF8DC	255,248,220			grey	#808080	128,128,128
	crimson	#DC143C	220,20,60			honeydew	#F0FFF0	240,255,240
	cyan	#00FFFF	0,255,255			hotpink	#FF69B4	255,105,180
	darkblue	#00008B	0,0,139			indianred	#CD5C5C	205,92,92
	darkcyan	#008B8B	0,139,139			indigo	#4B0082	75,0,130
	darkgoldenrod	#B8860B	184,134,11			ivory	#FFFFF0	255,255,240
	darkgray	#A9A9A9	169,169,169			khaki	#F0E68C	240,230,140
	darkgreen	#006400	0,100,0			lavender	#E6E6FA	230,230,250
	darkgrey	#A9A9A9	169,169,169			lavenderblush	#FFF0F5	255,240,245
	darkkhaki	#BDB76B	189,183,107			lawngreen	#7CFC00	124,252,0
	darkmagenta	#8B008B	139,0,139			lemonchiffon	#FFFACD	255,250,205
	darkolivegreen	#556B2F	85,107,47			lightblue	#ADD8E6	173,216,230
	darkorange	#FF8C00	255,140,0			lightcoral	#F08080	240,128,128
	darkorchid	#9932CC	153,50,204			lightcyan	#E0FFFF	224,255,255
	darkred	#8B0000	139,0,0			lightgoldenrodyellow	#FAFAD2	250,250,210
	darksalmon	#E9967A	233,150,122			lightgray	#D3D3D3	211,211,211
	darkseagreen	#8FBC8F	143,188,143			lightgreen	#90EE90	144,238,144
	darkslateblue	#483D8B	72,61,139			lightgrey	#D3D3D3	211,211,211
	darkslategray	#2F4F4F	47,79,79			lightpink	#FFB6C1	255,182,193
	darkslategrey	#2F4F4F	47,79,79			lightsalmon	#FFA07A	255,160,122

Color	Color name	Hex Value	RGB Value		Color	Color name	Hex Value	RGB Value
	lightseagreen	#20B2AA	32,178,170			pink	#FFC0CB	255,192,203
	lightskyblue	#87CEFA	135,206,250			plum	#DDA0DD	221,160,221
	lightslategray	#778899	119,136,153			powderblue	#B0E0E6	176,224,230
	lightslategrey	#778899	119,136,153			purple	#800080	128,0,128
	lightsteelblue	#B0C4DE	176,196,222			red	#FF0000	255,0,0
	lightyellow	#FFFFE0	255,255,224			rosybrown	#BC8F8F	188,143,143
	lime	#00FF00	0,255,0			royalblue	#4169E1	65,105,225
	limegreen	#32CD32	50,205,50			saddlebrown	#8B4513	139,69,19
	linen	#FAF0E6	250,240,230			salmon	#FA8072	250,128,114
	magenta	#FF00FF	255 0 255			sandybrown	#F4A460	244,164,96
	maroon	#800000	128,0,0			seagreen	#2E8B57	46,139,87
	mediumaquamarine	#66CDAA	102,205,170			seashell	#FFF5EE	255,245,238
	mediumblue	#0000CD	0,0,205			sienna	#A0522D	160,82,45
	mediumorchid	#BA55D3	186,85,211			silver	#C0C0C0	192,192,192
	mediumpurple	#9370DB	147,112,219			skyblue	#87CEEB	135,206,235
	mediumseagreen	#3CB371	60,179,113			slateblue	#6A5ACD	106,90,205
	mediumslateblue	#7B68EE	123,104,238			slategray	#708090	112,128,144
	mediumspringgreen	#00FA9A	0,250,154			slategrey	#708090	112,128,144
	mediumturquoise	#48D1CC	72,209,204			snow	#FFFAFA	255,250,250
	mediumvioletred	#C71585	199,21,133			springgreen	#00FF7F	0,255,127
	midnightblue	#191970	25,25,112			steelblue	#4682B4	70,130,180
	mintcream	#F5FFFA	245,255,250			tan	#D2B48C	210,180,140
	mistyrose	#FFE4E1	255,228,225			teal	#008080	0,128,128
	moccasin	#FFE4B5	255,228,181			thistle	#D8BFD8	216,191,216
	navajowhite	#FFDEAD	255,222,173			tomato	#FF6347	255,99,71
	navy	#000080	0,0,128			turquoise	#40E0D0	64,224,208
	oldlace	#FDF5E6	253,245,230			violet	#EE82EE	238,130,238
	olive	#808000	128,128,0			wheat	#F5DEB3	245,222,179
	olivedrab	#6B8E23	107,142,35			white	#FFFFFF	255,255,255
	orange	#FFA500	255,165,0			whitesmoke	#F5F5F5	245,245,245
	orangered	#FF4500	255,69,0			yellow	#FFFF00	255,255,0
	orchid	#DA70D6	218,112,214			yellowgreen	#9ACD32	154,205,50
	palegoldenrod	#EEE8AA	238,232,170					
	palegreen	#98FB98	152,251,152					
	paleturquoise	#AFEEEE	175,238,238					
	palevioletred	#DB7093	219,112,147					
	papayawhip	#FFEFD5	255,239,213					
	peachpuff	#FFDAB9	255,218,185					
	peru	#CD853F	205,133,63					

Transparency Opacity

Opacity = 0.0

Opacity = .2

Opacity = .4

Opacity = .6

Opacity = .8

Opacity = 1.0

Specifying the Background Image Size

During the writing of this book, a few browsers supported the *background-size* property, which enables the browser to reduce the image to specified dimensions. Assuming this property becomes a CSS standard, it enables you to upload a single image and use it as a background image for containers of different sizes. Here's an example (see Figure 16.9):

```
.tip {background-image:url('images/boat.jpg');
-moz-background-size:80%; background-size:80%; }
.content {background-image:url('images/boat.jpg');
-moz-background-size:90%; background-size:80%; }
```

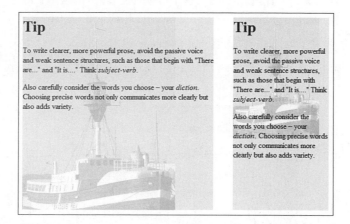

Figure 16.9: *Use the same image as the background for different-size boxes.*

Using Multiple Background Images

To add multiple images to a background, separate the background image declarations with commas. Suppose you want a different image to appear in each corner of the box. Your CSS style rule would look something like this:

```
body {height:400px;
background:url('images/blue.png') top left no-repeat,
url('images/green.png') top right no-repeat,
url('images/red.png') bottom left no-repeat,
url('images/yellow.png') bottom right no-repeat; }
```

Enabling the Background Image to Scroll with the Page

To make a background image stay put when a user scrolls up or down, use the *background-attachment* property and set its value to *fixed*, like this:

```
body {background-image:url('images/background.png');
   ➡ background-attachment:fixed; }
```

Controlling Image Opacity

If you use an image format that supports opacity, typically a PNG or GIF file, you can use the *opacity* property to make the image more or less transparent. Set the opacity value to something closer to zero for more transparency or closer to 1 for less transparency (more opacity). Here's an example that applies an opacity setting of 50% (see Figure 16.10):

```
body {background-image:url('images/background.png'); opacity:.5; }
```

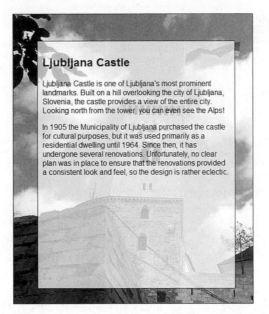

Figure 16.10: *You can make a PNG or GIF image more or less opaque.*

INSIDE TIP

Make separate classes for different degrees of opacity. For example:

```
.translucent-25 {opacity:25%; }
.translucent-50 {opacity:50%; }
.translucent-75 {opacity:75%; }
```

You can then apply opacity by adding the designated class to an element's opening tag; for example:

```
<img class="translucent-25"
  ➥ img src="images/background.png" />
```

Setting All Background Declarations in a Single Style Rule

To streamline your CSS, consider including all your background declarations in a single style rule in the following order:

- background-color
- linear-gradient or radial-gradient
- background-image
- background-size
- background-repeat
- background-attachment
- background-position

You don't need to add a declaration for each property, but you do need to include the declarations in the order listed. Here's an example:

```
background:#FFFAFA url('images/background.png') no-repeat center
  ➥ center; }
```

Dealing with Text Overflow and Wrapping

If a box contains more content than fits inside it, some of the content spills over the borders of the box. You can use the *overflow* property to add a scroll bar to the box to prevent this from occurring. The style declaration might look like this:

```
#sidebar {overflow:auto; }
```

The *overflow* property takes any of the following values:

- **hidden** does not display excess content.
- **scroll** displays the scroll bar regardless of whether the content fits.
- **auto** displays the scroll bar only when the content exceeds the box's capacity.

Specifying Text-Overflow Preference

During the writing of this book, a few browsers supported a new *text-overflow-props* property, which displays some indication near the bottom of a box, typically ellipses, when additional content is available but not shown. Here's an example:

```
.tip {width:120px; height:150px; text-overflow:ellipses; }
```

Opera supports this feature, but you need to use the property *-o-text-overflow*. Internet Explorer, Safari, and WebKit all use the simpler *text-overflow* (without "props"). Available values are *ellipsis* and *clip*. Clip is the default, which clips the text and doesn't show any indication it's been "clipped." The idea behind *text-overflow-props* is to provide additional options for how text overflow is indicated.

Breaking Long Words for a Better Fit

If you have narrow boxes, a situation could occur in which a word is wider than the box. When that happens, the word crosses the border, which looks lousy.

The CSS3 *word-wrap* property prevents this by enabling the browser to break long words and wrap them from one line to the next. This property takes either of two values: *normal* or *break-word*.

The Least You Need to Know

- To specify a box's dimensions, use the width and height properties.
- Here's the shorthand for adding a border:
  ```
  {border:width style color; }
  ```
- Padding is the space between the box and what's inside it.
- Margin is the space between the box and what's outside it.

- Add background color with the *background-color* property, and add a background image with the *background-image* property:

  ```
  body {background-image:url('images/background.png'); }
  ```

- If you're afraid that a box may contain more text than it can display, add *overflow:auto;* to its style rule to display a scroll bar if one is necessary.

Arranging and Rearranging Items on a Page

In This Chapter

- Positioning boxes on a page
- Making a box stay put, even as the user scrolls
- Laying one box on top of another
- Getting content to wrap around a box or image

You placed a box on a page. Now what? That box, along with any other boxes you've placed, line up shoulder to shoulder like passengers on an overcrowded bus. You need to take control of those boxes, position them where you want them to appear, wrap text around them when necessary, perhaps overlap boxes, and make all those boxes get along together.

The keys to taking control of boxes are the CSS *position* and *float* properties, along with a host of accompanying values. With the *position* property, you have the power to set a position type (static, fixed, or relative), specify a precise location for a box, and even layer boxes. The *float* property gives you even more control over a box's position in addition to controlling the way content flows around the box.

Specifying a Positioning Type

The first order of business is to specify a position type:

- Static
- Fixed
- Relative
- Absolute

The following sections describe each type and explain how to assign the various types to boxes.

Static

Unless you specify otherwise, *position:static* is the default setting. This essentially means you have no control over where the box appears. It appears in the normal flow. This may be what you want, especially if you're boxing a text element that should appear in the normal flow of the text.

Absolute

For absolute control over where a box appears, use *position:absolute*. Of course, after setting the position to absolute, you must enter additional specifications to indicate where you want the box to appear. In most cases, this means adding *top* and *left* properties to specify where you want the upper-left corner of the box positioned. Here's an example:

```
#sidebar {position:fixed; left:20px; top:100px; }
```

You can specify position using *left*, *right*, *top*, and/or *bottom* properties along with specific measurements.

Figure 17.1 shows absolute positioning used to move the image 20px down from the top. The image also has the *float:right* declaration that moves it just to the left of the header text.

INSIDE TIP

To find out more about float declarations, skip ahead to the last section in this chapter.

The box in this case is the image

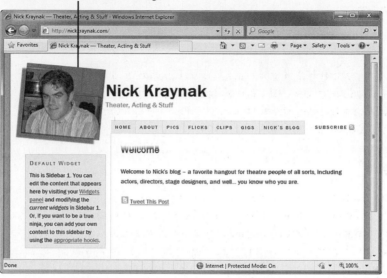

Figure 17.1: *Assign a box an absolute position.*

Relative

To establish a box position relative to the box's static position—where it normally would appear—use *position:relative*. As with absolute positioning, accompany the *position:relative* declaration with *top*, *left*, *right*, and/or *bottom* property declarations that indicate the direction and distance to move the element, like so:

```
#sidebar {position:relative; left:10px; top:10px; }
```

You rarely encounter relative positioning on web pages. Most developers simply use margins to position the element.

Fixed

To assign the box position relative to the browser window, use *position:fixed*. The box stays put even if the user scrolls down the page. You may want to use fixed positioning to keep a navigation element on-screen at all times, as shown in Figure 17.2, although I find this a little distracting.

Scroll down, and this navigation bar stays put

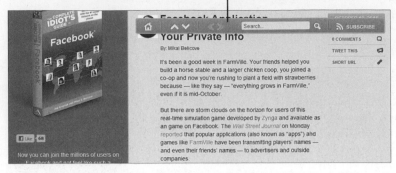

Figure 17.2: *Use the fixed position to keep a box on-screen at all times.*

WHOA!

Some sites use fixed positioning to keep an advertisement on-screen as you scroll, which is downright annoying.

Overlapping Elements for a Layered Effect

Whether an element's position is relative, absolute, or fixed, you can lay elements one on top of another, just as you can stack objects in a drawing program.

When layering elements, you need some control over the order in which they're stacked. Unless you specify otherwise, the browser determines the order based on the order of the elements in the HTML source code, the last element in the source code appearing in front of the others.

To control layering, use the *z-index* property with a numerical value. The element with the highest *z-index* property value appears on top. The one with the lowest value appears on the bottom. The following styles control the position and layering of the elements shown in Figure 17.3:

```
h1 {font-size:300%; position:absolute; left:100px; top:10px; }
h2 {font-size:200%; position:absolute; left:120px; top:70px; }
img {z-index:0; }
.inset {position:absolute; left:590px; top:190px; z-index:1}
```

Figure 17.3: *You can layer elements on a page.*

Floating Elements: It's Not What You Think

When you hear the word "float," you probably imagine objects floating above the page. Not in CSS. In CSS, float isn't up or down, it's left or right. Float a box left, and the content that follows it wraps around the right. Float a box right, and the content wraps around its left side. See Figure 17.4.

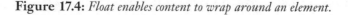

Figure 17.4: *Float enables content to wrap around an element.*

You typically use the *float* property to allow text to wrap around a figure, but you may use it for any block element. I like to use it for boxed tips.

NOTE

Consider creating two float classes for images—one that floats the image left and adds margin space to the right, and another that floats the image right and adds margin space to the left. You can then easily specify a float class by adding the desired class attribute to the image tag. Your float classes may look something like this:

```
alignleft {float:left; margin-right:6px; margin-bottom:4px; }
alignright {float:right; margin-left:6px; margin-bottom:4px; }
```

To align anything left or right, add the appropriate class attribute to the element's tag, like so:

```
<img class="alignleft" src="images/swan.gif" height="120px"
➥ width="100px" />
```

Floats occasionally cause problems with other nearby or containing elements, in which case you may need to clear a float. To clear a float, use the *clear* property and set its value to *left*, *right*, or *both*. This prevents nearby floating elements from floating to the left, right, or either side of the element with the *clear* property.

The Least You Need to Know

- Use *position:absolute* with *top, left, bottom,* and/or *right* declarations to precisely position an element on a page.
- Use *position:relative* with *top, left, bottom,* and/or *right* declarations to precisely position an element relative to where the box normally would appear.
- Use *z-index:#* to specify stacking order—the higher the number an element has, the closer to the front it appears.
- Use *float:left* to move an element to the left and wrap content around its right side.
- Use *float:right* to move an element to the right and wrap content around its left side.

Manipulating Page Layout

Chapter 18

In This Chapter

- Some design basics
- Topping off your page with a header
- Creating custom navigation bars
- Exploring layout column options
- Closing with a footer
- Using CSS3's flexible box model

One of the first tasks in designing a website is to establish the overall structure—the container that holds the content. The container typically accommodates a header that reaches completely across the page, a horizontal navigation bar above or below the header, one to four columns, and a footer. The overall structure really drives the design of everything else you include on the site.

This chapter shows you how to design aesthetically pleasing page layouts and style the various components that define your layouts.

Designing Attractive Page Layouts

Using CSS, you can position elements on web pages however you like. Before you start styling pages, however, you should have a page layout in mind so you know where everything needs to be.

Designing with a Sense of Symmetry ... or Not

When developing page layouts, strive to achieve symmetry—a balanced distribution of elements on the page, as shown in Figure 18.1.

Figure 18.1: *Strive to achieve a sense of symmetry and balance.*

You can use both symmetry and asymmetry in your design:

Horizontal symmetry: The left and right sides are like mirrored images of one another. For the most part, a person's face exhibits bilateral symmetry. On a web page, this doesn't mean the right side of a page must be a mirror image of the left side; it means the two sides must be balanced. If one side has a bunch of text, the other should have about as much text or an image or block of color to keep the page balanced.

Radial symmetry: A balanced arrangement of objects around an imaginary point in the middle of the page.

Asymmetry: Objects are balanced less by their position on the page and more by their size and color. For example, instead of horizontal symmetry with two fairly large shapes on the left and right side of the page, one side may contain several smaller elements that balance a fairly large element on the other side.

Adhering to the Rule of Thirds

In visual arts composition, follow the "rule of thirds." According to the rule of thirds, an image is divided into nine equal squares, like a tic-tac-toe grid, and important compositional elements must line up along these lines (see Figure 18.2). Images or layouts that adhere to this rule are thought to be more visually appealing and engaging.

Figure 18.2: *Follow the rule of thirds when designing your site.*

This doesn't mean your site needs to look like a tic-tac-toe grid. The rule allows for plenty of flexibility. For example, you may have a layout with a navigation bar in the left third of the grid and a large content area that consumes the other two thirds. Or you may want blog posts to appear on the left with one or two navigation bars on the right. You can even center your design in the middle of the grid and then work out toward the edges.

Drafting Page Layouts with Wireframing Tools

One of the best ways to plan your layout is to use a wireframing application—a graphics application specially designed for prototyping websites. Most wireframing tools perform two primary tasks: designing page layouts and developing flow charts for organizing pages. Most enable you to create and save your designs online so you can collaborate with others.

To plan your layout, you draw objects, including menu bars, buttons, blocks for text or images, drop-down lists, charts, and so on, on a blank canvas. You can then easily resize and rearrange objects. Figure 18.3 shows a sample page layout I created online for free with Mockingbird (gomockingbird.com).

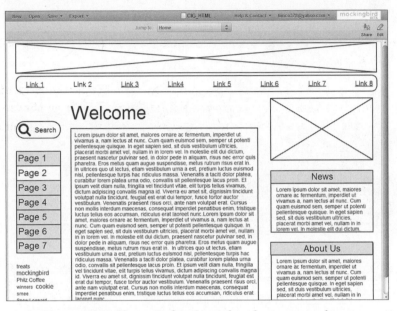

Figure 18.3: *Use a wireframing tool to plan your page layout.*

Take It from the Top: The Header

At the top of almost all sites is a header that brands the site. The header may include only text, only an image, or a combination of image and text. You can also set it up to change images over time or every time someone visits the page.

In the following sections, you discover how to use HTML and CSS to create different types of web page headers. Regardless of which type of header you create, bracket all elements that comprise the header between an opening and closing <header> tag, as explained in Chapter 4.

Using a Standard Text-Based Header

One of the easiest ways to add a header to your site is to use a text-based header. Add the header to your HTML source code where you want the header to appear (typically right after the opening <body> tag), and include the text you want to appear in the header. Keep in mind that you want to make the header a link so users can click it to return to the home page. Here's an example that includes a site title and tagline:

```
<header>
<a href="www.tornado-chasers.net"><h1>Tornado Chasers</h1>
<p>Specializing in joyrides throughout tornado alley!</p></a>
</header>
```

You can use CSS to style the header area and the elements in it individually. Here's an example that adds a yellow background to the header and padding above and below it, removes the margin from around the <h1> element and makes italic, and removes the underline from the link text and makes it green (see Figure 18.4):

```
header {display:block; margin:-8px; padding:2em;
    ➥ background-color:yellow; }
header h1 {margin:0px; font-style:italic; }
header a {text-decoration:none; color:green; }
```

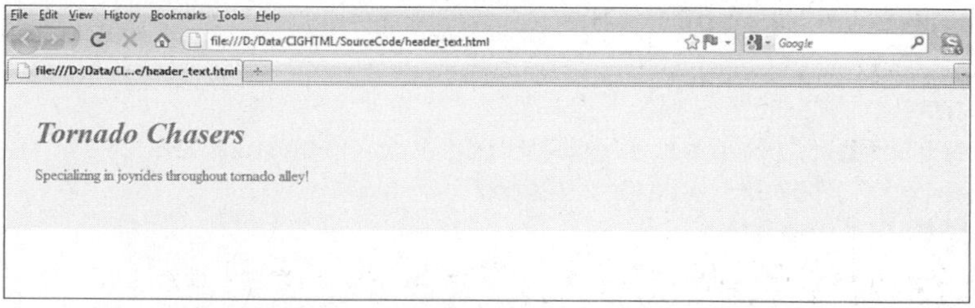

Figure 18.4: *This is a clickable text-based header.*

Making the Entire Header an Image

To use an image as your header (instead of text), you need an image of the desired dimensions. Consider using an application, such as BannerFans (bannerfans.com), to create and download a custom header image, as shown in Figure 18.5. You must then upload the header image to a folder on your web server so you can reference its location and name in your HTML.

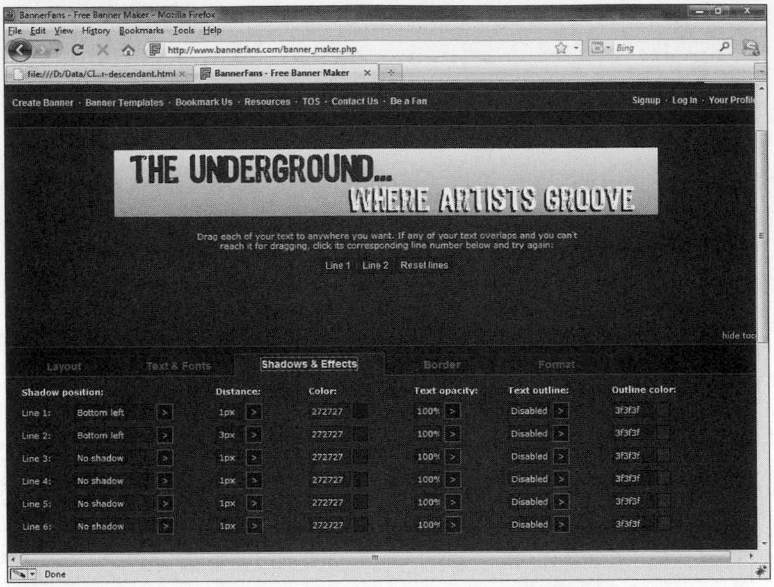

Figure 18.5: *Create a custom header image with bannerfans.com.*

Using a header image introduces an issue related to search engines. If you use only an image, search engines can't identify your site title from the image. To work around this, include text in the HTML and hide it using CSS. The HTML would look something like the following:

```
<header>
<a href="http://yoursite.com"><img src="images/header01.jpg"
 ➥ height="100px" width="925px" /></a>
<h1>Site Title</h1>
<h2>Site subtitle</h2>
</header>
```

Your CSS looks something like this:

```
header img {display:block; margin-left:auto; margin-right:auto;
 ➥ margin-top:-8px; border-style:none; }
header h1, header h2 {position:fixed; top:-2000px; }
```

The first style rule formats the header <img> element, making it a block element, centering it (by setting its left and right margins to *auto*), scooting it to the top (by subtracting 8px from the top margin), and removing any border that the link <a> tag would add around it.

The second style rule positions the header <h1> and <h2> elements way above the top of the page, so they don't appear but are still present for the benefit of search engines.

Mix and Match: Text and Graphics

You can mix text and graphics in the header in various ways. For example, you may include an image on the left with text on the right or a background image with text layered on top of it. Suppose you wanted a logo or photo on the left with the site title and subtitle on the right. Your HTML would look something like the following:

```
<a id="header-link" href="www.tornado-chasers.net">
<header>
<img src="http://joekraynak.com/images/joetiny.jpg" height="100px"
  ➥ width="97px" />
<h1>Tornado Chasers</h1>
<h2>Specializing in joyrides throughout tornado alley!</h2>
</header>
</a>
```

Your CSS would then need to float the image to the left and wrap text around the right side of it:

```
header {display:block; margin-left:auto; margin-right:auto;
  ➥ width:700px; }
header h1 {padding-top:1.2em; color:green; margin-bottom:0; }
header h2 {margin:0; font-style:italic; color:black; }
header img {float:left; margin-right:30px; border-style:none; }
#header-link {text-decoration:none; }
```

Adding a Horizontal Navigation Bar

You can easily create a navigation bar with HTML lists and links. To position that bar on a page and make it look attractive, however, you need CSS. To create a horizontal navigation bar, first create an unordered list of links (see Chapters 5 and 6). Your list may look something like the following.

```
<nav>
<ul class="nav-bar">
<li><a href="page1.html">Item 1</a></li>
<li><a href="page2.html">Item 2</a></li>
<li><a href="page3.html">Item 3</a></li>
<li><a href="page4.html">Item 4</a></li>
<li><a href="page5.html">Item 5</a></li>
<li><a href="page6.html">Item 6</a></li>
</ul>
</nav>
```

Using CSS, you can style your navigation bar however you like. The following CSS creates a solid gray bar with list items displayed in bold white text. When you mouse-over an item, it appears as a white tab with a black border and black text (see Figure 18.6).

```
ul.nav-bar {background:none repeat scroll 0 0 gray; font-weight:bold;
   ➥ padding:6px 0px; }
li {display:inline; }
a:link,a:visited {font-weight:bold; color:#FFFFFF;
   ➥ background-color:gray; text-align:center; padding:6px;
   ➥ text-decoration:none; }
a:hover,a:active {background-color:white; color:black;
   ➥ border-width:1px; border-top-style:solid;
   ➥ border-left-style:solid; border-right-style:solid; }
```

The first line creates the gray bar with bold text. The second line makes all the list items appear on one line. The third line controls the appearance of links when the mouse pointer is not over them. And the fourth line controls the appearance of links when the mouse is over the link.

Figure 18.6: *Create your own horizontal navigation bar.*

If you want to get a little fancier and make drop-down menus, you'll need to enlist some help from CSS3 transition and animation effects, as explained in Chapter 20.

Scoping Out Column Layout Options

Examine enough free and premium themes, and you soon discover that almost all of them are structured in some sort of column arrangement. These aren't table columns. They're boxes created with CSS style rules. Before you start fiddling with CSS, however, you need to decide on an overall structure for your site. The following sections lead you through the process of making this key decision.

Fixed-Width, Liquid, or Elastic?

You may be able to control the width of your web pages when designing them, but when others are viewing those pages, width is more a factor of the user's screen resolution and monitor and browser window size. Because of this, you should give some consideration to whether you want your column widths to remain fixed or to automatically adjust to accommodate different configurations.

You have five options:

Fixed-width: You specify the width of your columns, typically in pixels. Because pixel size may vary depending on the user's screen resolution, pages and the columns on those pages may appear wider or narrower. If, for example, you design a page to be 1,024 pixels wide, and someone viewing that page has a monitor resolution set to 800×600, the user will need to scroll to the right to see parts of the page off-screen. If the user views the page at a resolution of 1,600×900, the page will have a lot of white space off to the left and right.

Liquid: You specify the width of your columns as percentages. If the user views the page in a smaller window or at a lower resolution than how you designed the page to be viewed, the columns narrow but retain their relative widths. If the user views the page in a larger window or higher resolution, the columns widen. As column widths are adjusted, however, everything else remains the same, including image and font size.

Elastic: Elastic is similar to liquid except that when window size or screen resolution changes, everything changes size—column widths, text, graphics, navigation bars, and so on. To create an elastic design, you use the *em* unit for the column widths and the percentage unit for sizing other elements, including fonts.

Combination: You can combine different strategies; for example, you may want your left column width to remain the same while the right column remains liquid. You can do this by specifying a fixed width for the left column and *auto* for the right column.

{} **Flexible:** CSS3 introduces a flexible box model designed specifically for page layouts. With the flexible box model, browsers can resize boxes as in a liquid or elastic layout. During the writing of this book, the flexible box model was in draft mode and considered experimental, so I placed coverage of it at the very end of this chapter.

Creating a Fixed-Width Layout

Suppose you're creating a two-column layout with a page width of 1,024. You want one wide column on the left and two narrower columns on the right. You might tag the wide column as <article> and use <div> tags for the other two columns; for example, <div class="leftbar"> and <div class="rightbar">. You'd also want to wrap everything in a *container* div, so you can center it all within the browser window. Your CSS for setting the widths of these columns would look something like this:

```
#container {margin-left:auto; margin-right:auto; width:1024px;
  ➡ overflow:auto; }
.left-bar {float:left; width:160px; padding:10px; margin-left:25px;
  ➡ margin-top:25px; }
.right-bar {float:left; width:160px; padding:10px; margin-left:25px;
  ➡ margin-top:25px; }
article {float:left; width:544px; padding:10px; display:block;
  ➡ margin-left:25px; margin-top:25px; }
```

The first line creates a container for the other three elements. Setting the container's left and right margins to *auto* centers it in the browser window. Setting *overflow* to *auto* enables you to add a background to the container, if desired, that will show up behind the elements you "float" in the container.

The remaining three lines define the three blocks (columns) within the container. Each has the *float:left* declaration, which places the element as far left as possible and allows other elements that come after it to wrap around the right side of it. The *padding* declarations add space between each block's invisible border and the contents inside the block. The *margin* declarations add space above and to the left of each block.

The HTML for this layout looks like this:

```
<body>
<div id="container">
<article>Text for article goes here.</article>
<div class="left-bar">Text for left bar goes here. </div>
<div class="right-bar">Text for right bar goes here.</div>
</div>
</body>
```

Figure 18.7 shows the resulting layout. I added a *background-color* declaration to each block along with plenty of text to more clearly illustrate how the different blocks will appear. The blocks are 160px, 160px, and 544px wide, with four margins of 25px each (100px in all), and 10px padding on the left and right of each block (60px in all). Do the math, and you see that the space is equivalent to the width of the container:

$$544 + 160 + 160 + 100 + 60 = 1,024$$

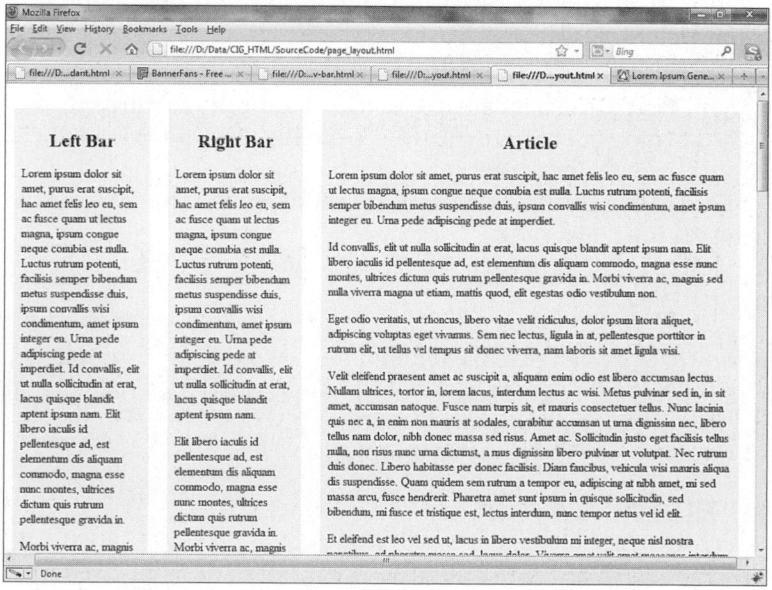

Figure 18.7: *A three-column layout created in CSS.*

Creating a Liquid Layout

To create a liquid layout, you merely specify element widths in percentages instead of pixels, so the percentage widths add up to 100 percent. To redo the design described in the previous section in percentage widths, you'd divide each pixel measurement by the total width: 1,024 pixels. This results in the following percentages: 52 percent (wide columns), 16 percent (each of two narrow columns), 1 percent (padding), and 2.5 percent (margins).

Because you're doing percentages instead of fixed measurements, you can set the container width to anything, or leave it blank to spread it out as much as possible. Your CSS might look something like this:

```
#container {margin-left:auto; margin-right:auto; overflow:auto; }
.left-bar {float:left; width:16%; padding:1%; margin-left:2.5%;
    ➥ margin-top:25px; }
.right-bar {float:left; width:16%; padding:1%; margin-left:2.5%;
    ➥ margin-top:25px; }
article {float:left; width:52%; padding:1%; margin-left:2.5%;
    ➥ margin-top:25px; }
```

Keep in mind that you can mix fixed and liquid layouts. For example, you can use a pixel setting for the left column so its width remains fixed while entering percentages for all other width settings.

Creating an Elastic Layout

To create an elastic layout, specify *all* dimensions in em units—widths, font sizes, image sizes … everything. Working in em units is tough because an em unit is relative to the font, so you may need to experiment quite a bit to get everything to look right. The reward for your efforts is that when someone zooms in or out on your site or changes the font size, your pages and everything on them scale accordingly.

Adding a Vertical Navigation Bar

As you might guess, you can stick anything in the columns (or boxes) you create, making them the perfect solution for building vertical navigation bars. Here's some HTML source code that's ideal for a vertical navigation menu:

```
<nav id="sidebar">
<h2>Main Menu</h2>
<a href="schools.html">Schools</a>
<a href="admin.html">Administration</a>
<a href="depts.html">Departments</a>
<a href="sports.html">Athletics</a>
<a href="calendar.html">Calendar</a>
<h2>Parents & Students</h2>
<a href="account.html">My Account</a>
<a href="handbook.html">Handbooks & Guides</a>
<a href="closings.html">Closings & Delays</a>
<a href="registration.html">Registration Forms</a>
</nav>
```

Add the following CSS to transform the HTML into an attractive sidebar for navigation:

```
nav#sidebar {display:block; background-color:yellow; width:150px; }
nav#sidebar h2 {background-color:purple; padding:6px; font-size:18px;
  ➥ color:yellow; }
nav a {display:block; padding:6px; }
nav a:link,a:visited {text-decoration:none;
  ➥ border-bottom-style:dotted; border-width:2px;
  ➥ border-color:purple; }
nav a:hover,a:active {background-color:purple; color:yellow; }
```

Wrapping It Up with a Footer

Every page should end in a footer. Footers typically include links to key sections of the site, copyright information, and perhaps contact information (such as a street address and phone number). You can place anything you want in the footer, and the HTML source code doesn't need to be anything special. Following is a sample with a few paragraphs and tags.

```
<footer>
<p><a href="home.html">Main Menu</a> | <a href="school.html">
    ➥ Schools</a> | <a href="admin.html">Administration</a> |
    ➥ <a href="sports.html">Athletics</a> | <a href="contact.html">
    ➥ Contact Us</a> | </p>
<p>2037 North Bridgeview Terrace * Indianapolis * Indiana * 46224</p>
<p>Phone:(555) 555-1212 * Fax:(555) 222-3333</p>
</footer>
```

If you'd like to center the footer and use a slightly smaller font, you may want to use some basic CSS to style it, like so:

```
footer p {font-size:.8em; text-align:center; }
```

Creating Newspaper Columns

{} If you're looking for a design that looks more like a magazine or newspaper layout, consider using the new CSS3 newspaper columns style. With newspaper columns, you specify the number of columns, the desired column width, and the gap between columns. The browser then renders the columns for you. You can even have the browser insert a horizontal line between columns. Here's sample CSS for the two-column arrangement, shown in Figure 18.8:

```
.news {column-count:3; column-width:175px; col-gap:20px;
    ➥ column-rule:2px solid black; }
```

You then need to bracket everything you want to be included in the multi-column layout with a <div class="news"> tag and a closing </div> tag.

During the writing of this book, support for the CSS multi-column feature was limited. You could get the feature to work in Firefox by adding *-moz-* before each property, as in

```
-moz-column-count:3
```

and in some other browsers by adding *-webkit-* in place of *-moz-*. Perhaps by the time you read this, more browsers will support this attractive feature.

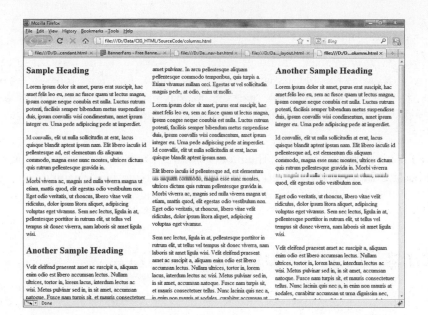

Figure 18.8: *With CSS multi-columns, you can create newspaper columns.*

Using CSS3's Flexible Box Model

CSS3's flexible box model is ideal for structuring pages. It enables you to treat every child of an element as a box within that element and arrange the children horizontally or vertically. Here's a very basic example in which the <body> element is used as a container for three children:

```
<body>
<div id="sidebar1">
<div id="sidebar2">
<div id="content">
</body>
```

Now let's use the CSS3 flexible box model to convert the three divisions within the body into flexible boxes:

```
body {display:box; box-orientation:horizontal; }
#sidebar1 {box-flex:0; width:180px; }
#sidebar2 {box-flex:1; min-width:180px; }
#content {box-flex:2; }
```

display:box tells the browser to treat the children of the <body> element as flexible boxes. *box-orientation:horizontal* arranges the boxes side by side; you could use *box-orientation:vertical* to stack the boxes instead. *box-flex:0* tells the browser not to treat the first sidebar as flexible; its width is fixed at 180px. *box-flex:1* tells the browser to make the second sidebar flexible, and the box has a minimum width of 180px. *box-flex-2* tells the browser to make the content box twice as wide as sidebar2.

Because the flexible box model was in draft mode during the writing of this book, prefixes were required to make the model work in browsers that support it. If the model is still in draft mode, you must add *-webkit-* for webkit-enabled browsers and *-moz-* for Firefox. Here, I added the prefixes for Firefox along with dimensions and shading:

```
body {display:-moz-box; -moz-box-orientation:horizontal; }
#sidebar1 {height:150px; background-color:#EEEEEE; -moz-box-flex:0;
➡ width:180px; }
#sidebar2 {height:150px; background-color:#DDDDDD; -moz-box-flex:1;
➡ min-width:180px; }
#content {height:150px; background-color:#CBCBCB; -moz-box-flex:2; }
```

Figure 18.9 shows the result. If you make the browser window larger, the two sidebars and content area widen. Make the browser window smaller, and the two sidebars and content area narrow.

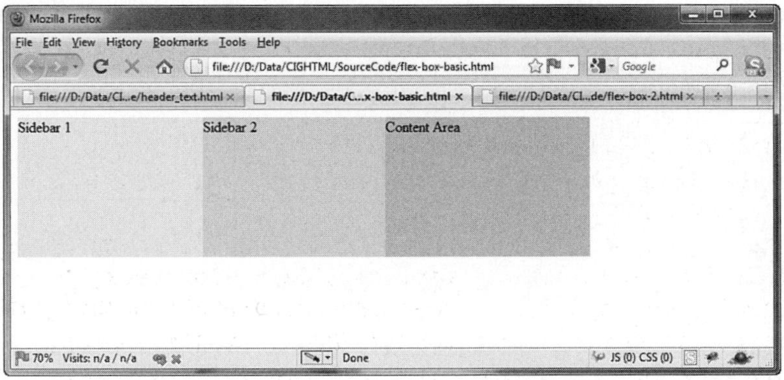

Figure 18.9: *Basic CSS3 flexible box layout.*

Suppose you want your page to consist of six boxes: a header, navigation bar, two sidebars, a content area, and footer. Your HTML might look something like this:

```
<body>
   <header>
       <h1>Site Title</h1>
       <p>Site Subtitle</p>
       <nav>
               <ul id="navbar">
               <li><a href="page1.html">Item 1</a></li>
               <li><a href="page2.html">Item 2</a></li>
               <li><a href="page3.html">Item 3</a></li>
               <li><a href="page4.html">Item 4</a></li>
               <li><a href="page5.html">Item 5</a></li>
               <li><a href="page6.html">Item 6</a></li>
               </ul>
       </nav>
   </header>
<div id="page">
   <div id="sidebar1">Sidebar 1</div>
   <div id="content">Content</div>
   <div id="sidebar2">Sidebar 2</div>
</div>
<footer>Footer</footer>
</body>
```

You can then use the CSS3 flexible box model to put everything in boxes. Here's an example, the result of which is shown in Figure 18.10:

```
header {background:#DDDDDD; display:block; margin-bottom:20px;
   ➥ padding:10px; }
nav {display:-moz-box; height:50px; width:100%; background:#C3C3C3; }
ul {display:-moz-box; -moz-box-flex:1; -moz-box-orient:horizontal;
   ➥ list-style-type:none; text-align:center; }
li {-moz-box-flex:1; min-width:40px; }
#page {display:-moz-box; -moz-box-flex:1; -moz-box-orient:horizontal;
   ➥ height:100%; width:100%; }
#sidebar1 {-moz-box-flex:1; background:#C3C3C3; padding:10px; }
#content {-moz-box-flex:3; padding:0 20px 10px 10px; }
#sidebar2 {-moz-box-flex:2; background:#EFEFEF; padding:10px; }
footer {color:white; background:#878787; display:block;
   ➥ margin-top:20px; padding:10px; text-align:center; }
header h1,p {text-align:center; }
a:link,a:visited {font-weight:bold; color:white; font-size:95%; }
a:hover, a:active {color:black; }
```

Figure 18.10: *Nest flexible boxes for a more complex CSS3 flexible layout.*

This example uses the flexible box model in two areas. The first is the navigation bar, which contains an unnumbered list with each list item acting as a flexible box. The second area to note is the <div id="page"> area, which contains three boxes: two sidebars and a content box arranged horizontally. The sidebars and content areas are flexible, with the content area taking up about 50 percent of the available space, the left sidebar taking up about 17 percent, and the right sidebar taking up the remaining 33 percent.

display:box, *box-orient*, and *box-flex* are three essential properties for working with flexible boxes, but several others may come in handy:

box-align: Controls alignment perpendicular to the orientation—horizontal alignment for vertical (stacked) boxes, and vertical alignment for horizontal (side-by-side) boxes. *box-align* properties are *start*, *end*, *center*, *baseline*, and *stretch*.

box-direction: Enables you to reverse the order of the boxes; instead of first to last, boxes appear last to first. Values are *normal* and *reverse*.

box-flex-group: Enables you to assign children to groups. All children that have the same *box-flex-group* number belong to the same group.

box-lines: Allows children in a group to be wrapped to two or more lines or columns. The default value is *single*. Use *box-lines:multiple* to allow children to wrap to multiple columns or rows, if necessary, to accommodate all children within the parent element.

box-ordinal-group: Provides more control over the arrangement of children than you get from *box-direction*. For example, the fifth child would normally appear fifth in the arrangement, but assign it a *box-ordinal-group* of 2, and it appears in the second spot.

box-pack: Opposite of *box-align*. Controls alignment in relation to the orientation— horizontal alignment for horizontal boxes, and vertical alignment for vertical boxes. *box-align* properties are *start*, *end*, *center*, and *justify*.

The Least You Need to Know

- Use the tic-tac-toe grid to ensure your page layouts are symmetric and well balanced.
- Create a prototype of your layout using a wireframing tool such as Mockingbird (gomockingbird.com).
- To create a horizontal navigation bar, make a list of links in HTML and then use CSS to make the list items inline elements:

```
li {display:inline; }
```

- To create a fixed-width layout, specify the widths of the elements that form the columns in pixels.
- After creating a footer, you can style the footer's paragraphs by using the *footer p* selector.
- Add *display:box* to an element's style declaration to treat the element's children as flexible boxes; use *box-orientation:vertical* or *box-orientation:horizontal* to arrange the children.

Sprucing Up Your Tables

Chapter 19

In This Chapter

- Targeting table elements for formatting
- Making things neat and tidy with borders
- Setting table width and height
- Arranging text within a table
- Colorizing your table

Tables are supposed to add order to the chaos of text by aligning entries in columns and rows. When you first create a table, however, it's anything but orderly. In fact, a table without formatting looks downright ugly.

All that's about to change. In this chapter, you discover how to take control of tables and their contents. You find out how to add borders and background colors, adjust column width and row height, add padding to give cell entries more breathing room, and more. (For guidance on creating tables, see Chapter 9.)

Targeting Table Elements with Selectors

HTML tables are comprised of numerous table tags, each of which you can use as a selector to apply styles to the table elements. Table 19.1 lists the selectors and explains the purpose of each, so you know which elements you can most easily target for formatting.

Table 19.1
Table Selectors

Use This Selector ...	To Apply Formatting To ...
table	The entire table
thead	The table heading
tbody	The body of the table
tfoot	The table's footer
th	Column headings
tr	Rows
col	Columns
td	Individual cells (data entries)
colgroup	Groups of columns
caption	Table caption

NOTE

As you focus on properties specific to tables, don't overlook standard CSS properties, such as those that apply formatting to text. You may want to choose a different font family for your table, specify different font sizes for table heading and data entries, use the *color* property to color text, make text bold or italic, and more. See Chapter 12 for more about formatting text with CSS styles.

Controlling the Borders

The first thing I like to do when formatting tables is to add borders so I can quickly glance at the table in a browser to identify its components.

Adding Borders

To add a border around a table or any of the elements within a table—including table headings, columns, and rows—use the CSS *border* property. To add a border around the entire table, for example, add the *border* property to the style declaration for the *table* selector, like this:

```
table {border:solid 1px; }
```

This places a 1-pixel border around the entire table, but not around any of the cells. To add a border around all the cells within a table, add the *border* property to the style declaration for the *table*, *td*, and *th* selectors, like so:

```
table, td, th {border:solid 1px; }
```

Unfortunately, when you add borders to table data entries, browsers insert a couple pixels of space between the cells, so your table ends up looking like the one in Figure 19.1. The next section shows you how to correct for this.

Q1 Results		
January	**February**	**March**
$100,000	$120,000	$116,050
$87,500	$89,350	$86,520
$12,500	$30,650	$29,530

Figure 19.1: *Borders around table and cells.*

Merging Table and Cell Borders

To remove the space between cells, you have two options: remove the space, or collapse the boundaries. To remove the space, add the *border-spacing:0px* declaration to the *table* selector's style rule, like this:

```
table, td, th {border:solid 1px; border-spacing:0px; }
```

This closes the gap, but you end up with a double-thick border between the cells, as shown in Figure 19.2.

Q1 Results		
January	**February**	**March**
$100,000	$120,000	$116,050
$87,500	$89,350	$86,520
$12,500	$30,650	$29,530

Figure 19.2: *Removing the gap results in a double-thick border.*

Setting *border-collapse* to *collapse* removes the spacing and collapses the borders, so the borders of the cells essentially overlap rather than butt up against one another, as shown in Figure 19.3. Add the *border-collapse:collapse* declaration to the style rule, like so:

```
table, td, th {border:1px solid black; border-collapse:collapse; }
```

Q1 Results		
January	February	March
$100,000	$120,000	$116,050
$87,500	$89,350	$86,520
$12,500	$30,650	$29,530

Figure 19.3: *Collapsed borders.*

WHOA!

Firefox handles the *border-collapse* property a little differently from most other browsers. As long as you have one style rule for *table*, *td*, and *th*, it works as expected. But if you have separate style rules for each of those selectors and add *border-collapse:collapse* to only the *table* selector's style rule, most of the borders disappear.

Specifying Table and Column Widths and Row Height

Tables flex to accommodate content. Rows are as tall as necessary to contain the entries at whatever font size is specified. The table and its columns expand as wide as the browser window allows—but you may have other ideas. The following sections explain how to take more control over table and column widths and row heights.

Establishing Table Width

To limit the width of your table, create or edit a style for the *table* selector to include the *width* property along with the desired width:

```
table {width:450px; }
```

Specifying Column Width

In tables, columns are generally as wide as the widest entry in the column, which makes it very difficult or impossible to predict just how wide columns will be. To enter precise column widths, create a column group that includes a <col> tag for each column. Place your group right after the opening <table> tag, like this:

```
<table>
<colgroup>
<col class="room-type">
<col class="price">
<col class="description">
</colgroup>
```

The <colgroup> tag is optional, but it may come in handy later. It enables you to apply formatting to all columns in the group. You can identify columns using either class or ID attributes.

Now, create a style to specify each column's width, like so:

```
.room-type {width:6em; }
.price {width:6em; }
.description {width:26em; }
```

Column widths are applied to the table, as shown in Figure 19.4.

Accommodations		
Room	**Price**	**Description**
Single	$75.00/ night	Our single rooms are designed for bargain hunters who just want to crash after a busy day at the beach. They include a double bed with a shared bathroom down the hall complete with shower.
Standard	$119.00/ night	Our standard rooms include a queen size bed, small bathroom with shower, TV, refrigerator, microwave oven, and a complimentary continental breakfast.
Deluxe	$149.00/ night	Our deluxe accommodations include a king size bed, bathroom with shower and bath, TV/DVD, refrigerator, microwave oven, and a breakfast buffet next door at the Sunshine cafe.

Figure 19.4: *Take control of column widths.*

Specifying Row Height

To have one or more rows of a specific height, create a style for the <tr> tag or a class style, and use the *height* property to set the row height. For example, to make all rows in a table the same height, create a style that looks something like this:

```
tr {height:3em; }
```

NOTE

Specifying a row height establishes a minimum height. If the content in one of the cells requires the row to be taller to accommodate it, browsers automatically increase the row height.

Aligning Text Within Cells

Columns and rows do most of the heavy lifting in aligning text in a table, but you can fine-tune the adjustment in several ways.

You can add the cellpadding attribute to the opening <table> tag and specify the amount of space between the cell contents and borders; for example <table cellpadding="8px">. This applies a uniform amount of padding to all cells. The drawback is that this is HTML, not CSS, so it doesn't carry the benefit of being able to change the cell padding for all tables on your site by editing a single style in a CSS file.

Use the *padding* property to add space between cell contents and borders. This enables you to use different amounts of padding for different cell elements; for example, you may want different amounts of padding for <th> and <td> elements. You can also specify different amounts of padding for the top, bottom, left, and right sides. See Chapter 16 for details about applying padding.

Use the *text-align* property to align text *left*, *right*, *center*, or *justified* inside the cells; for example, you may want to create a style rule such as *th {text-align:center; }* to center the heading at the top of each column.

Use the *vertical-align* property to align text vertically within a cell: *top*, *middle* (the default setting), *bottom*, or *baseline*. Baseline is nearly the same as top, although it may appear higher or lower depending on the font style and size and the line height.

Figure 19.5 shows a table formatted with uniform borders, headings centered atop the columns, table data entries vertically aligned at the top, and 8px padding all around. The CSS looks like this:

```
table {width:38em; font-size:22px; }
table, td, th {border:1px solid black; padding:8px;
  ➧ border-collapse:collapse; }
td {padding:8px; vertical-align:top; }
tr {height:1em; }
.room-type {width:6em; }
.price {width:6em; }
.description {width:26em; }
```

Accommodations		
Room	**Price**	**Description**
Single	$75.00/night	Our single rooms are designed for bargain hunters who just want to crash after a busy day at the beach. They include a double bed with a shared bathroom down the hall complete with shower.
Standard	$119.00/night	Our standard rooms include a queen size bed, small bathroom with shower, TV, refrigerator, microwave oven, and a complimentary continental breakfast.
Deluxe	$149.00/night	Our deluxe accommodations include a king size bed, bathroom with shower and bath, TV/DVD, refrigerator, microwave oven, and a breakfast buffet next door at the Sunshine cafe.

Figure 19.5: *Align text horizontally and vertically and add padding.*

Adding a Dash of Color

Color or shading not only improves the appearance of a table, but may also make a table easier to read. Many designers apply color to the table headings row and to alternating table data rows, as shown in Figure 19.6. To apply color, use the *background-color* property, as explained in Chapter 16. For example, to add color to the table heading row, create a style rule like this:

```
th {background-color:yellow; }
```

To add color to alternating rows, you have several options. You could add a class attribute to each odd or even <tr> tag and create a class style rule for the background color you want to apply, such as *.even {background-color:lightgray; }*.

You could use the selector *table tr:nth-child(odd)* and/or *table tr:nth-child(even)* to create a style rule that applies a specific background color to odd or even rows. For example, *table tr:nth-child(odd) {background-color:cyan; }* shades odd rows cyan. Unfortunately, this may not work in all web browsers.

Another option is to use JavaScript/jQuery, as explained in Chapter 22, to apply formatting to alternate rows. This may be the best option, because if you edit the table in a way that makes odd rows even and vice versa, the script automatically accommodates the change.

You can use these same techniques to apply background color to columns using *col* and *colgroup* or class/ID selectors for the style rules. The *background* properties, including *background-color* and *background-image*, and *width* property are the only properties you use with *col* and *colgroup*.

Accommodations		
Room	**Price**	**Description**
Single	$75.00/night	Our single rooms are designed for bargain hunters who just want to crash after a busy day at the beach. They include a double bed with a shared bathroom down the hall complete with shower.
Standard	$119.00/night	Our standard rooms include a queen size bed, small bathroom with shower, TV, refrigerator, microwave oven, and a complimentary continental breakfast.
Deluxe	$149.00/night	Our deluxe accommodations include a king size bed, bathroom with shower and bath, TV/DVD, refrigerator, microwave oven, and a breakfast buffet next door at the Sunshine cafe.

Figure 19.6: *Color or shading improves appearance and readability.*

NOTE

In addition to *background-color*, you can use *background-image* for any of the table elements, including the entire table.

The Least You Need to Know

- To add a border around a table and all the entries within it, create a CSS style like this:

```
table, td, th {border:solid 1px; border-collapse:collapse; }
```

- To set table width, add the *width* property to the *table* selector's style rule, like so:

```
table {width:500px; }
```

- To specify column widths, add a <col /> tag for each column following the opening <table> tag, like this:

```
<col class="price">
```

Then, create a style for each of the class or ID selectors, like so:

```
.price {width:6em; }
```

- To add space around entries in a table, use the *padding* property:

```
td, th {padding:8px; }
```

- To add color to cells, rows, or columns, edit or create a style for the *td*, *th*, *tr*, class, or ID selector for the element and use the *background-color:color* declaration to specify the color, like this:

```
th {background-color:#87CEFA; }
```

Stepping Up to More Advanced CSS

In This Chapter

- Swapping images on mouseovers
- Animating elements without complex scripts
- Keeping certain elements off-screen
- Creating CSS3 drop-down menus
- Making printable web pages

You know all you need to know about CSS to format pages, but you can do more with it to save time and deal with special situations, such as animating elements, creating your own drop-down menus, and generating print-friendly versions of web pages. This chapter introduces a few intermediate and advanced CSS techniques that may come in handy.

Executing an Image Rollover

With an *image rollover*, one image transitions into another whenever the user rests the mouse pointer on the image. Image rollovers are commonly used for buttons to indicate to a user that the mouse pointer is over the button and is ready to be clicked. The easiest way to do image rollovers is with CSS. Be sure you have two images that are the same dimensions and then use the following style rules to create your image rollover:

```
.button {width:100px; height:75px;
    ➥ background-image:url(/images/button.jpg); }
.button:hover {background-image:url(/images/button-hover.jpg); }
```

> **DEFINITION**
>
> An **image rollover** is a common special effect in which one image changes into another whenever the mouse pointer is over the image.

Hiding Stuff with the Display and Visibility Properties

The easiest way to keep elements from appearing on a page is to omit them from your source code. But suppose you want to include an element and keep it hidden. Maybe you have a page title that you want to include for search engine optimization (SEO) purposes but keep out of view so it doesn't conflict with your header image.

To hide an element but retain the space it occupies, set its *visibility* property to *hidden*, like so:

```
#logo {visibility:hidden; }
```

To hide an element and clear the space it occupies, set its *display* property to *none*, like this:

```
#logo {display:none; }
```

Because search engines may ignore elements hidden with the *visibility* or *display* properties, you may want to just shove an element off the left or right side of the screen (or even off the top or bottom) by giving the element a huge margin setting, like this:

```
#logo {margin-left:-9999em; }
```

Unless a visitor has a flat screen monitor as wide as a football field, they'll never see it, but search engines will.

Rotating, Scaling, Moving, and More with CSS Transform

Chapters 16 through 18 reveal a handful of techniques making the most of the CSS box model. One thing it doesn't mention is that in CSS3, you can *transform* boxes, including images. The CSS *transform* property enables you to rotate elements, scale them to different sizes, translate (move) them, and skew them so the boxes appear as though they're leaning (see Figure 20.1). Combine CSS transform with transitions and animations, as explained later in this chapter, and you have a powerful animation tool.

Original Translate Rotate Skew Scale

Figure 20.1: *Transform objects in CSS.*

The following sections explain how to put the CSS *transform* property into action. See "Animating Objects with CSS," later in this chapter, for details on how to create transitions and animations.

Rotating Elements

Using the CSS *transform* property, you can rotate images and boxed elements any number of degrees on a page in any direction. Rotate an image 90 degrees, for example, to place it on its side. Rotate it 180 degrees to flip it over.

To rotate an element, create a style for it using its tag, class, or ID selector. Here's an example for rotating an element 5 degrees counterclockwise, as shown in Figure 20.2:

```
.rotate (transform:rotate(-5deg); }
```

Figure 20.2: *This object is rotated 5 degrees counterclockwise.*

During the writing of this book, the rotation feature wasn't included in the official CSS3 specification. Until it is, include the property prefixes for the various web browsers that support the *transform* property:

```
.rotate {-webkit-transform:rotate(-5deg);
-moz-transform:rotate(-5deg);
-o-transform:rotate(-5deg);
 transform:rotate(-5deg); }
```

Unfortunately, during the writing of this book, Internet Explorer offered little support for CSS rotation. You could fairly easily rotate something in 90-degree increments, but that's nearly useless. For what it's worth, here's the style declaration for CSS rotation in Internet Explorer:

```
filter:progid:DXImageTransform.Microsoft.BasicImage(rotation=3);
```

You can set rotation equal to 1, 2, 3, or 4 representing 90, 180, 270, and 360 degrees, respectively. You can rotate objects in increments, but the code is so convoluted, it's not worth it. Hopefully, Internet Explorer 9 will support *transform:rotate*.

Scaling Elements: Bigger or Smaller

Use *transform:scale* declarations to make elements bigger or smaller. This enables you to use the same element—for instance, the same image—at different sizes. Here's an example for making an element 50 percent larger:

```
.scale50 {transform:scale(50); }
```

During the writing of this book, the scale feature wasn't included in the official CSS3 specification. Until it is, use the following style declarations to scale an element:

```
.scale50 {-webkit-transform:scale(-30deg);
-moz-transform:scale(-30deg);
-o-transform:scale(-30deg);
 transform:scale(-30deg); }
```

Translating Elements from Point A to Point B

Chapter 17 shows you how to position objects, but CSS3 also enables you to move an object the desired distance in the desired direction from its original starting point. At first glance, this might not seem like a big deal—after all, why wouldn't you just position the element where you wanted it in the first place? When combined with transitions and animations, however, the *translate* property can dynamically move an object across the screen when an event occurs, such as a user moving the mouse pointer over the object or clicking it.

The *translate* property uses *x* and *y* coordinates to move elements. You specify the coordinate (*x* or *y*) and the distance (a positive or negative value), and the browser moves the element the specified distance along the *x* or *y* axis in the specified direction, as shown in Figure 20.3. Here's an example that moves an element 100 pixels to the right (*x* axis) and 75 pixels down (*y* axis):

```
.translate100 {transform:translate (100px, 75px); }
```

To move an element left or up, use negative values.

If the *translate* property isn't supported in the current browsers, try the following style declarations:

```
.translate100 {-webkit-transform:translate (100px, 75px);
-moz-transform:translate (100px, 75px);
-o-transform:translate (100px, 75px);
 transform:translate (100px, 75px); }
```

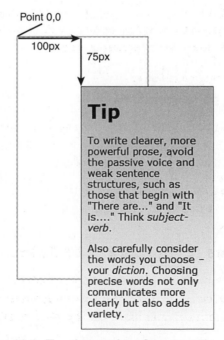

Figure 20.3: *Translate an object from point A to point B.*

Skewing Elements

In CSS3, you can skew elements so they appear as though they're leaning left or right. Here's an example that skews a text box 15 degrees clockwise:

```
.translateSkew {transform:skew(15deg); }
```

If necessary, use the prefixes for the various browsers: *-moz-*, *-webkit-*, and *-o-*.

Avoid overusing CSS skew. It's like italics—you don't make an entire page of text italic. Use skews sparingly, if at all.

Animating Objects with CSS

Two of the coolest new features of CSS3 are the *transition* and *animation* properties. These enable you to animate objects without the use of jQuery, JavaScript, Flash, or even animated GIFs. All you do is add the property to the object's style along with values that control the transition or animation. The following sections show you how.

> **WHOA!**
>
> During the writing of this book, *transition* and *animation* were available only in the CSS specification draft, so you had to add the draft prefixes *-o-* for Opera, *-webkit-* for webkit browsers, and *-moz-* for Firefox. Internet Explorer did not support transitions and animations. Hopefully, by the time you read this, all browsers will support these cool effects without the tweaks.

Creating Transitions

Transitions enable you to gradually change an element from one state to another when certain events occur, such as when a user places the mouse on the object or clicks it. To create a transition, here's what you do:

1. Create a style rule for the element's initial state that also contains the *transition* property and details the transition.

2. Create a style rule for the element's second (final) state, using a pseudo selector, and include properties to specify the location and appearance of the element in its final state.

Here's an example that transitions a red box (with the class="red-green" attribute) into a green box:

```
.red-green {height:100px; width:100px; background:red;
transition:all 2s ease-in-out; }
.red-green:hover {background:green; }
```

The first style specifies the properties of the element in its initial state. The *transition* declaration states that *all* properties are to be transitioned over the course of *2s* (2 seconds), easing into one property and out of the other.

The second style uses the pseudo class *hover*, so when the mouse is over the element, it transitions to green. (For more about using pseudo selectors to trigger changes in an element, see Chapter 10.)

You may need several *transition* declarations starting with *-o-*, *-moz-*, and *-webkit-* to get this to work in various browsers; for example:

```
.red-green {height:100px; width:100px; background:red;
-moz-transition:all 2s ease-in-out;
-webkit-transition:all 2s ease-in-out;
-o-transition:all 2s ease-in-out;
transition:all 2s ease-in-out; }
.red-green:hover {background:green; }
```

Instead of *ease-in-out*, you may use *linear*, *ease-in*, *ease-out*, and *cubic-bezier* (to define a custom effect, which is beyond the scope of this discussion). Try the different values to see which one you prefer. Instead of *all*, you can specify only those properties you want to include in the transition.

The *transition* property becomes a powerful animation tool when combined with the *transform* property. Here's sample CSS that transitions an element (with the class="rotate" attribute) smoothly from one position to another while rotating it 90 degrees and doubling its size:

```
.rotate {height:100px; width:100px; border:solid 1px black;
transition:all 2s ease-in-out; }
.rotate:hover {
transform:translate(100px,100px) rotate(90deg); scale(2); }
```

If you want your box to spin around a few times, use a rotation degree that's a multiple of 360, such as 720 or 1,440.

Creating Animations

Transitions may be sufficient for your animation needs, but if you need something more powerful, consider using a CSS animation. Animations tend to be smoother. They also enable you to use *tweens*, meaning that in addition to the start and end state of an element, you may add other states in be*tween*.

CSS animations are more involved than transitions, and during the writing of this book, browser support was scarce. If you'd like to try it, first describe the animation using the *@-webkit-keyframes* rule, like so:

```
@-webkit-keyframes fly {
0% {background-color:red; left:50px; top:100px; }
50% {background-color:green; left:200px; top:300px; }
100% {background-color:blue; left:400px; top:100px; }
}
```

This rule defines three keyframes. The object starts out red at coordinates 50px,100px; turns green as it travels to 200px,300px; and turns blue as it travels to 400px,100px. Now you must apply the animation to an element to provide additional instructions for the execution. Here's an example:

```
.bounce {
-webkit-animation-name:fly;
-webkit-animation-duration:4s;
-webkit-animation-direction:alternate;
-webkit-animation-timing-function:ease-in-out;
 width:200px; height:200px;
 background-color:blue; left:400px; top:100px;
 position:absolute; }
```

The first line establishes this as a class style rule, the second line calls the webkit keyframes rule "fly" into action, the third line specifies the duration of the animation, the fourth line specifies its direction, the fifth line specifies the timing function (in this case, ease-in-out), and the sixth line specifies the object's dimensions. The last two lines specify the object's final resting position and color.

Keep in mind that you must have an element on your web page that has the class="bounce" attribute for this to work.

Creating a CSS-Only Drop-Down Menu

Using straight CSS with the *:hover* pseudo class, you can create your own navigation bar drop-down menus. To keep this simple, I'm presenting minimal code. You can expand the HTML to include all the links and submenus you want and add style rules to make the navigation bar and drop-down menus appear however you want them to.

Here's the HTML (note that the closing tag for the third list item does not appear until after the sublist that follows it):

```
<nav>
<ul>
<li><a href="#">Item 1</a></li>
<li><a href="#">Item 2</a></li>
<li><a href="#">Item 3</a>
<ul>
<li><a href="#">Submenu Item 1</a></li>
<li><a href="#">Submenu Item 1</a></li>
<li><a href="#">Submenu Item 1</a></li>
</ul>
</li>
<li><a href="#">Item 4</a></li>
</ul>
</nav>
```

The CSS goes like this:

```
li {list-style:none; padding:10px; }
li ul {padding:0px; }
nav {z-index:4; display:block; }
nav li {float:left; }
nav li:hover {position:relative; }
nav li a {display:block; }
nav li ul {margin-top:-2px; display:none; }
nav li:hover ul {display:block; position:absolute; }
nav li ul li a {width:120px; }
```

WHOA!

This example uses the <nav> tag, which was not supported in all browsers during the writing of this book. If this doesn't work in Internet Explorer, replace <nav> with <div id="nav">. In the CSS, replace the *nav* with *#nav*. Or add the following to the top of your HTML document between the opening and closing <head> tags above any CSS tags:

```
<!--[if lt IE 9]>
<script src="http://html5shiv.googlecode.com/svn/trunk/
➥ html5.js"></script>
<![endif]-->
```

Figure 20.4 shows the completed drop-down menu.

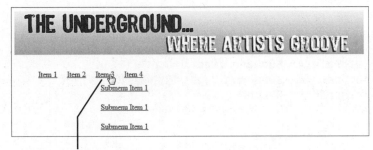

Hover over Item 3 to display drop-down menu

Figure 20.4: *Here's a CSS-only drop-down menu.*

To add some flair with CSS3, use the *transition* and *opacity* properties to the *nav li ul* and *nav li:hover ul* styles, like so:

```
nav li ul {margin-top:-2px; display:none;
opacity:0;
-moz-transition:all 1s ease-in-out;
-webkit-transition:all 1s ease-in-out;
-o-transition:all 1s ease-in-out;
transition:all 1s ease-in-out;
 }
nav li:hover ul {display:block; opacity:1; position:absolute; }
```

Creating Printable Versions of Web Pages

Web pages typically are packed with content visitors don't want or need when they choose to print the page—elements such as the page header, sidebars, and footers. To prevent these elements from appearing in the printed version, you may create a separate style sheet to control the appearance of elements in print.

> **WHOA!**
>
> If you're using a CMS such as WordPress to manage your site, check the theme you're using for a print.css file. In WordPress, log on, open the **Appearance** menu, click **Editor**, and check the Templates list (off to the right) for a file called print.css. If the theme already has a print.css file, you can edit it rather than starting from scratch.

To style pages for print, here's what you do:

1. Create a new text-only file and name it print.css. This will become a special cascading style sheet to format elements specifically for printing.

2. At the top of the new print.css style sheet, type the following:

```
/* Print Style Sheet */
@media print {
body {background:white; color:black; margin:0 }
}
```

3. For each element you don't want to print, include the *display:none* declaration, like so:

```
/* Print Style Sheet */
@media print {
body {background:white; color:black; margin:0 }
header, nav, footer, #sidebar-left, #sidebar-right
.advertisement .noprint {display:none;}
}
```

4. For each section you do want to include in the printed document, add the *margin-left:0* and *width* declarations along with any other style preferences:

```
/* Print Style Sheet */
@media print {
body {background:white; color:black; margin:0 }
header, nav, footer, #sidebar-left, #sidebar-right
  ➥ .advertisement .noprint {display:none;}
article, section {margin-left:0; width:auto; font-size:12px;
  ➥ border:none; }
aside {width:25%; float:right; font-size:11px; border:solid
  ➥ 1px #000000; }
}
```

5. Upload the print.css file to your web server. If you're using a CMS to manage your site, you typically place the file in the folder for the template you're using.

6. Include the following tag between the opening and closing <head> tags for the page, replacing "print.css" with the path and filename of the *print.css* file:

```
<link rel="stylesheet" href="print.css" type="text/css"
  ➥ media="print" />
```

If you're using a CMS to manage your site, you may need to insert the following tag into the *head* section of one of your template's PHP files (typically head.php):

```
<link rel="stylesheet" type="text/css" media="print"
href="<?php bloginfo('stylesheet_directory'); ?>/print.css" />
```

When you're done, open the page and try printing it. Depending on the results, you may need to make some adjustments to the print.css file.

Specifying Different Media Types

Just as you can create a different style sheet for applying print formatting, you can use other CSS media queries to customize web page layout and formatting for different devices, such as mobile devices, and display orientations—landscape or portrait. CSS2 introduced media types, but CSS3 pushes the concept further with *media queries*.

DEFINITION

A **media query** is a statement that instructs browsers to use a certain style sheet based on the capabilities of the device and/or browser displaying the page. The query consists of a media type and specifications for the device. For example:

```
@media screen and (orientation:portrait)
```

is for display of the page on a monitor when the browser window is taller than it is wide.

Media queries are used primarily to apply different styles to web pages for display on mobile devices, including the iPhone, Android, and BlackBerry. You can use media queries to check the width and height of the device or the browser window, the orientation (landscape or portrait), the screen resolution, and more.

The steps for using media queries are nearly the same as those for creating printable versions of web pages:

1. Create a new text-only file, and name it something like iphone.css. This will become a special cascading style sheet to format elements specifically for iPhones.

2. At the top of the new css file, type the media query you want to use. Because the iPhone has a display width of 480px, the media query (preceded by a comment) looks like this:

```
/* iPhone Style Sheet */
@media screen and (max-device-width:480px)
```

3. For any elements you want to exclude, add the *display:none* declaration, like so:

```
/* iPhone Style Sheet */
@media screen and (max-device-width:480px) {
footer {display:none; }
}
```

4. For each section you want to include, create a style:

```
/* iPhone Style Sheet */
@media screen and (max-device-width:480px) {
body {background-color:#ffffff; color:#000000; font-size:12px;
   ➥ margin:0; padding:0; }
nav ul {list-style:none; margin:8px; padding:0px; }
nav ul li a {background-color:#ffffff; border:1px solid
   ➥ #6c6c6c; color:#000000; display:block; font-size:16px;
   ➥ font-weight:bold; padding:12px 10px; text-decoration:none; }
}
```

5. Upload the iphone.css file to your web server. If you're using a CMS to manage your site, you typically place the file in the folder for the template you're using.

6. Include the following tag between the opening and closing <head> tags for the page, replacing "iphone.css" with the path and filename of the *iphone.css* file:

```
<link rel="stylesheet" href="iphone.css" type="text/css"
 media="" />
```

If you're using a CMS to manage your site, insert the following tag into the *head* section of one of your template's PHP files (typically head.php), replacing iphone.css with the path and filename of the *iphone.css* file:

```
<link rel="stylesheet" type="text/css" media="screen and
 (max-device-width:480px)"
href="<?php bloginfo('stylesheet_directory'); ?>/iphone.css" />
```

7. In this particular case, you also need to include the following tag between the opening and closing <head> tags at the top of the document so the Safari browser knows that the page is the width of the display and not the default 980 pixels wide:

```
<meta name="viewport" content="user-scalable=no,
 width=device-width" />
```

As you can see, styling for display on different devices can become very involved. In many cases, you may even want to streamline the content, essentially creating a version for display on standard PC monitors and another version for mobile browsers.

Styling Text for Speech Synthesis

To make your site more universally accessible, you may want to provide styles that tell browsers how to "read" the text to the user. Aural browsers convert documents to plain text and then use a screen reader to "read" the words aloud. All you need to do is create a style for all your text elements with properties specifying how you want the words and characters sounded out. Here's an example:

```
h1, h2, h3, h4, p {voice-family:female; voice-volume:medium;
 speech-rate:fast; pitch:low; }
```

CSS3 features numerous properties and associated values to control how speech is synthesized. For details, visit w3.org/TR/css3-speech.

The Least You Need to Know

- Changing an element's *visibility* property to *hidden* hides the element and retains the space the element occupies.
- Changing an element's *display* property to *none* hides the element and frees up the space the element occupies.
- To rotate a box in most browsers, create a class style such as the following, and add the class attribute to the element's opening tag:
  ```
  .rotate (-webkit-transform:rotate(-15deg);
  -moz-transform:rotate(-15deg);
  transform:rotate(-15deg);
  ```
- Use pseudo selectors and the *transition* property to create your own drop-down menus.
- To create a print version of a web page, create a separate print.css file containing the styles to format elements for printing and then link to print.css by inserting the following tag in the page's header area:
  ```
  <link rel="stylesheet" href="print.css" type="text/css"
  ➡ media="print" />
  ```

Making Your Pages More Dynamic and Interactive

CSS beautifies web pages, but it does little to enable users to interact with those pages. Part 4 reveals a few ways to make your site more dynamic and interactive.

Here, you discover the basics of using forms to collect data and how to use jQuery to dynamically change a page's contents and/or appearance in response to a user's actions. (jQuery is a collection of JavaScript scripts that makes programming web pages a whole lot easier.) Chapter 23 features a demonstration of HTML5's new canvas element to give you a basic understanding of how the canvas functions.

As a bonus, I reveal a couple tools that greatly simplify form building and design: Form Boss and PHP Form Generator. These tools not only enable you to create forms using HTML and CSS, but they also help generate the scripts required to process the form data. Form Boss can even help secure the data users enter.

Gathering Feedback and Other Data with Forms

In This Chapter

- Creating no-hassle forms with a form generator
- Building a form from the ground up
- Putting CSS to work on your form

You've encountered forms on the web. Visit Google, and you're greeted by a search form. To register online, order and pay for *anything*, and perhaps even schedule your next doctor's visit, you complete and submit a form. This is all fairly easy.

Life becomes more difficult when you're on the receiving end—when you need to create and use forms on your site to collect data. In this chapter, you discover how to create forms and learn the basics of processing form data. I show you the easy way to create and use forms first and then reveal some of what goes on behind the curtain, so you have a few tools to customize and troubleshoot forms if the need arises.

Wrapping Your Brain Around Forms

A form is a fill-in-the-blanks page that enables users to enter data. Form fields include text boxes, check box and radio button options, drop-down menus, dates, passwords, and e-mail, phone, and website addresses. Using HTML, you can create all these form fields and more. Creating the form isn't very difficult, as you'll see later in this chapter.

The challenging part comes in validating and processing the data and then doing something with it, such as sending it to yourself via e-mail or storing it in a database you can access. For this, you need a program or script that works behind the scenes.

Writing *PHP* scripts and creating *CGI* applications to process form data are beyond the scope of this book, but by using a form generator, you can easily clear that hurdle.

DEFINITION

PHP (short for hypertext preprocessor) is the most popular scripting language for processing form data and performing numerous other tasks that make web pages more dynamic and interactive. It's particularly well suited for managing the exchange of data between web pages and databases.

CGI (short for common gateway interface) is a scripting language commonly used for processing form data.

Taking the Easier Route

Creating a form and getting it to look pretty and function properly is a huge challenge. You need to know not only how to work with HTML form elements, but also how to style those elements with CSS, compose scripts to process the data, and—if you want entries stored in a database—how to set up a structured query language (SQL) database to receive the data. This is no small feat for rank beginners or even those who are more tech savvy and experienced. A better solution, especially if you need something more than a contact form, is to use a form generator.

With a form generator, you choose the fields to include on the form, specify field sizes, type field names and options, and fiddle with the layout. The form generator does the rest. Some form generators such as FormBoss (formboss.net) even handle the data processing for you and provide tools for more easily accessing the data and exporting it. Figure 21.1 shows a form being created in FormBoss.

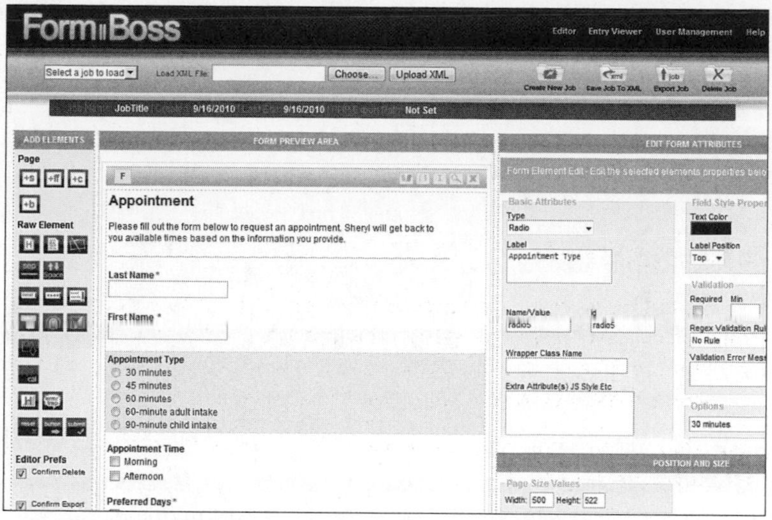

Figure 21.1: *Build a form in FormBoss.*

I've added forms to sites in all sorts of ways using all sorts of tools. The first step is to assess your needs. If you need something basic, such as a contact form, and you're using a CMS to manage your site, check for the availability of a secure contact form plug-in. Some contact form plug-ins include settings you can adjust or a style sheet you can edit to make your form fit in with your site's layout and color scheme.

If your needs are modest but you require something more than a contact form, consider building your own forms online for free using a tool such as phpFormGenerator (phpformgen.sourceforge.net), shown in Figure 21.2.

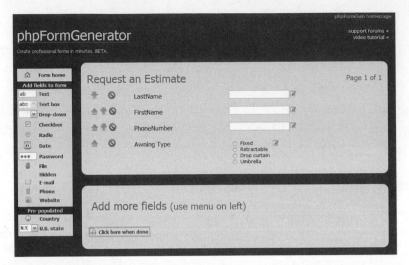

Figure 21.2: *phpFormGenerator builds the form and the PHP scripts for processing the data.*

If you need to process orders and online payments, check out turnkey e-commerce solutions available through your web hosting service. You may also want to check out what popular merchant services have to offer, including PayPal (paypal.com), eBay (ebay.com), and Google Checkout (checkout.google.com). PayPal now includes a feature that enables non-PayPal members to pay using a credit card.

If you need secure forms (for example, for a medical office), check online for secure form processing services. If you decide to fly solo, you probably need to contact your web hosting provider about upgrading to secure web hosting. You can then use a form generator, such as FormBoss, to create the secure forms you need.

INSIDE TIP

You can build forms online at phpformgen.sourceforge.net and download the source code for the form, but then you have to clear the hurdle of getting the form to work on your hosting service. Instead, see if your hosting service has an option for installing phpFormGenerator. If it does, install phpFormGenerator on your account and use it to create the forms you need. Your forms will then run on your sites without any additional configuration.

Building a Form by Hand

HTML enables do-it-yourselfers to code forms by hand. As mentioned earlier in this chapter, creating an HTML form isn't very difficult. Using about a dozen tags and another dozen or so attributes, you can build your own custom forms.

The following sections introduce you to the various form elements and their attributes. Even if you use a form generator to build your form, this information can come in handy if you need to troubleshoot or reconfigure a form.

Establishing the Overall Structure

The overall structure of a form consists of an opening and closing <form> tag that brackets one or more <input> tags along with at least one button—the Submit button. Here's the source code for a very basic form:

```
<form action='process.php' method='post' enctype='multipart/form-data'>
<label>Name:</label> <input type=text name='name' size=20>
<input type='submit' value='submit form'>
</form>
```

This form enables a user to enter his or her name and then submit it, as shown in Figure 21.3. Of course, until you have a process.php with instructions on what to do with that data, this form actually does nothing.

Figure 21.3: *A very basic form.*

The opening <form> tag typically includes the following three attributes:

action (a required attribute) indicates where to send the form data when the user submits it. Typically, you send the form data to a php script, such as process.php, which provides instructions on what to do with the data. You can also send the data to an HTML file for display or processing.

method (a required attribute) specifies how to send the form data. You have two choices here:

- *get* appends form data to the URL targeted in the *action* attribute, making it useful in cases when users may want to bookmark the result. For example, the Google search form uses the get method; if you perform a search, you'll see your search entry in the URL of the page results, and you can bookmark it. Drawbacks are that the amount of data is limited (to 2 kilobytes or 2,048 characters) and the get method is very insecure, making it a poor choice for collecting sensitive data, including passwords and credit card numbers.

- *post* has no data limitations and is more secure than the get method, but users cannot bookmark the form results.

enctype specifies how form data is encoded before being sent. You have three options here:

- *application/x-www-form-urlencoded* encodes all characters before the data is sent. This is the default, so if you omit the *enctype* attribute, this encoding is used.

- *multipart/form-data* does not encode characters. If your form allows users to upload files, this is the enctype to use.

- *text/plain* converts spaces to + signs but does not encode any other characters.

Other common attributes for the <form> tag are *name* and *ID*. *name* enables you to assign a name to the form, which comes in handy if you need to reference the form in a script. *ID* is useful for identifying the form so you can apply CSS styles to it.

Adding Labels and Fields to Your Form

When adding input fields to a form, you typically use two tags: <label> and <input>. <label> (a paired tag) displays a brief description of the field so the user knows what kind of input is required; for example <label>First Name</label> indicates that the input field requires the user to enter his or her first name. <input> (an unpaired tag) creates the text boxes and other fields that actually accept user input.

<input> almost always includes the type and name attributes (for example, <input type="text" name="firstname" />). Although type is not a required attribute, you should always include it to tell the browser the type of input required.

Many of the available types specify the type of input required, but a few actually cause the browser to display unique controls on the screen, including check boxes, radio buttons, and pop-up calendars from which to choose dates. See Figure 21.4.

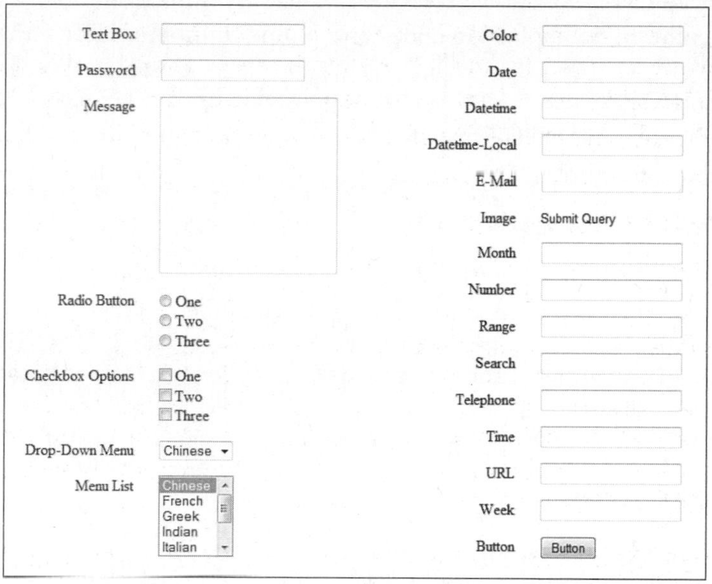

Figure 21.4: *You can use a variety of types of input fields.*

The name attribute helps identify the entries when you receive the data via e-mail or it's saved to a database. The name attribute is particularly important if you're saving data to a database because it specifies the column in which the data entry belongs.

The following sections show how to create various types of fields, including text boxes, text areas, check box and radio button options, and drop-down lists.

WHOA!

Labels can include spaces, but *names* must not have any spaces between them. For example, use *First Name* as the label, but *firstname* or *FirstName* as the name.

Adding a Text Box

Many fields on forms are simple text boxes used to collect entries such as a user's name, address, and telephone number. For text input, you typically specify the size of the text box and assign a name. You can also specify a maximum length for the entry, which can come in handy for zip codes and phone numbers. Here's an example:

```
<p><label>ZIP code</label></p> <input type="text" name="zip"
➡ size="5" maxlength="5" />
```

Adding a Password Box

A password box is nothing more than a text box in which the characters appear as asterisks as the user types the entry. Here's an example:

```
<p><label>Password</label></p> <input type="password" name="password"
➡ size="20" />
```

Adding a Text Area

A text area enables a user to type a somewhat lengthy entry. It's useful for contact forms in which you ask the user to send you a message. Instead of the <input> tag, you use the <textarea> tag and specify the height in rows and the width in columns:

```
<p><label>Message</label></p> <textarea rows="10" columns="20"
➡ maxlength="1000"></textarea>
```

INSIDE TIP

Although you can specify the dimensions of the text area with the rows and columns attributes, you may want to consider using CSS height and width attributes instead, especially if you're using several forms on your site that include text areas with the same dimensions. By using CSS, you can change the dimensions of all text-area elements at any time just by changing the style attributed to it.

Adding Check Box Options

In some cases, you may want users to select specific entries rather than typing whatever they want. In these cases, consider using check box or radio button options. What's the difference between the two? With check boxes, users can choose more than one option in a group. With radio button options (explained in the next section), users can choose only one option.

When creating a group of check box options, give every option in the group the same name, and always include the required value attribute. Here's an example:

```
<p><label>Favorite sports</label></p>
<input type="checkbox" name="sports" value="baseball" />Baseball<br />
<input type="checkbox" name="sports" value="football" />Football<br />
<input type="checkbox" name="sports" value="golf" />Golf<br />
<input type="checkbox" name="sports" value="soccer" />Soccer<br />
<input type="checkbox" name="sports" value="tabletennis" />Table
    ➡ Tennis<br />
<input type="checkbox" name="sports" value="tennis" />Tennis<br />
```

Figure 21.5 shows the check box list in a browser.

Figure 21.5: *Check box options.*

Adding Radio Button Options

Radio buttons force users to pick one option: Yes/No, True/False, favorite flavor, a political party, a candidate for election, … you name it. As with check box options, the value attribute is required. Here's an example:

```
<p><label>Which issue do you feel is most important?</label></p>
<input type="radio" name="issue" value="economy" />Economy<br />
<input type="radio" name="issue" value="education" />Education<br />
<input type="radio" name="issue" value="energy" />Energy<br />
<input type="radio" name="issue" value="environment" />Environment<br />
<input type="radio" name="issue" value="nationalsecurity" />National
    ➡ Security<br />
```

NOTE

With either the check box or radio button options, you can add the checked="checked" attribute to have an option selected by default. Businesses often use this on their sites to encourage (trick?) people into opting in to receive e-mail.

Creating a Menu

To create drop-down menus or lists of options, use the <select> tag along with <option> tags. Here's an example:

```
<p><label>What's your favorite ethnic food?</label></p>
<select name="ethnicfood">
<option value="chinese">Chinese</option>
<option value="french">French</option>
<option value="greek">Greek</option>
<option value="indian">Indian</option>
<option value="italian">Italian</option>
<option value="mexican">Mexican</option>
<option value="polish">Polish</option>
</select>
```

Figure 21.6 shows the menu in action.

What's your favorite ethnic food?

Chinese
Chinese
French
Greek
Indian
Italian
Mexican
Polish

Figure 21.6: *A drop-down form menu.*

You can add optional attributes to control the appearance of your menu and how it functions. Add selected="selected" to an option to preselect it. If this is omitted, the first option is the preselected choice.

Add the size attribute, and set it to the number of options you have to display all options without having to open a drop-down list; for example, if you have five options, add size="5". If you have five options and use something like size="3", three options appear in the box, along with a scroll bar on the right side of the box that enables users to bring the other options into view.

Allowing Users to Upload Files

With a form, users can send you files. For example, if you're using your form to collect information for a membership directory, you may want to enable users to send you digital photos of themselves to include in the directory.

First, be sure your opening <form> tag contains attributes that allow for file uploads. Specifically, it must include *enctype="multipart/form-data"*. Use the <input> tag with the type attribute set to *"file"*, and the accept attribute set to acceptable file types. Here's an example:

```
<input type="file" name="photo" size="30" accept="image/jpeg" />
```

WHOA!

Allowing users to upload files is somewhat risky, even if you restrict the upload to certain file types. Be sure the server-side script you're using (for example, a PHP script) includes something to validate the file to ensure it's an acceptable type and does not exceed a predetermined size. Consult a book on PHP to find out how to write a script that specifies a location for uploaded files and performs the necessary validation for secure uploads.

Adding Submit and Reset Buttons

All forms must include at least one button—a Submit button users can click to submit the data they entered. When a user clicks the button, the browser sends the data to the URL specified in the <form> tag's action attribute. To create a Submit button, you use the <input> tag and set the type attribute to *"submit"*. The <input> tag requires no additional attributes, but you probably want to include a name attribute to identify which button the user clicks. If you want the text on the button to be something other than Submit, you can add the value attribute.

Here's an example that changes the text on the button from Submit to Send:

```
<input type="submit" name="submit" value="Send" />
```

You may also want to include a Reset button users can click to clear all their field entries and start over. Here's sample source code for a Reset button:

```
<input type="reset" name="reset" value="startover" />
```

You can use the <button> tag in place of the <input> tag for the Submit and Reset buttons by including the type="submit" or type="reset" attributes. Unlike the <input> tag, <button> is a paired tag, so it enables you to add content and provides more flexibility in styling buttons.

INSIDE TIP

You can create your own Submit button; save it as a jpg, gif, or png file; and use it as your Submit button. To insert the button in your form, use the <input> tag with the type="image" attribute, the src attribute set to the location of the image on your web server, and the alt attribute set to alternative text to display if users can't see the button image. Here's an example:

```
<input type="img" src="images/submit.jpg" alt="Submit" />
```

Creating Other Form Fields

Although text boxes, check box and radio button options, drop-down lists, and the Submit button are the bread and butter of most forms, numerous other field types are available—many of which have been introduced in HTML5. Following are a list of values you can use with the type attribute to create a variety of data input fields (some of these may not be supported in all web browsers):

color lets the user specify a color.

date displays a pop-up calendar for selecting a specific date.

datetime displays a pop-up calendar along with a spin box for specifying the time in hours and minutes.

datetime-local is the same as datetime but for local dates and times.

email accepts only e-mail addresses that include the @ sign.

month displays a pop-up calendar for selecting a month.

number displays a spin box for entering a whole number.

range displays a slider for the user to drag to specify an imprecise number or selection.

search accepts search words and phrases.

tel accepts a telephone number.

time displays a spin box for specifying the time in hours and minutes.

url accepts only URLs that look like URLs; for example, google.com, not simply "google."

week displays a pop-up calendar for selecting a week.

Grouping Related Form Elements

If you have a long form, consider sectioning it off into groups of related fields. An online job application, for example, may have separate sections, including Personal Information, Work History, Education, and References. To group related fields, sandwich the fields between an opening and closing <fieldset> tag. You can label the group with a legend element. Here's an example:

```
<legend>Personal Information</legend>
<fieldset>
<p><label>First Name</label></p> <input type="text" name="firstname"
    ➥ size="20" />
<p><label>Last Name</label></p> <input type="text" name="lastname"
    ➥ size="20" />
<p><label>Street Address & Apt. #</label></p> <input type="text"
    ➥ name="address" size="30" />
<p><label>City or Town</label></p> <input type="text" name="city"
    ➥ size="20" />
<p><label>Zip</label></p> <input type="text" name="zip" size="5"
    ➥ maxlength="5" />
<p><label>Home Phone or Cell Number</label></p> <input type="tel"
    ➥ name="telephone" size="10" maxlength="10" />
<p><label>Birthdate</label></p> <input type="date" name="birthdate" />
</fieldset>
```

Figure 21.7 shows the result.

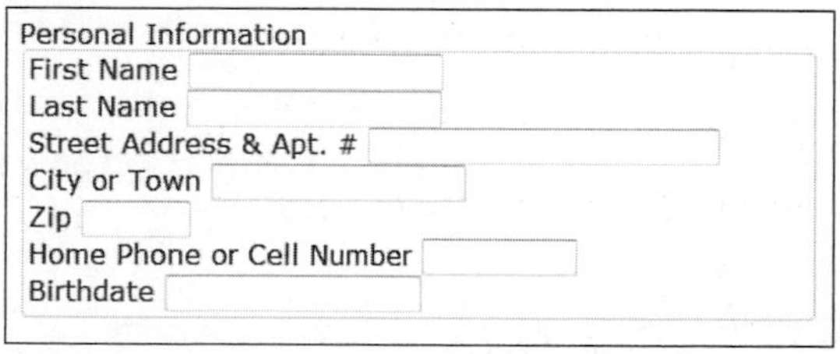

Figure 21.7: *Group fields to simplify data entry.*

Using Hidden Fields

The hidden attribute enables you to include data entries in the transmission the user doesn't see and/or didn't enter. For example, you may want a record of the date and time the form was submitted, and you don't want to bother asking the user to enter it. In such cases, simply add the hidden="hidden" attribute to the <input> tag.

Disabling Fields

Why include fields if you're just going to disable them? Well, you may want to disable certain fields to make them available only if the user chooses a specific entry in another field. For example, if you have radio button options for Male and Female, you may want to disable the Pregnant: Yes/No field and activate it only if the user chooses Female. You do this by adding the disabled="disabled" attribute to the <input> tag(s) for the field entries you want to disable.

Including Other Useful Attributes

Form elements support the standard HTML5 attributes, including ID, class, and accesskey and the event attributes. Form elements have several attributes designed solely for forms, however, which can come in very handy when you're building your forms. Table 21.1 lists and describes the most useful of the bunch not already covered in this chapter.

Table 21.1
Table Attributes

Attribute	Value	Description
autocomplete	*on* or *off*	When on, enables browsers to complete the form with the user's previous entries, if the user returns to the form.
autofocus	*autofocus*	Focuses on this specific field when the page loads.
form	*formname*	Identifies the forms to which the input field belongs.
formaction	*URL*	Overrides the form's action attribute.
formenctype	*application/ x-www-form- urlencoded multipart/form- data text/plain*	Overrides the form's enctype attribute.

Attribute	Value	Description
formmethod	*get post put delete*	Overrides the form's method attribute.
formnovalidate	*true false*	Overrides the form's novalidate attribute.
height	*pixels %*	Sets the input field's height.
list	*id of a datalist*	Tags a list of options.
max	*number*	Specifies the input field's maximum value.
min	*number*	Specifies the input field's minimum value.
multiple	*multiple*	Allows the user to enter more than one value.
pattern	*JavaScript Pattern*	Defines a pattern or format for the input field's value. For example, pattern="[0-9]".
placeholder	*text*	Provides a hint to help users decide what to enter.
readonly	*readonly*	Prevents a preexisting value in a field from being modified.
required	*required*	Specifies whether a field entry is required.
step	*number any*	Allowed for type=date, datetime, datetime-local, month, week, time, number, or range.
width	*pixels %*	Sets the width of an input field.

Spiffing Up Your Form with Some CSS

Forms look terrible without CSS. All the fields are scrunched up, and without some color, your entire form appears washed out. To bring your form to life, add some CSS style. Figure 21.8 shows a form without CSS.

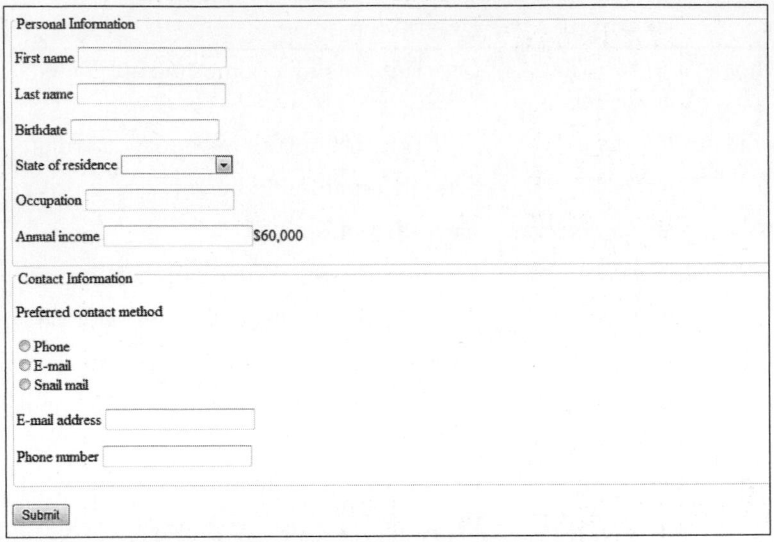

Figure 21.8: *A form before CSS.*

Adding a little style with CSS, you can make the form much more attractive and easier for the user to navigate and complete. Following is some sample CSS for formatting a form. The results are shown in Figure 21.9.

```
body { font-family:Verdana; font-size:0.95em; }
form { min-width:30em; max-width:40em; width:56em; border:1px solid
    ➥ #ccc; padding:.5em; }
label {display:block; float:left; width:10em; padding:0;
    ➥ text-align:right; }
select, options, input, textarea {margin-left:2em; }
.radio {display:block; padding-left:10em; }
legend {color:#fff; background:orange; padding:6px; border:0;
    ➥ font-weight:bold; }
fieldset {margin-top:15px; background:yellow; border:0; }
input:required {outline:1px red solid; color:red; }
.submit input {font-size:1.2em; color:#000; background:orange;
    ➥ border:2px outset #d7b9c9 }
p.submit {text-align:center; }
```

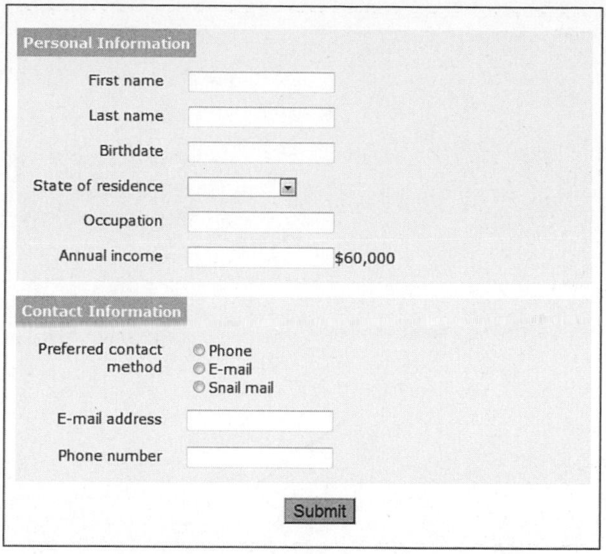

Figure 21.9: *Here's the same form after CSS.*

The Least You Need to Know

- Think outside the box to save time and aggravation. Use a form plug-in, generator, turnkey e-commerce solution, or phpFormGenerator to handle most of the work for you.

- Bracket your form with an opening and closing <form> tag, and include the essential attributes in the opening tag, like so:

```
<form action='process.php' method='post'
   ➠ enctype='multipart/form-data'>
```

- To label your fields, bracket each label between an opening and closing <label> tag.

- <input> is an unpaired tag that includes the type attribute, which specifies the input type, including text, password, radio, check box, date, time, e-mail, and file.

- Labels may include spaces. Input names may not.

- Use CSS to improve the layout and appearance of your form.

Getting Up to Speed on jQuery Basics

In This Chapter

- Understanding what jQuery is all about
- Setting up jQuery to do its thing
- Targeting elements for jQuery to act on
- Creating some cool special effects

jQuery is a web development tool designed to simplify the process of making web page elements more dynamic and interactive. Instead of writing your own complex JavaScripts, all you do is identify an HTML element you want jQuery to act on in some way and then specify the action. Some scripting is involved, but it's nothing compared to writing an entire script. For example, here's the script for making an HTML article element fade in:

```
$(document).ready(function() {
$('article').fadeIn();
});
```

$ stands for jQuery. The first and last lines bracket all jQuery statements and tell the browser to execute statements only when the document is ready, meaning it has loaded. The middle line instructs the browser to select all HTML article elements and run the fadeIn script from the jQuery library.

Using jQuery on your site is a two-step process:

1. Load the jQuery library.

2. Write jQuery statements, each of which consists of a selector, action, and parameters.

If you know how to work with CSS selectors, as explained in Chapter 10, you know at least half of what you need to know to start using jQuery. In this chapter, you get the other half.

Loading the jQuery Library

The jQuery library is a collection of JavaScripts, each designed to perform a specific task. Before your site can use anything from the library, your site needs to load the library. You can do this the easy way ... or the hard way.

The Easy Way

The easy way is to let Google handle it. The following code loads the library from Google's Content Delivery Network (CDN):

```
<script type="text/javascript" src="https://ajax.googleapis.com/ajax/
    libs/jquery/1.4.3/jquery.min.js"></script>
```

Insert the code right before the </head> tag at the top of each web page. If you're using a CMS to manage your site, you may need to place the tag in the header.php file, as shown in Figure 22.1, or your template may have a special area for adding scripts to the header. Your CMS will then insert the code at the top of every page. See Chapter 11 for more about customizing a theme.

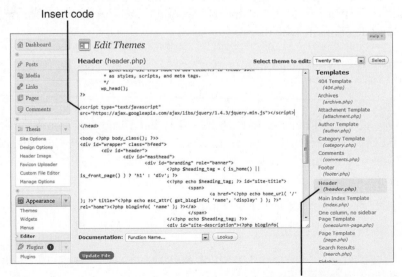

Figure 22.1: *Add the script to the head of your web pages.*

Note that this code loads version 1.4.3. To find out which is the most recent version of the library, go to code.google.com/apis/libraries/devguide.html, scroll down to the Libraries section, and look for jQuery. From there, you can copy and paste the path to the file.

INSIDE TIP

Consider dropping the number at the end of the version number. For example, instead of 1.4.3, use 1.4. Your site will then automatically load the most recent 1.4 version. Drop the 4, too, using only the number 1, and your site will load the most recent 1 version; for example, 1.4.6, 1.5.0, 1.6.2 … whatever it happens to be. The only trouble with this approach is that something in the jQuery library might change somewhere down the line and render one of your jQuery statements inoperable.

The Hard Way

The hard way consists of downloading the library, uploading it to your site, and adding a bit of code at the top of the source code for your web pages that loads the library from your server.

To download the jQuery library, go to jquery.com, and click the big **Download(jQuery)** button. This displays the jQuery library, as shown in Figure 22.2. It might not look like much, but this little text file packs a lot of punch. Use your browser's **Save** command to save the file to a folder on your computer. You may want to save it in the same folder that contains your web documents.

Figure 22.2: *Download the jQuery library.*

You'll need the jQuery library in two places—on your computer (assuming you're developing your web pages on your computer) and on your site. (See Chapter 1 for details on uploading files to your server.)

With the jQuery library file in place, you now have to link to it from your web pages. Use one of the following codes, replacing the *src* address with the path to the jquery.min.js file. Insert the code right before the </head> tag at the top of each web page. The first code is similar to what you would use to link to the library on your server. The second is more similar to what you would use if you're linking to the file on your computer.

```
<script type="text/javascript" src="http://yoursite.com/jQuery/
➥ jquery.min.js"></script>
<script type="text/javascript" src="file:///C:/Web/Pages/jQuery/
➥ jquery-1.4.3.min.js"></script>
```

If you're using a CMS to manage your site, you may need to place the tag in the header.php file, as shown in Figure 22.1, or your template may have a special area for adding scripts to the header. Your CMS will then insert the code at the top of every page. See Chapter 11 for more about customizing a theme.

INSIDE TIP

If you're developing your site on your computer and then uploading it to your server, download the library to run on your computer as you develop your site.

Adding a Couple More Essential Codes

You're not done yet. You have two more codes to insert. First, insert opening and closing JavaScript <script> tags immediately after the </script> code for loading the jQuery library. You should now have something like this:

```
<script type="text/javascript" src="https://ajax.googleapis.com/ajax/
  ➡ libs/jquery/1.4.3/jquery.min.js"></script>
<script type="text/javascript">
</script>
```

Between the opening and closing tags you just added, add the document-ready jQuery statement. You should now have something that looks like this:

```
<script type="text/javascript" src="https://ajax.googleapis.com/ajax/
  ➡ libs/jquery/1.4.3/jquery.min.js"></script>
<script type="text/javascript">
$(document).ready(function() {

});
</script>
```

Now this is very important: *all* the other jQuery statements described in this chapter must be embedded in the document-ready statement. In other words, they must be inserted where you see that blank line in the preceding code.

Now you're ready to play.

Constructing jQuery Statements

Every jQuery statement consists of the following four components:

- **jQuery** or **$** (for short) indicating that what's about to come is a jQuery statement.

- Selector that targets the element to which the jQuery action applies.

- Action that specifies an action/script from the jQuery library.

- Parameters that influence exactly what the action does. Sometimes, parameters aren't needed, but you still designate a place for them with ().

Here's an example:

```
$('article').fadeIn('slow')
```

$ signals that this is a jQuery statement, ('article') targets <article> elements, .fadeIn is the jQuery fade-in script, and ('slow') is the parameter. Remember, this statement must be embedded in the document-ready statement, so what you now have is something like this in the head section of the web page:

```
<script type="text/javascript" src="https://ajax.googleapis.com/ajax/
  ➡ libs/jquery/1.4.3/jquery.min.js"></script>
<script type="text/javascript">
$(document).ready(function() {
$('article').fadeIn('slow')
});
</script>
```

For fadeIn to work, the element must not be displayed at first, so you'd need to add the *display:none* to the article style in your CSS to make this work. The page will load without the article showing, and the article will then fade in. For more about creating and editing styles, check out the chapters in Part 3.

In this particular example, the document-ready event is what triggers the fade in. If you don't want the action to *fire* on document ready, you must specify the event that fires the statement.

DEFINITION

Fire means to execute an action or run a script.

Here's an example in which clicking an element with the class="disappear" attribute, causes the paragraph text to fade out:

```
$('.disappear').click(function() {
$('p').fadeOut();
});
```

Again, you must remember to embed this statement in the document-ready statement, like so:

```
<script type="text/javascript" src="https://ajax.googleapis.com/ajax/
➥ libs/jquery/1.4.3/jquery.min.js"></script>
<script type="text/javascript">
$(document).ready(function() {
$('.disappear').click(function() {
$('p').fadeOut();
});
});
</script>
```

Note that }); appears twice at the end. Every open statement must be closed.

The following sections provide more in-depth coverage of selectors, events, and actions.

Targeting HTML Elements

One of the keys to using jQuery effectively is knowing how to use selectors to target elements. The most common selectors are HTML tags and CSS classes and IDs. Fortunately, jQuery uses the same notation for the various elements, classes, and IDs as HTML and CSS do. All you do is insert the selector with single quotation marks between parentheses. Following are examples of a tag, ID, and class selector:

('p')

('#content')

('.fade-in')

WHOA!

You may run into trouble using some HTML5 elements as selectors in some browsers. Some workarounds are available on the web, including html5shiv, which enables Internet Explorer to recognize HTML5 elements. Check out code. google.com/p/html5shiv. The other option is to bracket the content with <div> tags, add a class or ID attribute to the opening <div> tag, and use the class or ID as your selector—but this sort of defeats the purpose of HTML5.

To select more than one element, include a selector for each element, separated by commas, like so:

('p,h1,h2,ul,.button,#content')

You may also want to get more selective with your selectors. Suppose you want to add a color or shading to alternating rows in a table. To do this, you could use the jQuery *even* filter:

('tbody tr:even')

This instructs the browser to perform whatever jQuery action you decide to execute on even rows in the table's body. Other filters include :first, :last, :odd, and :eq(#), where # is whichever one you specify, such as 4 for the fourth row.

Complete coverage of selectors would fill a chapter or two. jQuery has dozens of selectors. For a complete list, visit api.jquery.com/category/selectors.

Targeting 'this'

You know how to target elements by using various selectors, but you also need to know how to target 'this', which refers to the element involved in the event that triggered the action. For example, if the event consists of the user clicking a tab, 'this' refers to the tab. You can then create jQuery statements specifically for modifying the appearance or behavior of that tab, as shown here:

```
$('.tab').click(function() {
$('#content').fadeIn();
$(this).css('font-weight','bold');
});
```

With this code in place, after the user clicks an element that includes the class="tab" attribute, the tab's text becomes bold.

Triggering Scripts with Events

An *event* is an occurrence that triggers a jQuery action, such as the page loading completely or a user clicking a button. You already encountered a few events in this chapter: .ready, .fadeIn, and .fadeOut. jQuery has more than 50 events. This chapter covers several of the more common events, including .click, .mouseover, and .hover. You can find a complete list at jquery.com.

When constructing jQuery statements, the event is preceded by a selector, which identifies the element involved in the event. The following selector-event combination tells the browser to fire the action whenever an element with the class="button" attribute is clicked:

```
$('.button').click(function() {
});
```

Of course, this statement is incomplete because no action is specified. That's the subject of the next section.

Specifying jQuery Actions

jQuery features many actions for manipulating elements on web pages. Some of these are attributes that get and set attributes of elements, such as .removeAttr(), .addClass(), and .removeClass(). Others are classified as effects adding animated effects, including .fadeIn() and .fadeOut(). What's important is that these actions or methods or commands or whatever you want to call them enable you to manipulate elements and styles.

To specify a jQuery action, you type the desired action followed by a selector that targets the element, like so:

```
.css('background-color','#cccccc');
```

This instructs the browser to add the *background-color:#cccccc* declaration to the element's style.

The following sections show you how to put it all together—to write jQuery statements that combine selectors, events, and actions to change elements on your site, making your web pages much more dynamic.

Adding and Removing a Class Attribute

CSS enables you to control nearly every characteristic of an HTML element, including its size, position, and color. jQuery gives you control over CSS. Together, CSS and jQuery give you the power to dynamically control the look and layout of every element on a page. You do this by adding class attributes to targeted elements or removing existing attributes.

Suppose you want to give users the option of zooming in to display text 20 percent larger than normal. You can do this by adding a class attribute to the element's opening tag, but first create the desired class style in your site's style sheet file. It may look something like this:

```
.large {font-size:120%; }
```

You also need an element on the web page the user can click to zoom in. This can be as simple as a word or paragraph with a unique class attribute your jQuery statement can target. It doesn't need to be a hyperlink. Here's an example:

```
<p class="zoom">Zoom</p>
```

Next, add your jQuery statement, which may look like this:

```
$('.zoom').click(function() {
$('article').addClass('large');
});
```

To toggle the zoom in and then back to normal size, replace .addClass with .toggleClass:

```
$('.zoom').click(function() {
$('article').toggleClass('large');
});
```

Now the user can click to zoom in and click again to zoom out to normal size text.

When adding classes, just remember that the class itself must exist in the style sheet.

This merely scratches the surface of what you can do with the .addClass, .removeClass, and .toggleClass commands. These are a few of the most powerful and commonly used jQuery commands.

NOTE

You can apply CSS with jQuery's .css command, too. For example, to add the 120 percent zoom using the .css command, your jQuery statement would look like this:

```
$('.zoom').click(function() {
$('article').css('font-size','120%');
});
```

Doing More with jQuery

You can do much more with jQuery than merely adding and removing classes. You can add and remove HTML, hide and show elements, slide elements up or down (as in a drop-down menu), and much more. The following sections show you how to execute a few of these moves.

Hiding and Showing Elements

You can magically make elements appear and disappear with the .show() and .hide() commands. The .show() command is very useful if you want to tuck something out of the way but give visitors the option to view it.

First, tuck the element out of the way by adding the *display:none* declaration to its style rule (or create a new style rule for the element that contains *display:none*). Create an element the user can click to show the element, and give it a unique class attribute you can target, such as class="showtime". Now you're ready for your jQuery statement:

```
$('.show').click(function() {
$('article').show();
});
```

The .hide() command works the same way, only in reverse. You don't want the element to have a default style of *display:none*, because you want it to be visible when the page loads. You can also use the .toggle() command to toggle the element's status to show or hide.

Adding and Removing Elements

In addition to being able to add and remove classes to HTML tags, jQuery can add and remove HTML, meaning you have the power to create web pages dynamically. To add an HTML element, place the source code along with an indication of where you want the element placed in your jQuery statement, like this:

```
$('.view-tip').click(function() {
$('<div class="tip"><p><strong>Tip</strong></p><p>Be sure to change
➥ the filter on your furnace every month. In addition to extending
➥ the life of your furnace, this significantly improves its
➥ efficiency.</p>')
.insertAfter('article');
});
```

To remove elements, use the .remove() command targeting the element's tag or one of its ID or class selectors. To be more selective, you can use the *:contains* filter, like so:

```
$('.tip').remove(':contains("Caution")');
```

This would remove only those items with the class attribute of *tip* that contain the word "caution."

Creating a Sliding Panel

A sliding panel is an animation effect that gradually reveals or conceals an element by raising or lowering the bottom of it, sort of like a projector screen. This effect is often used for drop-down menus, but you can use it to animate the display of any element on a page.

Although you can use the .slideUp() and .slideDown() commands, you may find the .slideToggle() most useful. Here's an example of .slideToggle() for revealing and concealing an image:

```
$('.slide-button').click(function() {
$('.slide').slideToggle('slow', function() {
});
```

Moving an Object Across the Page

You can use jQuery's .animate() command to move objects on a page. This is one of the more complex maneuvers because .animate() requires several parameters to specify direction, distance, and speed. Here's a very simple example of .animate() you can use to move an image across the screen 100 pixels to the right:

```
$('img').click(function(){
$('img').animate({'left':'+=100px'}, 'slow');
});
```

To make this work, you must also create an image style that includes the *position:absolute* declaration. You may also want to include *top* and *left* declarations to specify the image's starting point. Your style will look something like this:

```
img {position:absolute;
left:75px; top:100px; }
```

In this example, clicking the image triggers the .animate() action, which then adds 100 pixels to the image's left margin and moves the image slowly from point A to point B. If you keep clicking the image, it continues to move 100 pixels with each click.

The Least You Need to Know

- To make the jQuery library available on your site, add the following code to the top of the source code for your web pages:

  ```
  <script type="text/javascript" src="https://ajax.googleapis.
  ➥ com/ajax/libs/jquery/1.4.3/jquery.min.js"></script>
  <script type="text/javascript">
  $(document).ready(function() {
  });
  </script>
  ```

- Be sure all your jQuery statements are on the blank line after the document-ready statement.

- Start with the styles you want to apply and then write the jQuery statements to apply those styles.

- jQuery statements are in the following format, starting with an event that triggers an action:

  ```
  $(document).ready(function() {
  $('#content').fadeIn();
  });
  ```

Transforming Your Page into a Canvas

In This Chapter

- The basics of HTML5's canvas element
- Specifying your canvas dimensions
- Drawing lines, rectangles, curves, and other shapes
- Adjusting fill and stroke colors, line widths, and more
- Adding images to your canvas

The HTML5 <canvas> tag packs a lot of punch. It enables you to place a drawing surface anywhere on a page and then draw and arrange shapes on it to create illustrations. You can then use CSS to position the canvas, scale it, and more.

As you'll see in this chapter, canvas is a powerful tool, but it's not practical unless it's part of a web-based application. The purpose of canvas is to facilitate the creation of web-based applications that draw on pages dynamically. For example, using canvas in tandem with JavaScript, you can create an application that gathers data, such as stock prices, and renders a graph in real time.

Creating powerful web-based applications is beyond the scope of this book, so this chapter focuses exclusively on canvas. I cover the basics of displaying a canvas on a page and drawing various lines and shapes on it.

Prepping Your Canvas

Before you can start drawing anything, you need to define your canvas area. All you do is insert an opening and closing <canvas> tag with a unique ID attribute and the desired dimensions.

```
<canvas id="illustration" height="300px" width="400px"></canvas>
```

If you don't specify dimensions, the default dimensions are used: 300 pixels wide by 150 pixels high.

Not all browsers support the <canvas> tag, so add some fallback content between the opening and closing <canvas> tags. This may be some sort of static image or graph or text that provides a description of the content or data being shown.

Adding Some Basic JavaScript

You're going to be drawing on the canvas using JavaScript, so you need to set the stage by adding opening and closing <script> tags in the head area of the page's HTML source code that specify the script type as "JavaScript". Use the following source code to replace *illustration* with the ID you attributed to your canvas:

```
<head>
<script type="text/JavaScript">
window.onload = function() {
var canvas = document.getElementById('illustration');
var context = canvas.getContext('2d');
//ADD ALL DRAWING METHODS AND PROPERTIES HERE
}
</script>
</head>
```

As you proceed through this chapter, insert all drawing commands for this canvas where indicated.

Styling Your Canvas

Your canvas is a block element you can style as you do any other block element. For example, you can add a background color or image, place a border around the canvas, specify its position, and more. For now, create a style for your canvas that adds a dotted black border around it. You can use an external style sheet, as explained in Chapter 10, or create an internal style sheet by placing the following code right before the closing </head> tag:

```
<style type="text/css">
canvas {border:1px dotted black; }
</style>
```

Open the HTML document in a web browser that supports canvas, and your blank canvas should appear in all its glory, as shown in Figure 23.1.

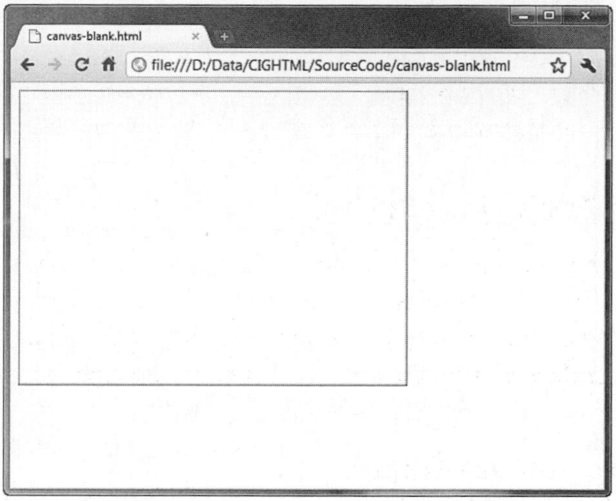

Figure 23.1: *Starting with a blank canvas.*

Drawing Lines, Curves, and Basic Shapes

You don't see it, but your canvas is like a huge sheet of graph paper—a grid comprised of dots (pixels) arranged in columns and rows, as shown in Figure 23.2. Columns of pixels run up and down along the *y* axis, while rows run across the canvas along the *x* axis. Positions on the grid are described using *x,y* coordinates, with the point in the upper-left corner of the canvas being 0,0. As you move down and to the right, the numbers go up.

You'll be using coordinates to draw objects on the canvas. To draw a straight line, for example, you specify *x,y* coordinates for the two end points. To draw a circle, you specify coordinates for its center and a measurement for the radius. The following sections show you how to draw shapes and specify their dimensions.

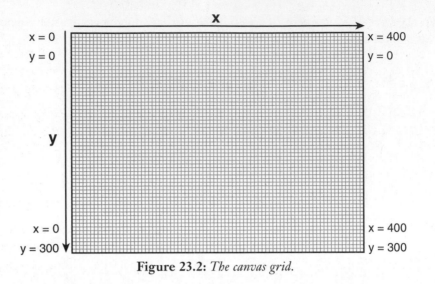

Figure 23.2: *The canvas grid.*

Drawing Lines

To draw lines on the canvas, move to the point where you want the line to start, draw a line to where you want the line to end, and add your stroke to fill in the line. Here's an example:

```
context.beginPath();
context.moveTo(20,40);
context.lineTo(250,40);
context.stroke();
```

Unless you specify otherwise, the line you draw is 1px wide and black. You can change the color, width, and style of the line prior to drawing it. See "Taking Control of Colors, Line Styles, and Gradients," later in this chapter, for details.

Remember that whatever you're drawing must be within the draw function, so you should now have a script that looks like this:

```
window.onload = function() {
var canvas = document.getElementById('illustration');
var context = canvas.getContext('2d');
//ADD ALL DRAWING METHODS AND PROPERTIES HERE
context.beginPath();
context.moveTo(20,40);
context.lineTo(250,40);
context.stroke();
}
```

Drawing Paths

When drawing a line or series of lines, you're actually drawing *paths*. A path consists of one or more lines, arcs, and/or other shapes, and it may be open or closed. A closed path is simply one that ends where it began. Drawing a path is a five-step process:

1. Specify a stroke and fill color … assuming you want something other than black. See "Taking Control of Colors, Line Styles, and Gradients," later in this chapter, for details.

2. Begin the path with *beginPath()*.

3. Draw lines and shapes, as explained in the previous and following sections.

4. *Optional:* close the shape. If you use the *closePath* method to close the shape, canvas draws a line from the endpoint of the last shape to the path's starting point. (Shapes are automatically closed if you specify a fill for the shape.)

5. Use the stroke and/or fill method to produce the shape.

Here's a sample script for drawing the triangle shown in Figure 23.3:

```
context.fillStyle = "#ADFF2F";
context.strokeStyle = "#008000";
context.beginPath();
context.moveTo(20,20);
context.lineTo(150,20);
context.lineTo(20,150);
context.closePath();
context.stroke();
context.fill();
```

In this example, instead of *context.closePath()*, you could use *context.lineTo(20,20)*, which would end the last line where the first line began and close the shape.

Figure 23.3: *A closed shape with stroke and fill.*

NOTE

After specifying a stroke or fill color, the color remains in effect until you change it.

You may add lines and shapes to the path you created. All lines and shapes after the *beginPath* method contribute to forming a single shape. To create a separate group of lines and shapes, enter a new *beginPath* method.

Drawing Rectangles

Drawing closed shapes—including rectangles—is a snap, because you don't need to deal with closing the shape. With rectangles, all you do is specify the coordinates for the upper-left corner of the rectangle along with the rectangle's width and height. With canvas, you can draw three types of rectangles: filled, outline only, and clear (no line, no fill). Here's an example that creates all three types with the "clear" rectangle on top of the filled rectangle (see Figure 23.4):

```
context.fillStyle = "#00FF00";
context.strokeStyle = "#000000";
context.strokeRect(0,0,200,150);
context.fillRect(20,20,160,110);
context.clearRect(40,40,120,70);
```

Figure 23.4: *Stroke, fill, and clear rectangles.*

These three methods insert rectangles as separate shapes on the canvas. Another option is to draw a rectangle using beginPath and then add the stroke and/or fill, like this:

```
context.beginPath();
context.rect(20,20,160,110);
context.stroke();
context.fill();
```

Drawing Circles and Arcs

To draw a circle or arc, specify the *x* and *y* coordinates of the center point, the radius measure, the start and end angles, and the direction in which to draw the arc. The expression goes like this:

```
arc (x, y, radius, startAngle, endAngle anticlockwise)
```

x, *y*, and radius are fairly obvious. The two angle settings specify the length of the arc in radians. The *radian* provides a way to convert an angle measure into a length measurement. For example, a 90-degree angle is approximately 1.6 radians. Multiply that number by the radius of the circle, and you get an actual distance of the arc in centimeters, inches, pixels, or whatever unit you're working in.

Working in radians is great as long as you can visualize a radian's length in proportion to the circle. The circumference of a circle is $2\pi r$, so a circle has 2π radians. A half circle is π radians. Because π is about 3.14, a half circle is about 3.14 radians, and a full circle is about 6.3 radians. Another way to look at it is that a radian is approximately 57 degrees. Here's the code for creating an arc that's about a quarter of the circle's total circumference:

```
context.arc(100, 100, 75, 0, 1.6, false);
```

If you prefer to work in degrees (with a little more precision), JavaScript provides a conversion factor: *radians = (Math.PI/180)*degrees*. Here's the code for that same quarter arc using the conversion statement:

```
context.arc(100, 100, 75, 0, (Math.PI/180)*90, false);
```

Unless you specify otherwise, the start angle is 0, as if both hands on a clock are pointing east to 3. The arc is drawn clockwise from this point, as shown in Figure 23.5, which shows two 90-degree arcs—one filled and one not. To create only the arc (without any fill), see "Adjusting Transparency," later in this chapter. To draw the arc counterclockwise from this point, change the value for *anticlockwise* from *false* to *true*.

Figure 23.5: *90-degree arcs.*

As you draw circles, keep the following radian orientations in mind:

Radian	Degrees	Direction
0	0	East
Math.PI/2	90	South
Math.PI	180	West
Math.PI*3/2	270	North

Drawing Bézier Curves

A Bézier curve is a mathematical curve defined by two endpoints and one or two control points for shaping the line. Canvas supports two types of Bézier curves: *quadratic* (one control point) and *cubic* (two control points).

Drawing Bézier curves is challenging because coordinate values don't exactly help you envision the shape of the curve. If you want to give it a go, here are the formats for drawing quadratic and cubic curves:

```
quadraticCurveTo(cp1x, cp1y, x, y)
bezierCurveTo(cp1x, cp1y, cp2x, cp2y, x, y)
```

For the quadratic curve, you specify the coordinates of the control point (cp1x, cp1y) and the end point (x, y). For the cubic curve, you specify the coordinates of two control points followed by the coordinates of the line's end point. Here's the script for creating the cubic curve shown in Figure 23.6:

```
context.beginPath();
context.moveTo(20,100);
context.bezierCurveTo(50, 25, 75, 125, 150, 125);
context.stroke();
```

Figure 23.6: *A Bézier curve.*

Taking Control of Colors, Line Styles, and Gradients

Like a graphics program, canvas gives you control of stroke and fill styles, line widths and styles, gradients, and more. You may have noticed a couple of these options in the scripts you encountered earlier in this chapter. The following sections provide additional details.

Specifying a Stroke and Fill Color

Unless you specify otherwise, every line and shape you create is black, inside and out. To change that, set the strokeStyle and fillStyle attributes to the desired colors. Use any of the CSS color names or codes, as explained in Chapter 13. These may include color names, hex codes such as *#66FF66*, or RGB values such as *rgb(145,175,44)*. Wherever you want to change colors, use the *fillStyle* and/or *strokeStyle* properties to set your preferences, like so:

```
context.fillStyle = "#F8F8F8";
context.strokeStyle = "#0000FF";
```

These new colors become the colors for all shapes you draw from this point in the script to the end or to the point at which you change the colors again.

Adjusting Transparency

When layering objects, you may want to adjust transparency so you can see through an object to the background or to the object behind it. You have two options here. You can enter a transparency setting using the *globalAlpha* property or using the *rgba* function to specify transparency for the *fillStyle* and/or *strokeStyle* properties. The rgba approach enables you to set transparency separately for strokes and fills.

Figure 23.7 shows transparency in action. Starting with the upper-left rectangle and moving down and to the right, the rectangles have an opacity of .2, .4, .6, .8, and 1.

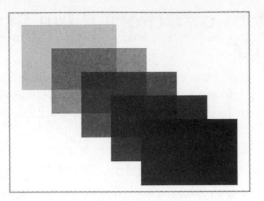

Figure 23.7: *Make shapes semi-transparent.*

To draw semi-transparent shapes to the canvas, insert the *globalAlpha* property in the script where you want to start drawing transparent shapes, and set it to the desired opacity, with 0 being fully transparent and 1 being fully opaque. Here's an example:

```
globalAlpha = ".65";
```

To take the rgba transparency approach, use the *rgba* function with four color values. The fourth value specifies the transparency level. Here's an example:

```
context.fillStyle = "rgba(255, 0, 0, .65)";
```

Specifying a Line Width and Style

When you start drawing lines and shapes, canvas defaults to using lines that are 1 pixel wide with square ends. You can take control of your lines by adjusting various line styles, including line width, cap (ends), and corners.

To set the line width, insert the *lineWidth* property where you want the line width to change, and specify the desired thickness in pixels, like so:

```
context.lineWidth = "2";
```

Canvas also enables you to specify the style for the ends of the line using the *lineCap* property. You have three options: *butt* (the default setting), *round*, and *square*. Butt caps are square. To produce round caps, canvas places a little half circle at the ends of the line to round them off. To produce square caps, canvas adds a small rectangle to the ends of the lines—they look like butt ends, but the line is a little longer as a result of the added caps.

The *lineJoin* and *miterLimit* properties provide control over the appearance of joined lines. You can set lineJoin to *round*, *bevel*, or *miter* to produce the different effects shown in Figure 23.8.

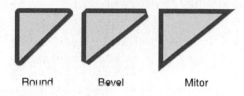

Round   Bevel   Mitor

Figure 23.8: *Different lineJoin settings in action.*

To produce the miter effect, canvas extends the outside edges of both lines to the point at which they meet to form a nice, sharp corner. If thick lines meet at an extremely sharp angle, however, the miter effect isn't very aesthetically pleasing. To prevent this, add a *miterLimit* property, like so:

```
miterLimit="8"
```

This squares off any edges that look more like spikes than corners, giving the corners a smoother appearance.

Adding Gradients

In addition to filling shapes with solid colors, you can fill them with *gradients*. To use a gradient, you must first create it. To create a *linear gradient*, add the linear gradient method, like so:

```
var lgrad = context.createLinearGradient(125,0,125,250);
```

The first two values are the coordinates of the starting point, and the last two values are the coordinates of the ending point. This particular gradient is set to start at the top and blend the colors down to the bottom.

To create a *radial gradient*, add the radial gradient method, like so:

```
var rgrad = context.createRadialGradient(50,50,20,75,75,75);
```

The first three values establish the center point and radius of the first circle, and the second three values establish the center point and radius of a second circle.

Now you're ready to add the colors you want to fade into one another by adding *color stops*. Here's the code for a linear gradient that blends yellow to green to blue from top to bottom:

```
var lgrad = context.createLinearGradient(125,0,250,250);
lgrad.addColorStop(0,"yellow");
lgrad.addColorStop(.7,"green");
lgrad.addColorStop(1,"blue");
context.fillStyle = lgrad;
```

The numbers represent where each color is its most intense. In this case, yellow starts at the beginning (0) and blends with green until it's all green 70 percent down the page and then green blends with blue down to the bottom (1), at which point it's pure blue.

Adding Other Images to Your Canvas

You can place images on your canvas as part of your drawing. This is especially useful if you're creating a dynamic image—for example, a graph that updates automatically when new values are available. You could place a blank graph in the background and then have a web-based application plot data on the graph.

Importing an Image

You can use JavaScript in various ways to import images. The easiest way is to include the image on the same page and use the *document.getElementByTagName* or *document. getElementById* method. You must be sure the image is fully loaded before trying to place it on the canvas, so use the *window.onload* event to add it. The following code shows how to load an image that's on the same page and has the id="graph" attribute, and then how to draw the image to the canvas.

```
<head>
<script type="text/JavaScript">
window.onload = function() {
var canvas = document.getElementById('illustration');
var context = canvas.getContext('2d');
var image = document.getElementById('graph');
context.drawImage(image, 0, 0);
};
</script>
</head>
```

Of course, somewhere in the body of your web page document, you need to include HTML tags for the canvas and the image, wherever you want each of them to appear, like so:

```
<canvas id="illustration" height="200px;" width="200px"></canvas>
<img id="graph" width="100px" height="145px" src="images/graph.jpg" />
```

Resizing an Image

As you're drawing the image to the canvas, you can specify parameters to have the image scaled down or up. Here's what the *drawImage()* method used in the previous section would look like with additional parameters for resizing the image:

```
context.drawImage(image, 0, 0, 175, 150);
```

Here, *image* identifies the image to insert, the first two numbers specify the coordinates for the upper-left corner of the image, and the last two values represent the desired width and height, respectively.

> **WHOA!**
>
> Be careful when scaling bitmapped images, such as JPEGs. You might want to resize the image in a graphics program first to determine width and height values that won't cause the image to appear overly distorted, grainy, or blurry.

Cropping an Image

As you're drawing the image to the canvas, you can specify parameters to have the image cropped or—as JavaScript refers to it—*sliced*. Slicing is a two-step operation. First, the source image is cropped to a rectangle of specified dimensions. Then, the cropped image is positioned on the canvas and its dimensions are set. The *drawImage* method for slicing an image looks like this:

```
context.drawImage(image, 240, 220, 486, 348, 100, 100, 486, 348);
```

The first two values specify the upper-left corner of the rectangle for cropping the source image. The second two values specify the width and height of that rectangle, respectively (see Figure 23.9). The next two values are the *x* and *y* coordinates on the canvas where the upper-left corner of the image will be placed. The last two values are the image's dimensions, as illustrated in Figure 23.10.

Figure 23.9: *Slice and draw an image to the canvas, part 1.*

Figure 23.10: *Slice and draw an image to the canvas, part 2.*

The Least You Need to Know

- To establish a canvas, place the following code between the opening and closing <head> tags on the page and insert all other drawing methods and properties where indicated:

```
<script type="text/JavaScript">
window.onload = function() {
var canvas = document.getElementById('illustration');
var context = canvas.getContext('2d');
//ADD ALL DRAWING METHODS AND PROPERTIES HERE
}
</script>
```

- Specify stroke and fill styles before drawing the object:

```
context.fillStyle = "#F8F8F8";
context.strokeStyle = "#0000FF";
```

- Here's how to insert a canvas:

```
<canvas id="illustration" height="250px;" width="250px">
  ➡ </canvas>
```

- To draw a line, use this code:

```
context.beginPath();
context.moveTo(20,40);
context.lineTo(150,40);
context.stroke();
```

- Here's what you need to draw a rectangle:

```
context.strokeRect(0,0,200,150);
```

- And this code draws a circle:

```
context.arc(100, 100, 75, 0, (Math.PI/180)*90, false);4
```

Testing and Fine-Tuning Your Site

Your site may look and function just fine on your computer in your browser of choice, but how will it function in the real world, where visitors access it using different browsers and even mobile devices? Will your pages load quickly enough to keep impatient visitors from wandering off? And how will your pages fare with search engines?

The chapters in Part 5 help you answer all those questions and more. Here you test your site in multiple browsers, discover strategies to make your pages more attractive targets for search engines, and pick up a few tricks for optimizing your site's performance. Here you discover a host of valuable, free tools to optimize performance and search engine optimization (SEO). I reveal websites where you can test the speed at which pages load and troubleshoot speed bumps. I also steer you toward a few browser add-ons that evaluate your site for performance and SEO issues.

By the end of this part, you'll have complete confidence that your site is ready for prime time.

Taking Your Site for a Test Drive

In This Chapter

- Checking and double-checking your site
- Testing your site in different web browsers
- Ensuring your site is accessible to all
- Evaluating your forms

Your web pages may look great and function impeccably in the web browser you use, but that doesn't mean they will in other browsers. How can you be sure your site looks right, functions properly, and is universally accessible on all browsers? You can never be 100 percent certain, but you can run a few tests to be sure your site conforms to the latest standards, and looks right and functions well on a majority of systems. This chapter shows you how.

Validating Your Web Pages

HTML5 and CSS3 are standards designed to ensure reliability and some degree of consistency among web browsers. Assuming everyone plays by the rules, your web pages should look right and function well in every browser used to access your site. Validating your web pages means making sure you're playing by the rules and that your pages don't contain any code that might compromise their display in a wide range of browsers.

The following sections introduce you to several tools for ensuring that your pages conform to the latest HTML and CSS standards and contain no broken links.

Validating the HTML

The World Wide Web Consortium (W3C) is the organization responsible for organizing the development of web standards, including HTML and CSS. W3C provides several handy tools for validating pages, including its HTML Validator.

To validate a page, go to validator.w3.org. Click in the **Address** box, type or paste the address of the page you want to validate, and click **Check**, as shown in Figure 24.1. Validator checks the page to ensure that the markup (source code) complies with the standard specified in the page's document type declaration (DTD). (See Chapter 4 for details about the DTD.)

If you're developing pages offline to upload later, you can upload the files to the validator. Click the **Validate by File Upload** tab, use the controls to upload the file you want to check, and run the validator on it.

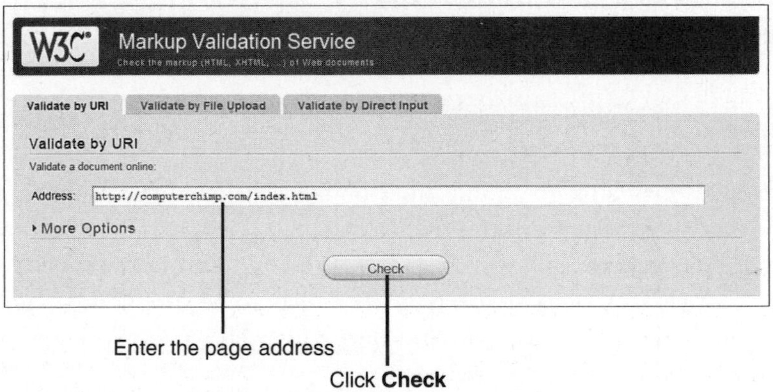

Enter the page address

Click **Check**

Figure 24.1: *The W3C HTML Validator.*

After the HTML Validator completes its tests, it displays a report, like the one shown in Figure 24.2, highlighting any validation errors. Fix the problems and then click the **Revalidate** button to run the checks again.

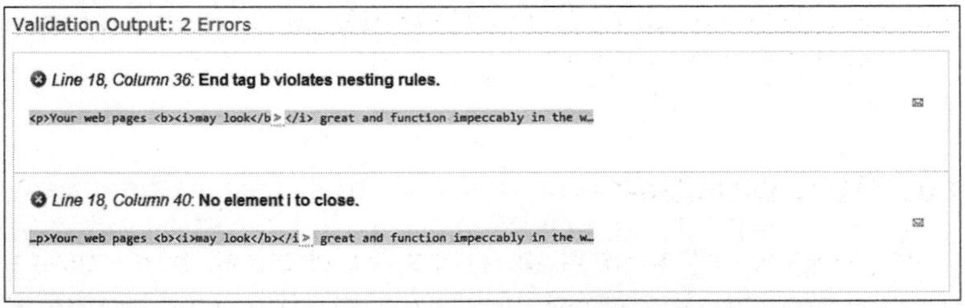

Figure 24.2: *HTML Validator identifies problems in the HTML source code.*

Validating the CSS

W3C also provides a CSS validator. To validate a page's CSS, go to jigsaw.w3.org/css-validator, click in the **Address** box, type or paste the address of the page you want to validate, and click **Check**. Validator checks the page to ensure that the CSS complies with the standard specified in the page's DTD.

After the CSS Validator completes its tests, it displays a report, like the one shown in Figure 24.3, highlighting any validation errors. Fix the problems and then click your browser's **Back** button and click **Check** to run the checks again.

W3C® The W3C CSS Validation Service	
W3C CSS Validator results for http://nickkraynak.com (CSS level 2.1)	

Jump to: Errors (19)　Warnings (125)　Validated CSS

W3C CSS Validator results for http://nickkraynak.com (CSS level 2.1)

Sorry! We found the following errors (19)

URI : http://nickkraynak.com/wp-content/themes/graphene/style.css

286	.post	Property -moz-border-radius-topright doesn't exist : 30px 30px
287	.post	Property -webkit-border-top-right-radius doesn't exist : 30px 30px
288	.post	Property border-top-right-radius doesn't exist in CSS level 2.1 but exists in : 30px 30px
292	.one_column .post	Property -moz-border-radius-topright doesn't exist : 0 0
293	.one_column .post	Property -webkit-border-top-right-radius doesn't exist : 0 0
294	.one_column .post	Property border-top-right-radius doesn't exist in CSS level 2.1 but exists in : 0 0
690	#comments li.depth-1	Property -moz-border-radius-topright doesn't exist : 30px 30px
691	#comments li.depth-1	Property -webkit-border-top-right-radius doesn't exist : 30px 30px
692	#comments li.depth-1	Property border-top-right-radius doesn't exist in CSS level 2.1 but exists in : 30px 30px
791	#commentform	Property -moz-border-radius-topright doesn't exist : 30px 30px
792	#commentform	Property -webkit-border-top-right-radius doesn't exist : 30px 30px
793	#commentform	Property border-top-right-radius doesn't exist in CSS level 2.1 but exists in : 30px 30px

Figure 24.3: *CSS Validator identifies problems in style sheets.*

WHOA!

Be sure to check any forms on your site to ensure they're functioning properly. For example, if your site has a contact form, complete it, submit it, and check your e-mail to be sure you received it. If your forms don't work, visitors may have no way of contacting you to let you know.

Checking for Broken Links

You don't want to send visitors down dead ends, so check all the hyperlinks on your site. If you have only a few links, you can do it yourself. If you have numerous links on a page, consider having the W3C Link Checker check them for you.

Assuming you already ran the HTML and CSS validators, you know the drill. Go to validator.w3.org/checklink, click in the **Address** box, type or paste the address of the page you want to check, and click **Check**. Link Checker tests the links and displays a report indicating any problems, as shown in Figure 24.4.

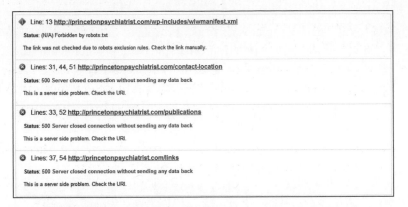

Figure 24.4: *The W3C Link Checker tests your links for you.*

Be aware that the link check may take considerably more time than HTML or CSS validation because Link Checker must visit all the pages and other resources the page links to, including images on the page and CSS files that contain style rules for the page.

Viewing Your Website in Different Browsers

The same web page looks different when displayed in different browsers or even different versions of the same browser. This is to be expected. You want to be sure your site's appearance is acceptable in at least the top three or four browsers, including mobile web browsers: Mozilla Firefox, Internet Explorer, Google Chrome, Safari, and Opera, in that order last I checked. (For the latest browser stats, check out w3schools. com/browsers/browsers_stats.asp.)

You can download all these browsers for free and check every page on every one of them, but tools are available that perform the checks for you and consolidate the results. Some of these tools have the added benefit of being able to test pages in popular mobile devices or simulators. Following are some cross-browser testing tools you might want to check out:

- At Browser Shots (browsershots.org), you type the address of the page, choose the browsers you want to check, and click **Submit**. In a matter of seconds or minutes or hours—depending on how busy the site is—Browser Shots displays thumbnail screen shots of the page in different browsers, as shown in Figure 24.5. Click a thumbnail image to see a larger version.

- Spoon Browser Sandbox (spoon.net/browsers) enables you to run different browsers without having to install them.

- BrowserSeal (browserseal.com) is an application that runs on your computer. It includes standalone versions of all the top browsers, including Opera Mini. Because it's not a web-based service, no subscription is required.

Plenty of other cross-browser testing tools are available, many of them web-based services that range in price from free to up to $1,000 per year.

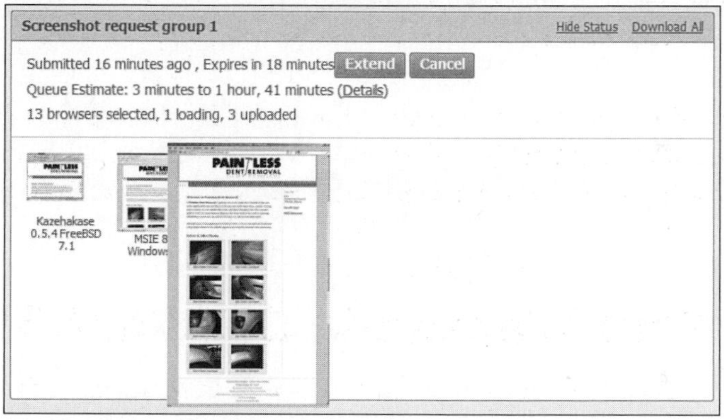

Figure 24.5: *Browser Shots shows the page in different browsers.*

Another way to test mobile sites is to use a mobile emulator (simulator) for the device/browser on which you want to test your pages. Simulators are either web based, like the Opera Mini Simulator shown in Figure 24.6, or applications you install and use on your computer. Following is a list of popular mobile emulators and information on where to find them:

- **BlackBerry Smartphone Simulators:** us.blackberry.com/developers/resources/simulators.jsp

- **iPhone Web Simulator:** marketcircle.com/iphoney

- **Opera Mini Simulator:** opera.com/mobile/demo

- **Nokia Simulator:** Visit forum.nokia.com and explore the available development tools

- **Yospace Smartphone Emulator:** yospace.com/index.php/spedemo.html

- **Android Emulator:** developer.android.com/guide/developing/tools/emulator. html

Figure 24.6: *Opera Mini Simulator in action.*

INSIDE TIP

If you're using a CMS to manage your site, mobile plug-ins may be available that configure your site automatically for display on various mobile devices. These plug-ins typically include a separate CSS file you can edit to customize the appearance of your pages.

Checking Your Site Accessibility

In addition to overseeing the development of HTML and CSS standards, W3C offers Web Content Accessibility Guidelines for "making web content accessible to a wider range of people with disabilities, including blindness and low vision, deafness and hearing loss, learning disabilities, cognitive limitations, limited movement, speech disabilities, photosensitivity, and combinations of these."

Your site should adhere to these guidelines. Fortunately, a few accessibility testing sites are available to lend a hand. Following are three of the best:

- **Functional Accessibility Evaluator:** fae.cita.uiuc.edu

- **Web Accessibility Evaluation Tool:** wave.webaim.org

- **HERA:** sidar.org

These tools work the same way as the validation tools described earlier in this chapter. You plug in the address of the page you want to check, click a link or button to execute the test, and use the results to attend to problem areas.

Your website needs to be accessible to all users, including those with visual or hearing impairments. Figure 24.7 shows sample results from the Functional Accessibility Evaluator.

Summary Report

Untitled Report   2010-11-11 15:14
Ruleset: 1004-1 (current)
URL: http://computerchimp.com/

Evaluation Results by Best Practices Main Category

Category	Status	% Pass	% Warn	% Fail
Navigation & Orientation	Almost Complete	96	0	3
Text Equivalents	Partially Implemented	50	25	25
Scripting	Complete	100	0	0
Styling	Complete	100	0	0
HTML Standards	Complete	100	0	0

Note: % Pass includes N/A results.

Evaluation Results by Best Practices Subcategory

Category/Subcategory	% Pass	% Warn	% Fail
Navigation & Orientation			
Titles (title & h1)	100	0	0
Subheadings (h2..h6)	100	0	0
Navigation Bars	100	0	0
Form Control Labels	80	0	20
Default Language	100	0	0
Data Tables	100	0	0
Access Keys	100	0	0
Frames	100	0	0

Figure 24.7: *How accessible is your site?*

Dealing with Web Browser Compatibility Issues

The web is in a constant state of flux. Different browsers and even different versions of the same browser vary in their support for the latest HTML and CSS standards. HTML5 and CSS3 compound the problem by being so new and perhaps even in development as you read this.

Making a site cross-browser compatible and future-proofing it can be a very complicated chore in itself, but you can employ a few basic strategies without too much effort, as explained in the following sections.

> **INSIDE TIP**
>
> FindMeByIP has an excellent browser compatibility chart at findmebyip.com/litmus. If that page is no longer available, search the web for "HTML5 compatibility chart," "HTML5 support chart," "CSS3 support chart," or a similar search phrase to find out which features are supported in various browsers and versions of those browsers.

Adding HTML5 Support to Browsers

Most current browsers have fairly wide support for HTML5 elements or at least recognize the tags, so you can target elements with CSS styles. Internet Explorer 8 and earlier versions are the most notable exceptions. To work around this problem, you can use JavaScript to "create" new elements that the Internet Explorer can recognize.

The easiest way to do this is to reference a JavaScript file on Google that contains scripts for creating all HTML5 elements. To reference the JavaScript file, include the following code between the opening and closing <head> tags on each page of your site:

```
<!--[if lt IE 9]>
<script src="http://html5shiv.googlecode.com/svn/trunk/html5.js">
    ➥ </script>
<![endif]-->
```

If you're using a CMS, such as WordPress, you may need to paste the code into the header.php file or a comparable file. The CMS will then include the code in the head section of every page on your site.

The first line is a conditional "if" statement telling the browser that if it is a version earlier than Internet Explorer 9, the browser should run the script to create the HTML5 elements. If the browser is version 9 or later, it doesn't run the script.

Using Browser Prefixes

Some browsers that support the latest CSS styles may require a browser prefix before the CSS property until the browser officially supports that property:

> **-moz-** for Mozilla Firefox
>
> **-webkit-** for WebKit browsers including Safari and Google Chrome
>
> **-o-** for Opera

When using newer styles that certain browsers don't officially support, include the browser prefixes, as in this example:

```
aside {
border-radius:5px;
-moz-border-radius:5px;
-webkit-border-radius:5px;
-o-border-radius:5px;
}
```

Always include the property without the prefix as well, so as browsers officially adopt the style, your styles will continue to function.

Throughout this book, I point out instances when you may need to include browser prefixes.

Using Conditional CMS Statements

If you know that a certain browser doesn't support the CSS property you want to use, include a conditional "if" statement that specifies different formatting for that browser. You often see conditional statements for various versions of Internet Explorer, because it often plays by different rules. Following are some examples of conditional statements:

> **[if IE]** targets all versions of Internet Explorer.
>
> **[if IE 7]** targets only Internet Explorer 7.

[if gt IE 7] targets all versions of Internet Explorer greater than version 7.

[if lte IE 7] targets Internet Explorer 7 and earlier versions.

[if ! Gecko] targets all browsers except Gecko-based browsers, including Firefox and Camino.

Conditional operators include lt (less than), lte (less than or equal to), eq (equal to), gt (greater than), and gte (greater than or equal to). To reference different browsers, use the designations shown in Table 24.1.

Table 24.1
Browser Designations for Conditional Statements

Designation	Browser
IE	Internet Explorer
Gecko	Gecko-based browsers, including Firefox and Camino
WebKit	WebKit-based browsers, including Google Chrome and Safari
SafMob	Mobile Safari
Opera	Opera
IEMac	Internet Explorer for the Mac
Konq	Konqueror
IEmob	Internet Explorer mobile
PSP	Playstation Portable
NetF	Net Front

To use a conditional statement to specify formatting for a browser, start with the conditional statement followed by the CSS style rule. Here's an example:

```
aside {
width:350px;
[if lt IE9] width:450px;
}
```

In this example, an aside is 350px for all browsers except Internet Explorer 8 and earlier, in which case the aside element is 450px wide.

INSIDE TIP

Because Internet Explorer tends to stray from the mainstream, some developers create a separate CSS style sheet specifically for it. If you choose to take this approach, include the conditional "if" statement in the <head> section of all web page documents, like so:

```
<!--[if IE]>
<link rel="stylesheet" type="text/css" href="ie.css" />
<![endif]-->
```

This tells Internet Explorer to use a different style sheet, so the style sheet itself doesn't require any if statements. For more about style sheets, see Chapter 10.

Using Browser and Feature Detection

In the past, many developers used browser detection to identify each user's browser and then serve up specific content or CSS formatting for different browsers. With so many browsers and browser versions being used on the web and the ever-evolving nature of the web, this practice has become obsolete. Now, most developers use *feature detection.*

Feature detection tests whether a browser supports a specific HTML element, CSS style, or other web standard. If the browser supports the feature, the browser can proceed. If it doesn't support the feature, the source code either adds the feature in some way or instructs the browser to use something else instead, such as a different style sheet.

Feature detection requires a script that queries the browser for the presence of specific features and returns a value of true if the browser supports the feature or false if the browser doesn't. Additional code in the script uses the true or false value to tell the browser how to proceed.

Scripting for feature detection is beyond the scope of this book. If you need to include feature detection on your site, I recommend checking out api.jquery.com/jQuery.support for instructions on using the jQuery.support utility to perform feature detection. The utility includes a collection of scripts that greatly simplify the process. For more about jQuery, see Chapter 22.

NOTE

As you might guess, testing for all available features would involve writing dozens of scripts. Fortunately, you don't have to test for everything. You can omit testing for HTML elements and CSS styles that are widely supported and any elements and styles you're not using on your site. Include feature tests for only those elements and styles that have trouble running on certain browsers.

The Least You Need to Know

- Validate your pages at validator.w3.org to ensure conformity with the HTML standard you're following.

- Validate your CSS at jigsaw.w3.org/css-validator to ensure compliance with CSS standards.

- Be sure your site looks right in at least the top five web browsers: Firefox, Internet Explorer, Google Chrome, Opera, and Safari.

- You may use various mobile browser emulators to check your site's appearance and functionality on mobile devices.

- Evaluate your site's accessibility at fae.cita.uiuc.edu or any of several other accessibility test sites.

- To start using the latest web standards while you're waiting for web browsers to fully adopt those standards, use browser prefixes, conditional statements, and feature detection as workarounds.

Boosting Your Site's Search Engine Ranking

In This Chapter

- Helping search engines discover and index your site
- Identifying areas for improvement
- Making your site's content attractive to search engines
- Creating internal and inbound links
- Using meta tags to tell search engines about your pages

After investing considerable time and effort in creating a website, you want to be sure web users can find it. When users search for specific words and phrases related to your site, you want your site to appear in the search results—preferably on page one, and ideally at the top of page one.

I can't promise you a #1 search engine ranking, but I can offer guidance to boost your ranking and ensure that your site is properly indexed by the major search engines and directories. That's what this chapter is all about.

What Do Search Engines Look For?

To boost your site's search engine ranking, you must first recognize the purpose of search engines: to help people find what they're looking for—the best information, guidance, products, services, and so on, that match a specific search entry. It's not about your site. It's all about serving users' needs.

So how do search engines determine which pages best serve a user's specific needs? By examining and evaluating numerous factors on an ever-changing list. These factors are likely to include the following.

Keywords in domain name: You don't want a domain name that's crazy long, but it's best to include at least one word in it, preferably the first word, that matches the word most users are likely to use to find your site.

Keywords in site title: Your site title must contain words that match the words in the user's search entry.

Keywords in page's filename: A page's filename should indicate what that page is about.

Meta keywords and descriptions: Meta keywords and descriptions give you the opportunity to tell search engines what your site is about. (More about meta keywords and descriptions later in this chapter.)

Keywords in content: Specifically, keywords in <h1>, <h2>, and <h3> headings, paragraphs, lists, blockquotes, and any other content the user can read. Keyword prominence is also a consideration; a keyword in a heading, for instance, carries more weight than the same keyword embedded in a paragraph.

Keyword density: This is the ratio of the number of times a keyword appears to the total number of words on the page.

Keywords in images and videos: Search engines may not be able to identify the "content" of an image or video by examining the file, but they can gather clues from the filename and the alt attribute you use to describe the image or video.

Number and quality of inbound links: Think of inbound links (links from other sites to yours) as referrals that boost your site's standing in the community. Inbound links carry a lot of weight, especially if highly ranked sites link to your site. For more about links, see "Implementing a Savvy Linking Strategy," later in this chapter.

Relevance of internal and external links: Internal links are those used to navigate your site. External links are those that link your site out to other sites. Both types of links should be relative to the content on your site.

Freshness of content: Fresh content trumps older content, and indicates that the page is being maintained. One great way to continuously add fresh content is to include a blog as part of your site and post to it at least two times per week.

Performance: A page that takes more than a few seconds to load may negatively affect a user's experience and, as a result, the page's search engine rank.

Sitemap and robots.txt file: A sitemap tells search engines what to index, whereas a robots.txt file tells them what *not* to index. Both files help focus a search engine's efforts on relevant content.

WHOA!

Don't try to trick your way to a higher search engine ranking. Keyword stuffing (cramming keywords in pages, meta tags, footers, and so on), using link farms for inbound links, posting lots of comments in forums and on blogs to link to your site, and other shenanigans are likely to do more harm than good. Search engines will penalize your site for engaging in bad SEO practices.

Performing an SEO Audit of Your Site

You can hire search engine optimization (SEO) services to audit your site and provide guidance on how to improve your site's search engine ranking, but you can also do it yourself using free tools and services available via the web. One of my favorite tools is the SEO Doctor add-on for the Mozilla Firefox web browser.

You can download and install Firefox for free at mozilla.com/firefox. To download and install the SEO Doctor add-on, first run Firefox, and then perform the following steps:

1. Click **Tools, Add-ons**.

2. Click **Get Add-ons**.

3. Click in the search box, type **SEO**, and press **Enter**.

4. Click **SEO Doctor** and click **Add to Firefox**.

5. Click **Install Now**.

6. When prompted, restart Firefox.

After installing SEO Doctor, an icon for it appears in the lower-left corner of the Firefox window, as shown in Figure 25.1. Open the page you want to check, and click the SEO Doctor icon to view the stats for this page. SEO Doctor examines several factors that contribute to the page's SEO and displays a list of them. Click a factor to view additional details and recommendations.

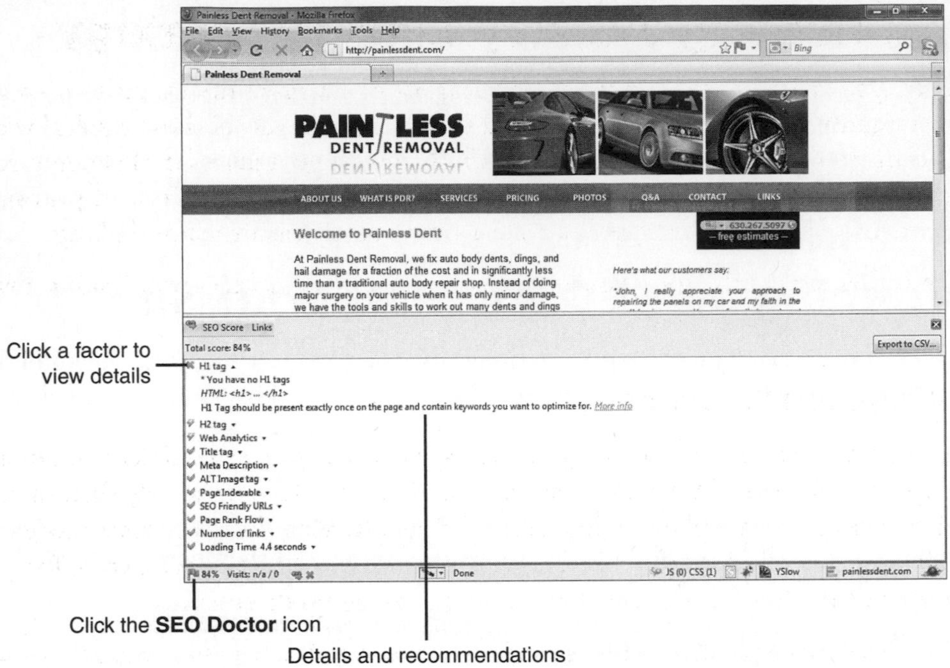

Click a factor to view details

Click the **SEO Doctor** icon

Details and recommendations

Figure 25.1: *SEO Doctor performs an SEO audit and offers suggestions.*

Keying in on Page and Post Titles and Page Content

Search engines generally give the most weight to keywords in titles and content, so those should be your areas of focus as well. Be sure every page has a unique title. To add a title, insert it between the opening and closing <head> tags and bracket it with opening and closing <title> tags, like so:

```
<title>Care and Feeding of True Chameleons and Other Reptiles</title>
```

Use keywords in your title that match what users are likely to search for to find pages like this, and be sure the keywords match keywords on the page itself. In addition, try to limit each title to no more than 60 characters.

Implementing a Savvy Linking Strategy

After you launch a site, it quickly becomes part of a community of websites—a global community (the World Wide Web) and the community of websites that deal with a specific topic, product, service, and so on. By raising your status in that community, you improve your search engine rank. For example, if every site that's in your site's community links to your site, your site should quickly earn the top ranking.

To earn a high ranking for your site, develop and implement a savvy linking strategy, starting with internal links.

Creating Internal Links

Internal links point to pages on your site, as opposed to external links that point to pages on *other* sites. When creating internal links, develop a relatively shallow navigation structure that makes all pages on your site reachable from the main navigation bar or one of its submenus. The deeper the structure (the more submenus, for example), the less likely search bots are going to dig up those pages.

Also, use text-based links in your navigation bar. Buttons may look nicer, but search engines can't read buttons.

Optimize anchor text with keywords. Anchor text is what the user clicks to activate the link. Use descriptive keywords in your anchor text that's consistent with the name of the page it links to.

Finally, add contextual links to pages you want ranked higher. A *contextual link* is one that's embedded in the content. For example, if you want to call attention to a page on your site about bicycle repair and another page on your site mentions "bicycle repair," link that mention of "bicycle repair" to the page dedicated to that topic.

WHOA!

Don't use keywords or phrases to the point that your use of them seems unnatural. Users won't like it, nor will search engines. Focusing on keywords does not mean *exclusively* focusing on keywords. Your primary focus should be to serve the needs of your intended audience. Do that well and you'll earn a higher search ranking.

Generating Inbound Links

Generating inbound links is tough because few website owners are eager to dilute their standing in the community by linking out to other sites. The best approach is to make your site so incredibly interesting that everyone *wants* to link to it—in other words, *earn* your inbound links.

To do this, you might want to try the following techniques: add your site address to all your online profiles and accounts, including Facebook, LinkedIn, and any professional organizations you belong to—assuming they provide that opportunity. For example, you can create a Google Profile that includes a link to your site.

Also, post a press release or two that links back to your site, or offer to write an article for a reputable and preferably prominent online journal or newsletter related to your site's content.

When you post comments on other sites, blogs, and forums, include a link to your site when it makes sense to do so and when the other sites allow it. Don't overdo this. Obvious self-promotion is spamming and quickly tarnishes your site's reputation.

You could also add your business listing to online directories and include your site's address.

Creating a business page or group on Facebook with a link to your site is another option.

Finally, you could submit your site for consideration in reputable specialized web directories relevant to your site's content.

Avoid the temptation to buy inbound links, randomly exchange links, list your site in directories built solely for generating inbound links, or engage in other tactics to trick your way to a higher ranking. These methods usually do more harm than good.

INSIDE TIP

If you have a business, add a listing for it to Google Local (local.google.com) and be sure to include the address of your business's website. When users perform a search related to products and services your site mentions, Google often displays Google Local entries at the top of the list, especially if the user specifies a location in the search that's in the vicinity of your business, such as a matching zip code or city name. Also consider creating a listing on yelp (yelp.com).

Attending to External Links

External links are those that link your pages to pages on other sites. In terms of SEO, external links tend to have the opposite effect on search engine rankings: the more your site links out to other sites, the less important your site appears to be. External links, however, may help search engines do a better job of indexing your site, assuming you link to sites in the same category as yours.

If you feel the need to link to other sites, here are a few tips:

- Keep external links to a minimum.

- Link only to reputable, prominent sites.

- Link to sites that are relevant to the content on your site.

- Avoid placing external links on every page—for example, in a footer or sidebar that appears on every page. You may want to create a Links or Other Resources page for links to external sites.

Rolling Out a Sitemap and Robots.txt File

Every site should have a sitemap and a robots.txt file to instruct search bots on what to index and what not to index. The following sections explain how to create each of these files.

> **INSIDE TIP**
>
> If you're using a CMS to manage your site, the CMS may generate a robots.txt file automatically, and plug-ins may be available for generating a sitemap, such as Google XML Sitemaps for WordPress. You can also find plenty of sitemap generators on the web.

Making Your Own Site Map

A sitemap is nothing more than a text file that indicates the location and name of each page you want indexed and its relative importance. The contents of the file look like this, but typically list more pages than shown in the following.

```
<?xml version="1.0" encoding="UTF-8"?>
<urlset xmlns="http://www.google.com/schemas/sitemap/0.90">
<url>
<loc>http://yoursite.com/about.html</loc>
<priority>0.9</priority>
</url>
<url>
<loc>http://yoursite.com/contac.html</loc>
<priority>0.9</priority>
</url>
</urlset>
```

Create your sitemap in any text editor, and save it as sitemap.xml. Upload the file to your site's root directory, which is where search engines will look for it.

Creating a Robots.txt File

Your site may consist of dozens or even hundreds of files you don't need or want a search engine to index. For example, WordPress creates and uses numerous directories packed with files that are not related to the content of the site. If search engines were to sift through all those folders and files to find the HTML documents, they would waste time and bandwidth, possibly slowing down your site and skipping files that really should be indexed.

A robots.txt file is a text file that contains directives on which search bots can access your site and which pages they're allowed to index. A typical robots.txt file looks something like this:

```
User-agent:*
Disallow:/cgi-bin
Disallow:/wp-admin
Disallow:/wp-includes
Disallow:/wp-content/plugins
Disallow:/wp-content/cache
Disallow:/wp-content/themes
Disallow:/trackback
Disallow:/comments
Sitemap:http://yoursite.com/sitemap.xml
```

The first line in this case addresses the instructions to all user agents (search bots). The last line tells search engines where to find the sitemap that tells them what to index. All the lines in between tell the search engines what not to index—in this case, the contents of several directories that do not contain web pages.

Submitting Your Site for Indexing

Search bots are constantly on the prowl for new sites and content; the major search sites—including Google, Yahoo!, and Bing—are almost certain to discover your site without your help. Still, you should check the Open Directory (dmoz.org) to be sure your site is listed, and submit it for consideration if it's not. Open Directory is *the* place to be listed, because hundreds of other sites consult it for their listings.

To submit your site, go to dmoz.org and search for it by address. If a link to your site doesn't appear, go to dmoz.org/docs/en/add.html and follow the instructions to be sure your site is suitable for inclusion in the directory. If it is, suggest that it be added.

If you feel you must add your site to Google, you can do so at google.com/addurl. To add a site to Yahoo!, go to dir.yahoo.com, navigate to the category best suited for your site, click the **Suggest a Site** link (upper right), and follow the on-screen cues to complete the operation. You can submit your site to Bing at bing.com/webmaster/SubmitSitePage.aspx.

SEO Meta Tag Do's and Don'ts

You can and should add *meta tags* to every web page to provide search engines with keywords and a description of each page; for example:

```
<meta name="description" content="Tips and tricks on how to grow
➥ vegetables, including tomatoes, green peppers, and strawberries
➥ in hanging containers." />
<meta name="keywords" content="grow tomatoes, grow green peppers,
➥ grow strawberries, hanging containers" />
```

Insert meta tags between the opening and closing <head> tags near the top of the page.

DEFINITION

A **meta tag** is part of a web page's HTML source code that's not displayed on the page but works behind the scenes to provide browsers and search engines with information about the page, including keywords and a page description.

In the past, web developers abused meta tags, stuffing them with keywords to attract search engines and artificially obtain higher search engine rankings. In response, search engines have reduced the importance of meta tags and may even penalize sites for meta tag abuse. The following sections provide guidance on how to use meta tags properly and avoid common mistakes.

Meta Tag Do's

Although meta tags are less powerful than they once were, you should still use them, so do …

- Use meta tags.
- Limit meta keywords to no more than 10.
- Limit meta descriptions to no more than 160 characters.
- Include keywords in both the meta keywords and meta description tags.
- Be sure your meta keywords and description align with the page's contents.
- List the most important keywords first.

Meta Tag Don'ts

When adding meta tags to your pages, avoid the following common mistakes. Don't …

- Stuff meta tags with keywords.
- Repeat keywords.
- Use keywords in meta tags that aren't included in the page contents.

> **INSIDE TIP**
>
> If you're using a CMS to manage your site, plug-ins may be available to simplify the process of adding meta data to pages and posts. In addition, some themes may have built-in SEO features that include options for adding meta keywords and descriptions.

Using Google Webmaster Tools to Improve SEO

Google offers a free service called Webmaster Tools that provides detailed reports about site and page visibility on Google. Webmaster Tools can help you verify that your sitemap and robots.txt files are functional and accessible to search bots, caution you about inaccessible pages, and provide valuable SEO statistics, including a record of which keywords and phrases people use most often in reaching your site.

To get started, head to Google and create a free Google account if you don't already have one. Then, add and verify your site:

1. Go to google.com/webmasters, click **Sign in to Webmaster Tools**, and log in to your Google account.

2. Click **Add a site**, type the URL of the site you want to add, such as http://www.yoursite.com/, and click **Continue**. The Site verification page appears.

3. Select the verification method you want and follow the on-screen instructions.

Now when you log in to Webmaster Tools, the opening page displays a link for your site. Click the link, and a dashboard appears, providing an overview of your site's stats along with links for viewing more detailed information, as shown in Figure 25.2.

At first, your dashboard doesn't contain this much data; Google gathers the data over time. For now, just be sure your sitemap status has a green check mark indicating that the sitemap exists and is accessible.

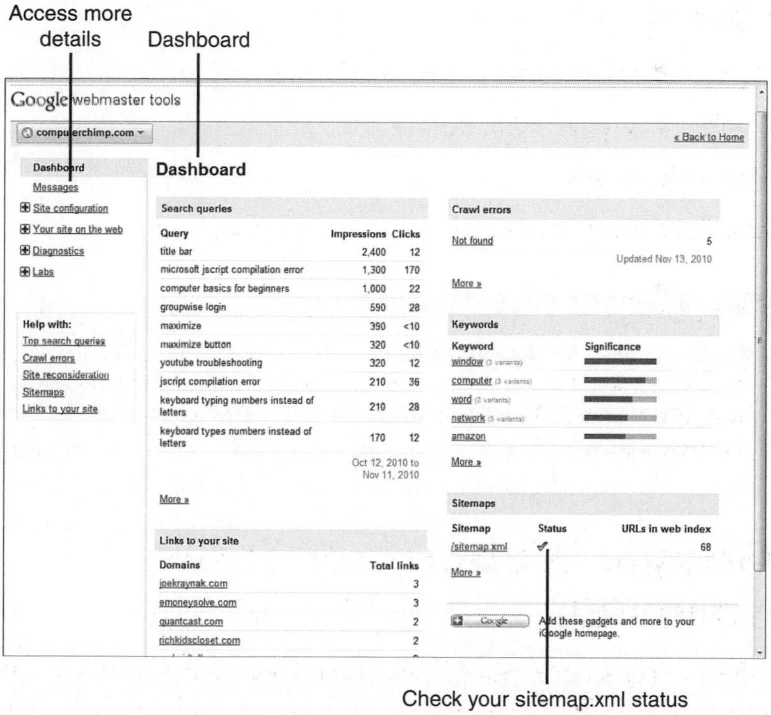

Figure 25.2: *The Google Webmaster Tools dashboard.*

For even more details about your web pages, check out Google Analytics at google.com/analytics. You add a short script to the bottom of your pages, and Google Analytics tracks activity on those pages and presents data and statistics, including the number of visitors per day (see Figure 25.3).

Figure 25.3: *Google Analytics tracks traffic on websites.*

Checking Page Rankings for Specific Keywords

You may find it useful or at least interesting to know where certain pages appear in the search results for specific keywords and phrases. For example, if you've created a site to promote your paintless dent auto body repair business in Villa Park, Illinois, where does your site's home page appear when someone Googles "paintless dent repair villa park"?

You can find plenty of page-rank checkers on the web, but one of my favorites is an add-on for Firefox called Rank Checker. To download and install it, fire up Firefox and go to tools.seobook.com/firefox/rank-checker. Click the **Download Now** button and follow the on-screen instructions to download and install Rank Checker. (You'll need to supply a valid e-mail address to obtain login information for accessing the download.)

After installing Rank Checker, run Firefox and perform the following steps to check your site's ranking for specific keywords and phrases:

1. Click the **Rank Checker** icon (in the lower-right corner of the Firefox window). This opens a separate Rank Checker window, as shown in Figure 25.4.

2. Click in the **Domain** box, and type your site's domain name.

3. Click in the **Keyword** box, type a keyword or phrase, click **Add**, and repeat this step for each keyword or phrase you want to check.

4. Click **Start**, near the lower-left corner of the window. Rank Checker checks your page rank for the keywords and phrases you entered. This may take several seconds. It then displays its results, as shown in Figure 25.4.

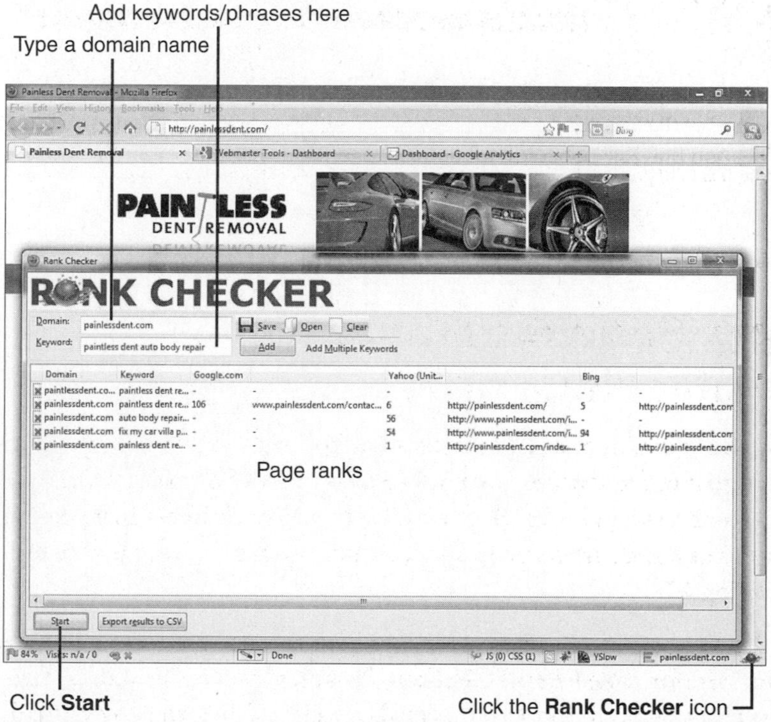

Figure 25.4: *Check your search engine page rank for specific keywords and phrases.*

The Least You Need to Know

- Focus on page titles and content. Nothing contributes more to SEO than compelling and relevant content.
- Design your site with a shallow navigation structure to accommodate search engine bots.
- Be sure all your page titles, content, and links are keyword optimized.
- Add a sitemap and robots.txt file to your site's root directory to instruct search engines on what to index and what not to index.
- Be sure every page has a keyword and description meta tag, but don't overuse keywords.
- Open a free Google account and use Google's Webmaster Tools to improve SEO.

Making Your Pages Load Faster

In This Chapter

- Checking the speed of page loading times and hunting down bottlenecks
- Making photos and other images leaner and faster
- Caching CMS-generated pages to reduce load times
- Reducing JavaScript drag
- Working with HTTP request and DNS lookup issues

The web provides on-demand access 24/7, and web users are very demanding. If a page takes more than a few seconds to load, users are likely to click the **Back** button and try the next link in the list of search results. Because of this, search engines are likely to subtract points if your pages take too long to load.

This chapter is designed to help you make your pages load faster. Here, you discover how to test your pages to see just how long they take to load and to diagnose potential speed bumps. You also pick up several techniques to improve your site's performance.

Testing Web Page Loading Times

One way to test web page loading times is to use a stopwatch. A better way is to test your site online at Pingdom Tools, where you not only find out how long a page takes to load, but also access a list of each page's components and how long it takes each of them to load.

To test a page's loading time, head to tools.pingdom.com, type the address of the page you want to test, and click **Test Now**, as shown in Figure 26.1. Pingdom Tools loads the page, which may take several seconds, and displays the test results. The results may provide some indication of problem areas, such as large images that are bogging down your load times.

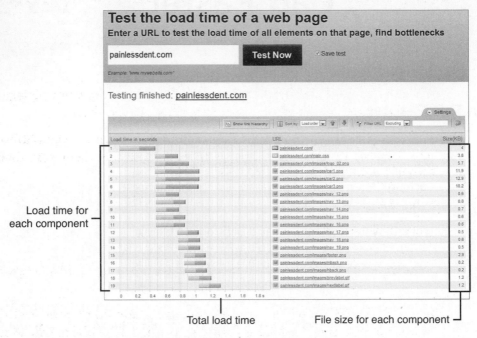

Figure 26.1: *Test web page loading times.*

Identifying Bottlenecks

Pingdom Tools and similar test sites reveal the big picture, but they provide little insight into what you can do to make your pages load faster. For that, you need a better tool, such as Google Page Speed or Yahoo!'s YSlow. To use either of these tools, you must have the Mozilla Firefox browser, which you can download and install at mozilla.com/firefox. The Firebug add-on must also be installed; see Chapter 11 for details on installing Firebug.

You can then run Firefox and install the Page Speed or YSlow add-on. The steps for installing YSlow are very similar to those for installing Firebug. You run Firefox and then use its Tools, Add-ons command to search for and install it. The process for installing Page Speed is a little different because it doesn't show up in a Firefox Add-on search. You need to go to Google to get it:

1. Use Firefox to go to code.google.com/speed/page-speed.

2. Click **Page Speed Downloads**.

3. Click the **Install Page Speed** button. The Software Installation dialog box appears indicating that you're about to install page-speed.xpi.

4. If Firefox displays a warning bar near the top of the window, click **Allow**. The Software Installation dialog box appears, indicating that you're about to install page-speed.xpi.

5. Click **Install Now**.

6. Click **Restart Firefox**.

After Firefox restarts, you can use Page Speed to identify issues that may be slowing down your page loads. Here's how:

1. Open the page you want to test in Firefox, and wait until it's fully loaded. When a page is done loading, Firefox displays "Done" in the middle of its status bar (at the bottom of the window).

2. Click the Firebug icon (at the right end of the status bar; it looks like a bug) or click **Tools, Firebug, Open Firebug**.

3. Click the **Page Speed** tab.

4. Click **Analyze Performance**. Page Speed analyzes the page and displays its results, as shown in Figure 26.2.

5. Click a plus sign next to an issue to view more details.

Page Speed tab

Click for details

Firebug icon

Figure 26.2: *Here are the Page Speed results.*

Page Speed lists several issues you may know little or nothing about. The following sections shed light on the most common issues and provide guidance on how to address them.

Reducing HTTP Requests

Hypertext transfer protocol (HTTP) requests are calls to the server for files needed to render a web page. Generally, the more HTTP requests, the more time is required to render the page. To reduce the number of HTTP requests, consider the following:

Simplify your site's design: For example, instead of using small graphics for navigation buttons, rely on text links, which are better for SEO purposes anyway. Another option is to use an image map instead of multiple small images, as explained in Chapter 7.

Combine files: You can combine the contents of two or more CSS files into a single CSS file and include all JavaScript scripts in a single script file. If you do this, be sure to delete any <style> tags at the top of your web documents that refer to CSS files no longer in use and any <script> tags that refer to script files no longer in use.

Combine images with CSS sprites: With CSS sprites, you combine several images and then refer to those images in your CSS via their *x,y* coordinates. See "Using CSS Sprites," later in this chapter, for details.

Use CSS3 for special effects: CSS3 supports many features that enable you to reduce your use of images for shadows, buttons, gradients, and so on. This not only reduces the number of HTTP requests but also the bandwidth for downloading images.

Streamlining Images

Image files tend to be larger than text files of the HTML and CSS variety, so they take longer to download. Because images contribute so much to the visual appeal of a site, you probably don't want to eliminate them completely, but you can make images leaner so they load faster. The following sections offer a few strategies for reducing image-related page load delays.

Reducing Image File Sizes

Large, high-quality images can slow down your site considerably. Consider reducing the size and quality of images to improve page load speed. You can use just about any photo editor or graphics program to adjust image size and quality. Here's how you do it in Picasa, which you can download for free from picasa.google.com:

1. Open a photo or other JPEG image in Picasa.

2. Click **Export**.

3. Select a folder in which to store the exported file.

4. Drag the **Resize** slider to the left to reduce the size of the image.

5. Open the **Image Quality** list and choose a lower-quality setting.

6. Click **Export**.

Tiny images with average quality aren't always a good idea. Users may want larger, higher-quality images, and smaller images may not help as much with search engine optimization (SEO). For the best of both worlds, consider using *thumbnail* images.

To use a thumbnail, create two versions of the image—a small, lower-quality version to display on the page, and a larger, higher-quality image. Then, make the small image link to the larger image. (See Chapter 7 for details on making an image a clickable link.)

If you're using a CMS such as WordPress to manage your site, it may include a feature that creates thumbnails for you. When inserting an image into a post or page, look for a thumbnail option.

Specifying Image Dimensions

One way to make your page *seem* to load faster is to specify image dimensions so browsers can display the page with placeholders for the images while they download. This gives users quicker access to the contents on the page so they can proceed without having to wait for the images. Whenever you insert an image, add height and width attributes to the image tag to specify the image's actual dimensions. See Chapter 7 for details.

Using CSS Sprites

CSS sprites is a technique that enables you to consolidate several small images into one big image and then use CSS to display one of the smaller images wherever you need it to appear. Here's how it works:

1. The sprite is essentially a grid with its upper-left corner positioned at a point with coordinates $x,y = 0,0$, as shown in Figure 26.3.

2. You place images on the sprite, with the upper-left corner of each image a specific distance, in pixels, from $x,y = 0,0$.

3. Using HTML and CSS, you create a box where you want the image to appear—a box with the same dimensions as the image. The browser moves the sprite up and to the left to align the upper-left corner of the image on the sprite with the upper-left corner of the box. This displays the image inside the box and hides all other images positioned outside the box.

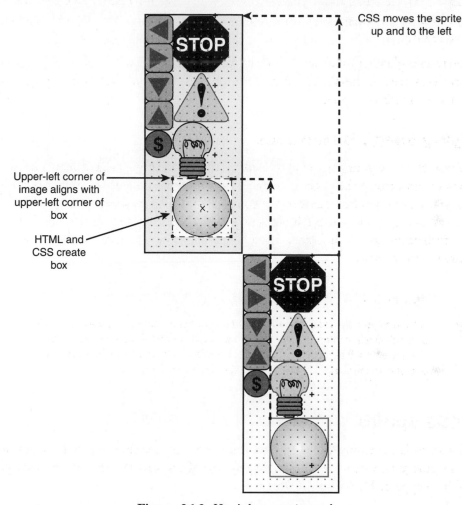

CSS moves the sprite up and to the left

Upper-left corner of image aligns with upper-left corner of box

HTML and CSS create box

Figure 26.3: *Here's how a sprite works.*

You can use just about any graphics program to create your sprite as long as the program enables you to determine each image's dimensions and the x,y coordinate of its upper-left corner. Create a new image, and use the options in your graphics program to display its grid and set the units to pixels. Also be sure the upper-left corner of the grid has the x,y coordinates of 0,0 and that numbers increase as you move to the right and down.

Paste or draw any images you want to include on the sprite. They can be very close, but the imaginary box around an image should not overlap a neighboring image. Click an image and then jot down its dimensions and the x,y coordinates of its upper-left corner. Repeat this step for all images that comprise the sprite.

x, y coordinates of the image's upper-left corner

Image dimensions

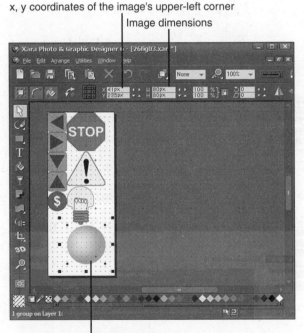

Click an image on the sprite

Figure 26.4: *Here's a sample sprite.*

Create a 1px×1px transparent gif or png image, which is what you'll use to pull the sprite onto your web page. Now you're ready to create the CSS and HTML for putting your sprite to work.

Create a CSS class called "sprite" that loads the transparent image; for example:

```
.sprite {background:url('images/mySprite.png'); }
```

Use the *background-position* property to specify the number of pixels each image needs to shift up and to the left, and use the height and width attributes to specify each image's dimensions, like so:

```
/* Button */
.left {background-position:0px 0px; height:40px; width:40px; }
.right {background-position:0px -41px; height:40px; width:40px; }
.down {background-position:0px -82px; height:40px; width:40px; }
.up {background-position:0px -123px; height:40px; width:40px; }
.dollar {background-position:0px -164px; height:40px; width:40px; }
/* Icon */
.stop {background-position:-41px 0px; height:80px; width:80px; }
.caution {background-position:-41px -81px; height:71px; width:80px; }
.bulb {background-position:-41px -153px; height:80px; width:56px; }
.ball {background-position:-41px -235px; height:80px; width:80px; }
```

Use HTML img tags along with the CSS classes you created to load images where you want them displayed on your page, like this:

```
<img src="images/1x1.png" class="sprite ball" alt="Ball" />
```

This particular tag loads the transparent .png image and assigns it two classes:

- *sprite* designates the file mySprite.png as the background image.

- *ball* moves the sprite 41 pixels left and 235 pixels up, and displays the image in a box that's 80 pixels high by 80 pixels wide.

INSIDE TIP

You may be able to save some time and frustration by using a sprite-creation tool. For example, at spriteme.org, you can access a tool that enables you to open a page in your browser and click a button to build the sprite and generate the required CSS for you.

Adding an HTTP Expires Header

The Expires header tells web browsers how long to store objects in their cache before refreshing those objects. You typically set expiration dates for images, CSS files, and scripts, so browsers won't download these items again on recent return visits to the site. To add an HTTP Expires header, log in to your web hosting account and use its file manager to open the .htaccess file, located in the root directory of your site. You can then add your HTTP Expires header, which looks something like this:

```
# Expires header
ExpiresActive On
ExpiresByType image/gif "access plus 2 months"
ExpiresByType image/png "access plus 2 months"
ExpiresByType image/jpg "access plus 2 months"
ExpiresByType image/jpeg "access plus 2 months"
ExpiresByType image/ico "access plus 2 months"
ExpiresByType text/css "access plus 2 months"
ExpiresByType text/js "access plus 2 months"
```

This tells browsers that for each type of file listed in the Expires header, the browser should continue to load files from its cache when available instead of downloading the files, as long as the files in the cache are not more than two months old. You can enter Expires periods in days, months, or even years.

> **WHOA!**
>
> Be careful when editing the .htaccess file. Errors could make your site inaccessible. Consider backing up the file to your computer before editing the original, just in case.

Caching CMS-Generated Pages

One of the drawbacks of maintaining a site using a CMS is that the CMS must assemble the page when a browser calls for it, which takes additional time and consumes additional resources on the web server. To avoid this, consider installing a cache plug-in, such as W3 Total Cache for WordPress.

A cache plug-in retains a copy of each page when the page is first loaded and then delivers that page when a browser calls for it. This can slash page load times and help conserve valuable web server resources.

Gzipping Components

Gzip is a utility that compresses and decompresses files on the fly. A browser that supports Gzip signals to the web server that it supports Gzip. The web server then sends compressed versions of files, which the browser decompresses upon receipt.

Before doing anything with Gzip compression, test your site to determine whether files are already being compressed:

1. Point your web browser to gidnetwork.com/tools/gzip-test.php.

2. Enter the address of the site you want to test for Gzip compression in the **Web Page URL** box.

3. Click **Check**.

4. Note the result.

5. If your site shows it's not using GZip compression, add the DEFLATE command to your .htaccess file; for example:

```
AddOutputFilterByType DEFLATE text/html text/plain text/xml
➥ text/css text/javascript application/x-javascript
```

Retest your page, as instructed in steps 1 and 2. If the page is still not compressed, search your hosting provider's help system or the web to find information about how to enable Gzip or whichever compression utility your hosting provider uses.

Moving CSS to Beginning and JavaScript to End

Another way to make your pages appear to load faster is to place the CSS <style> tags at the beginning and the JavaScript <script> tags at the end, when possible. This ensures that the CSS loads first, giving the browser what it needs to display the page. JavaScript tends to take longer to load and isn't always essential for displaying the page, so it can take its time while the user checks out the page.

Placing CSS at the beginning is always a good idea, but placing JavaScript at the end is not always the best move. Some scripts may need to load earlier for the page to function properly. Try moving one JavaScript at a time to the beginning and testing the page to be sure the move is acceptable.

Minifying CSS and JavaScript

If you're trying to cut every single millisecond out of your page load times, you can try minifying CSS and JavaScript. Minifying consists of removing everything unnecessary, including comments, spaces, and tabs. Be careful with this strategy. Minifying makes the file contents very difficult to read. Do this only after you're done tweaking your CSS and scripts, and have decided you never again will need to edit them. Or at least make backups before minifying files.

Page Speed can help you minimize JavaScript and CSS. Perform the Page Speed analysis, as instructed earlier in this chapter. Then, click the **plus sign** next to one of the Minify options (Minify CSS, Minify JavaScript, or Minify HTML). Next to each file you want minimized, click the **Save As** link and follow the on-screen cues to save the minified versions to your computer. You can then replace the nonminified versions with these new streamlined versions. Be sure the minified versions have the same filenames as the originals.

> **INSIDE TIP**
>
> The latest, greatest tool in speeding up websites is the content delivery network (CDN)—a collection of web servers in numerous locations designed for speedy delivery of web content. A CDN determines the quickest route between one of its servers and the browser requesting the page, and delivers the page from that server. To learn more, search the web for CDN providers and check out what's involved.

The Least You Need to Know

- Test web page loading times at Pingdom Tools (tools.pingdom.com).
- To identify issues that may be slowing down your page load times, install the Google Page Speed add-on for Firefox and use it to evaluate your pages.

- To reduce the number of HTTP requests, consolidate CSS into one file, JavaScript into another, and small images into a sprite.

- Add an Expires header to your site's .htaccess file so browsers can load pages from their cache rather than from your web server on return visits.

- If you're using a CMS to manage your site, install a cache plug-in so the CMS doesn't need to generate a fresh page for every request.

- Always place CSS <style> tags at the top of your web pages and, when possible, JavaScript <script> tags at the end.

Glossary

absolute URL   An address to an Internet resource that indicates its location regardless of the current location.

achromatic   No color—black and white, or grayscale.

analogous   Neighboring colors on the color wheel.

attribute   Text added to an HTML tag that further describes an element's properties.

background   The color or image that appears behind an HTML element's contents.

base URL   An Internet address that designates the starting point for all relative URLs on a page.

Bézier curve   A mathematical curve defined by two endpoints and one or two control points for shaping the line.

block element   A web page component that appears on its own line.

blog   An online journal in which you post content regularly that others can comment on.

blogging platform   Software that typically resides online and enables you to create, design, and manage your blog.

border   A line that defines an element's perimeter.

box model   The CSS system that governs the behavior of elements and the space around and inside them.

canvas   An HTML5 element that enables scripts to draw on web pages in real time—for example, plotting data on a graph as the page receives data from an online source.

CDN (content delivery network)   A collection of web servers in numerous locations designed for speedy delivery of web content. A CDN determines the quickest route between one of its servers and the browser requesting the page and delivers the page from that server.

CGI (common gateway interface)   A scripting language commonly used for processing form data.

character entity   An HTML code that represents a character you can't simply type on a web page.

class selector   An entry at the beginning of a style rule that targets an HTML element that has a specific class attribute.

CMS (content management system)   A tool that simplifies the creation and management of websites, enabling developers to log in and update their websites online.

color scheme   Color combinations intended to appear harmonious.

complementary   Two colors directly opposite one another on the color wheel that contrast in a harmonious way.

contextual link   A hyperlink embedded in the content of a web page, instead of in a navigation bar or button.

CSS (cascading style sheets)   A set of formatting rules for controlling the appearance and layout of HTML documents that enable developers to separate formatting from content. Separating formatting from content facilitates the process of changing the design without having to change settings on every single web page. CSS3 is the most recent version.

declaration   A component of a CSS style rule that specifies how a given property of that element should appear. A declaration consists of two parts: one of the element's properties, such as height, and the property's value, such as 150px.

deprecated   No longer in use. As HTML evolves, new elements are added and elements that have fallen out of favor are deprecated.

DNS (domain name server) lookup   The act of matching a domain name to the number that actually represents the computer on which that domain resides.

domain name   A string of characters that represents the location of a group of related resources on the Internet.

DTD (document type declaration)   A tag at the beginning of a document that indicates the document type.

element   A component of a web page, such as a paragraph, heading, or image.

embed code   An HTML tag that enables you to include an external resource on a web page, such as a YouTube video.

event   An occurrence that triggers an action to occur on a web page.

event attribute   HTML text added to a tag that ties the element to an incident, such as a click or mouseover.

fire   To execute an action or run a script.

float   A CSS property that enables you to position an HTML element all the way to the left or right of neighboring elements.

font family   A set of typefaces that appear similar regardless of size, weight, color, or style.

font style   A quality that enhances the appearance of text, such as bold or italic.

FTP (file transfer protocol)   Rules that govern the exchange of files over the Internet.

gradient   Two or more colors that gradually blend into one another.

hexadecimal (hex) code   A series of six letters and/or numbers that represent a color. Letters are A through F and numbers are 0 to 9. Each of the three sets of two characters represents a value for red green blue (RGB).

hotspot   An area on an image that functions as a hyperlink.

HTML (hypertext markup language)   A collection of standard tags and rules for identifying web content in a way that enables web browsers to render web pages properly. HTML5 is the most recent version.

HTML editor   A software application for creating and editing web pages.

HTTP (hypertext transfer protocol) request   A call for a specific web resource, such as a page or image.

hue   The characteristic that makes a color the color it is, such as blue, red, or green.

hyperlink   An HTML element users may click to access a different resource or site.

ID selector   An entry at the beginning of a style rule that targets an HTML element that has a specific ID attribute.

image rollover   An image that changes appearance in some way when the mouse pointer is over it.

inline element   A web page component that appears in the normal content flow, such as bold text within a paragraph.

JavaScript   A programming language that helps developers make web page content more dynamic and interactive.

jQuery   A library of scripts that simplifies the process of developing dynamic and interactive content for web pages.

keyword   A word or phrase on a web page that best describes the page's content. Search engines use keywords to identify and index web pages.

link   *See* hyperlink.

margin   The space outside an HTML element.

meta tag   A type of HTML tag not normally visible to users that passes information to web browsers and/or search engines.

monochromatic   One color, in addition to black, white, and gray.

nest   To place one element inside of another.

outline   A line outside an element's border that typically denotes that the element is selected or active in some way.

padding   The space between an element's boundaries and the content inside it.

paired tag   A type of HTML tag that requires an opening tag to mark where the element begins and another tag that marks where it ends—for example, <b>this text is bold</b>.

path   One or more lines in an HTML5 canvas drawing that consists of arcs and/or other shapes.

PHP (hypertext preprocessor)   The most popular scripting language for processing form data and performing numerous other tasks that make web pages more dynamic and interactive. It's particularly well suited for managing the exchange of data between web pages and databases.

presentation attribute   HTML text added to an HTML tag solely to control the appearance of an element.

presentation tag   An HTML tag, such as <b>, used solely to control the appearance of an element.

property   A characteristic of an element, such as height, width, or color.

protocol   Rules that govern the transfer of data.

pseudo class   A string added to a selector that enables you to apply different formatting to an HTML element based on its context or state, such as whether the mouse pointer is over it.

radian   A unit that converts an angle measure into a length measurement along the circumference of a circle. The circumference of a full circle, 360 degrees, is 2π radians.

relative URL   An address to an Internet resource that indicates its location relative to the current directory.

saturation   The intensity of a color—its purity and strength in the absence of white or black.

selector   An entry at the beginning of a style rule that targets specific HTML tags, attributes, classes, or IDs.

SEO (search engine optimization)   The use of various techniques to make a website more attractive to search engines and improve a site's ranking in search results.

SGML (Standard Generalized Markup Language) A set of rules that govern the creation of markup languages.

source code Computer-related instructions written in a format human beings can understand. In regard to HTML and CSS, source code tells browsers how to render a page.

split complementary A color scheme that uses a color and the two colors adjacent to its complementary color.

sprite A collection of images stored in a single file, each of which is referred to by the *x,y* coordinates of its upper-left corner.

style rule A CSS entry that applies formatting to one or more HTML elements. A style rule consists of two parts: a *selector* that targets the element and a *declaration* that specifies the formatting for that element.

subdomain A domain subdivision having the same domain name with a prefix tacked on to it.

syntax Rules that govern the arrangement of words or codes.

tag An HTML code characterized by one or more characters sandwiched between angle brackets, like this: <body>.

tag selector An entry at the beginning of a style rule that targets an HTML element's tag.

tetradic A color scheme that uses two pairs of complementary colors.

theme A collection of styles that control the appearance and layout of web pages and everything on those pages. You can totally change the appearance and layout of a site simply by choosing a different theme.

thumbnail A smaller version of an image the user can click to view the larger, higher-quality image.

triadic A color scheme that uses three colors equidistant on the color wheel.

unpaired tag An HTML tag that flies solo, requiring no closing tag to mark the end of the element—for example, the <img /> tag.

URI (uniform resource identifier)   *See* URL (uniform resource locator).

URL (uniform resource locator)   An address for a specific resource, such as a web page or an image, on the Internet.

validate   To check whether web page source code conforms to a given specification.

value   (1) A characteristic of a property—for example, the value for the color property is a specific color, such as red, blue, or chartreuse. (2) The quality that determines how light or dark a color appears.

visual editor   An HTML editor that keeps the HTML tags hidden and displays pages as they will appear in a web browser.

web hosting provider   A business that provides a place on the Internet for websites and blogs.

web server   A computer on the Internet that stores files that comprise a website and makes those files accessible to web browsers.

widget   A component easily added to a website without having to know how to write the program or script to create it. You can add widgets to sidebars on your site to display a calendar, clock, links to your favorite pages, search boxes, advertisements, and just about any other web page content you can imagine.

wireframe   A model of a web page without content used to visualize the overall layout of the page.

XML (eXtensible Markup Language)   A set of rules for encoding electronic documents. XML is used to create other markup languages. XML is a simplified version of SGML developed for use in marking up online documents.

z-index   A CSS property that enables you to define the order in which layered elements are stacked.

HTML Tags and Attributes Quick Reference

HTML5 Tags

Tag	Description
<!--...-->	Hidden comment
<!DOCTYPE HTML>	Document Type Declaration (DTD)
<a>	Hyperlink
<abbr>	Abbreviation
<address>	Address
<area>	Area inside image map
<article>	Defines an article
<aside>	Tangential content
<audio>	Audio content
<b>	Bold
<base>	Designates directory from which other directories' locations are referenced
<bdo>	Direction of text display
<blockquote>	Quoted material
<body>	Body element
 	Line break
<button>	Push button
<canvas>	Dynamic drawing area
<caption>	Table caption
<cite>	Citation of source
<code>	Computer code text

continues

HTML5 Tags (continued)

Tag	Description
<col>	Table column
<colgroup>	Table column groups
<command>	Command button
<datalist>	Drop-down list
<dd>	Definition description
<del>	Deleted text
<details>	Element details
<dfn>	Definition term
<div>	Section in a document
<dl>	Definition list
<dt>	Definition term
<em>	Emphasized text (typically italic)
<embed>	External content (such as a YouTube video)
<fieldset>	Grouping of form elements
<figcaption>	Figure caption
<figure>	Grouping of elements, including figure caption, typically to explain parts of a document
<footer>	Footer (content placed at bottom of every page)
<form>	Form
<h1> to <h6>	Heading levels 1 to 6
<head>	Information about the document
<header>	Header (content placed at the top of every page)
<hgroup>	Group of headings
<hr>	Horizontal rule
<html>	HTML content
<i>	Italics
<iframe>	Inline frame
<img>	Image
<input>	Input field

Tag	Description
<ins>	Inserted text
<kbd>	Keyboard text
<keygen>	Generated key in form
<label>	Label for form control
<legend>	Title in fieldset
<li>	List item (used with <ol> or <ul>)
<link>	Resource reference (typically used to link HTML documents to style sheets)
<map>	Image map
<mark>	Marked text
<menu>	Menu list
<meta>	Meta information
<meter>	Measurement within a predefined range
<nav>	Primary page navigation area
<noscript>	Area where scripts are prohibited from running
<object>	Embedded object
<ol>	Ordered (numbered) list
<optgroup>	Option group
<option>	Option in a drop-down list
<output>	Output text
<p>	Paragraph
<param>	Object parameter
<pre>	Preformatted text
<progress>	Progress bar
<q>	Short quotation
<rp>	What to show browsers that don't support the ruby element
<rt>	Details about ruby element
<ruby>	Ruby annotations
<s>	Corrected text (usually use <del> instead)

continues

HTML5 Tags (continued)

Tag	Description
<samp>	Sample computer code
<script>	Script
<section>	Section of page or article
<select>	Selectable list
<small>	Small text
<source>	Media resources
<span>	Selection of words or characters
<strong>	Strong (typically bold) text
<style>	Inline style definition
<sub>	Subscripted text
<summary>	Header of a <detail> element
<sup>	Superscripted text
<table>	Table
<tbody>	Table body
<td>	Table data (cell)
<textarea>	Text area (for long entries on a form)
<tfoot>	Table footer
<th>	Table column heading
<thead>	Table column heading group
<time>	Date/time
<title>	Document title (appears in browser window's title bar)
<tr>	Table row
<ul>	Unordered list
<var>	Variable
<video>	Video
<wbr>	Possible line break

Standard Attributes

Attribute	Value	Description
accesskey	character	Denotes keyboard shortcut to access element
class	classname	Assigns element a classname corresponding to classname in style sheet
contenteditable	true, false	Specifies whether user can edit the content
contextmenu	menu_id	Identifies context menu for an element
data-	value	Creates new attribute you define
dir	ltr, rtl	Sets text direction left to right or right to left
draggable	true, false, auto	Specifies whether user can drag the element
hidden	hidden	Hides element irrelevant to user
ID	id	Assigns element a unique ID corresponding to ID in style sheet
item	empty, url	Group elements
itemprop	url, group value	Group items
lang	language_code	Denotes language for an element's content
spellcheck	true, false	Indicates whether element must have its spelling or grammar checked
style	style_definition	Assigns inline style to an element
subject	id	Identifies element's corresponding item
tabindex	number	Sets the tab order of an element
title	text	Provides extra information about an element

Event Attributes: Window Events (For Use with <body> Tag)

Attribute	Run Script ...
onafterprint	after document is printed
onbeforeprint	before document is printed
onbeforeonload	before document loads
onblur	when window loses focus
onerror	when error occurs
onfocus	when window gets focus
onhaschange	when document has change
onload	when document loads
onmessage	when message is triggered
onoffline	when document goes offline
ononline	when document comes online
onpagehide	when window is hidden
onpageshow	when window becomes visible
onpopstate	when window's history changes
onredo	when document performs a redo
onresize	when window is resized
onstorage	when document loads
onundo	when document performs undo
onunload	when the user leaves document

Event Attributes: Form Events (Typically for Use with Form Elements)

Attribute	Run Script ...
onblur	when element loses focus
onchange	when element changes
oncontextmenu	when context menu is triggered
onfocus	when element gets focus
onformchange	when form changes
onforminput	when form gets user input
oninput	when element gets user input
oninvalid	when element is invalid
onselect	when element is selected
onsubmit	when form is submitted

Event Attributes: Mouse-Triggered Events

Attribute	Run Script ...
onclick	on mouse click
ondblclick	on mouse double-click
ondrag	when element is dragged
ondragend	at end of drag operation
ondragenter	when element is dragged to valid drop target
ondragleave	when element leaves valid drop target
ondragover	when element is dragged over valid drop target
ondragstart	at start of drag operation
ondrop	when dragged element is dropped
onmousedown	when mouse button is pressed
onmousemove	when mouse pointer moves
onmouseout	when mouse pointer moves off element
onmouseover	when mouse pointer moves over element
onmouseup	when mouse button is released
onmousewheel	when mouse wheel is rotated
onscroll	when element's scrollbar is scrolled

Event Attributes: Keyboard-Triggered Events

Attribute	Run Script ...
onkeydown	when key is pressed
onkeypress	when key is pressed and released
onkeyup	when key is released

Event Attributes: Media Triggered Events (Including Audio, Video, and Images)

Attribute	Run Script ...
onabort	on abort event
oncanplay	when media can start play, but may need buffering delay
oncanplaythrough	when media can play to the end, without buffering
ondurationchange	when length of media is changed
onemptied	when media resource element becomes empty (due to errors)
onended	when media reaches end
onerror	when error occurs during loading of element
onloadeddata	when media data is loaded
onloadedmetadata	when duration and other media data is loaded
onloadstart	when browser starts to load media data
onpause	when media data is paused
onplay	when media data is ready to start playing
onplaying	when media data starts playing
onprogress	when browser gets media data
onratechange	when media data's speed changes
onreadystatechange	when ready-state changes
onseeked	when media element's seeking ends
onseeking	when media element's seeking begins

Attribute	Run Script ...
onstalled	when getting media data stalls
onsuspend	when browser stops getting media data before operation is completed
ontimeupdate	when media changes playing position
onvolumechange	when media changes volume or volume is set to "mute"
onwaiting	when media is stopped but ready to resume

CSS Quick Reference

This CSS quick reference is divided into two parts. The first part lists CSS properties and their corresponding values. The second part presents pseudo classes, units, and colors.

Many of the groups begin with the shorthand entry, which enables you to specify several values for a single property. For example, instead of entering the following border declarations:

```
{border-width:1px; border-style:solid; border-color:blue; }
```

You can enter the shorthand version that includes all three properties:

```
{border:1px solid blue; }
```

In this appendix, the shorthand property looks like this:

border   border-width
                                 border-style
                                 border-color

When using the property, however, you would replace "border-width," "border-style," and "border-color" with their corresponding values.

CSS values appear in normal type, like this:

```
thin | medium | thick
```

You type these values as is. The vertical line (|) stands for "or," meaning you use only one of the properties.

Values that appear in italics function as placeholders for specific entries; for example, in place of %, you type a percentage; for *color*, you type a color name, hex value (such as #00ff00), or rgb value; for *length*, you type a measurement, such as 4px or 1em.

You may also notice some funky entries with square brackets, question marks, and ||, such as this:

box-shadow   inset? || [*length*{2,4} || *color?*]

The question mark indicates that the entry is optional. For example, in this listing, "inset" is an option you can use to display the shadow inside the box instead of outside it. Specifying a color is also optional. The square brackets group entries. For example, if you see something like [top | center | bottom] || [left | center | right], you can specify top, center, or bottom and left, center or right. The || means and/or. Curly brackets indicate the number of entries—in the box-shadow listing, you can include two to four length entries, with the first two numbers specifying the horizontal and vertical offsets of the box-shadow, the optional third number for the blur radius, and the optional fourth number for the spread radius.

CSS Properties and Values

Animation

Properties	Values
animation	*animation-name* *animation-duration* *animation-timing-function* *animation-delay* *animation-iteration-count* *animation-direction*
animation-name	none | name
animation-duration	*time*
animation-timing-function	ease | linear | ease-in | ease-out | ease-in-out | cubic-Bézier (*number,* *number, number, number, number*)
animation-delay	*time*
animation-iteration-count	inherit | number
animation-direction	normal | alternate
animation-play-state	running | paused

Background

Properties	Values
background	*background-image* *background-position* *background-size* *background-repeat* *background-attachment* *background-origin* *background-clip* *background-color*
background-image	url(*url*) | none
background-position	top left | top center | top right | center left | center center | center right | bottom left | bottom center | bottom right | *x% y%* | *x-pos y-pos*
background-size	auto | cover | contain | *length* | %
background-repeat	repeat | repeat-x | repeat-y | no-repeat
background-attachment	scroll | fixed
background-origin	border-box | padding-box | content-box
background-clip	border-box | padding-box | content-box | no-clip | *length* | %
background-color	*color* | transparent
background-break	bounding-box | each-box | continuous

Border and Outline

Properties	Values
border	*border-width* *border-style* *border-color*
border-width	thin | medium | thick | *length*
border-style	none | hidden | dotted | dashed | solid | double | groove | ridge | inset | outset
border-color	*color*
border-break	*border-width* *border-style* *border-color* close

continues

Border and Outline (continued)

Properties	Values
border-bottom	*border-bottom-width* *border-style* *border-color*
border-bottom-color	*border-color*
border-bottom-style	*border-style*
border-bottom-width	thin I medium I thick I *length*
border-collapse	collapse I separate
border-image	url(*url*) [*length*{2,4} stretch I repeat I round] I none
border-left	*border-width* *border-style* *border-color*
border-left-color	*border-color*
border-left-style	*border-style*
border-left-width	thin I medium I thick I *length*
border-right	*border-width* *border-style* *border-color*
border-right-color	*border-color*
border-right-style	*border-style*
border-right-width	thin I medium I thick I *length*
border-top	*border-width* *border-style* *border-color*
border-top-color	*border-color*
border-top-style	*border-style*
border-top-width	thin I medium I thick I *length*
border-radius	*border-top-right-radius* *border-bottom-right-radius* *border-bottom-left-radius* *border-top-left-radius*
border-top-right-radius	*length*

Properties	Values
border-bottom-right-radius	*length*
border-bottom-left-radius	*length*
border-top-left-radius	*length*
outline	*outline-color* *outline-style* *outline-width*
outline-color	*color*	invert
outline-offset	inherit	*length*
outline-style	none	dotted	dashed	solid	double	groove | ridge	inset	outset
outline-width	thin	medium	thick	*length*

Box Properties

Properties	Values
box-shadow	inset?		[*length*{2,4}		*color?*]	none
display	none	inline	block	box	inline-block	list-item | run-in	compact	table	inline-table	table-row-group | table-header-group	table-footer-group	table-row | table-column-group	table-column	table-cell	table- caption	ruby	ruby-base	ruby-text	ruby-base-group | ruby-text-group
overflow	visible	hidden	scroll	auto	no-display	no-content 	[*overflow-x*		*overflow-y*]
overflow-style	auto	marquee-line	marquee-block
overflow-x	visible	hidden	scroll	auto	no-display	no-content
overflow-y	visible	hidden	scroll	auto	no-display	no-content
visibility	visible	hidden	collapse

Columns

Properties	Values
columns	*column-width* *column-count*
column-width	auto | *length*
column-count	auto | *number*
column-fill	auto | balance
column-gap	normal | *length*
column-rule	*column-rule-width* *column-rule-style* *column-rule-color*
column-rule-width	thin | medium | thick | *length*
column-rule-style	border-style
column-rule-color	*color*
column-span	1 | all

Dimensions

Properties	Values
height	none | *length* | %
max-height	none | *length* | %
max-width	none | *length* | %
min-height	none | *length* | %
min-width	none | *length* | %
width	none | *length* | %

Flexible Box

Properties	Values
box-align	start | end | center | base-line | stretch
box-direction	normal | reverse | inherit
box-flex	*number*
box-flex-group	*integer*

Properties	Values
box-lines	single I multiple
box-ordinal-group	*integer*
box-orient	horizontal I vertical I inline-axis I block-axis I inherit
box-pack	start I end I center I justify

Fonts

Properties	Values
font	*font-style* *font-variant* *font-weight* *font-size/line-height* *font-family* caption I icon I menu I message-box I small-caption I status bar
font-style	normal I italic I oblique I inherit
font-variant	normal I small-caps I inherit
font-weight	normal I bold I bolder I lighter I 100 I 200 I 300 I 400 I 500 I 600 I 700 I 800 I 900 I inherit
font-size	xx-small I x-small I small I medium I large I x-large I xx-large I smaller I larger I inherit I *length* I %
font-family	*family-name* I *generic-family* I inherit
font-size-adjust	none I inherit I *number*
font-stretch	normal I wider I narrower I ultra-condensed I extra-condensed I condensed I semi-condensed I semi-expanded I expanded I extra-expanded I ultra-expanded I inherit

Gradients

Property	Syntax
background	-moz-linear-gradient([*point* II *angle*,]? *stop, stop* [,*stop*]*)
	-webkit-gradient(linear, *point1, point2*, from(*color*), to(*color*))
	-moz-radial-gradient(*point1, radius1, point2, radius2*, from(*color1*), to(*color2*))
	-webkit-gradient(*radial, point1, radius1, point2, radius2*, from(*color1*), to(*color2*))

Grid Positioning

Properties	Values
grid-columns	none	inherit	[*length*	*percentage*	*relative length*]
grid-rows	none	inherit	[*length*	*percentage*	*relative length*]

Hyperlinks

Properties	Values
target	*target-name* *target-new* *target-position*
target-name	current	root	parent	new	modal	*string*
target-new	window	tab	none
target-position	above	behind	front	back

Line Box

Properties	Values
alignment-adjust	auto	baseline	before-edge	text-before-edge	middle	central	after-edge	text-after-edge	ideographic	alphabetic	hanging	mathematical	*length*	%
alignment-baseline	baseline	use-script	before-edge	text-before-edge	middle	central	after-edge	text-after-edge	ideographic	alphabetic	hanging	mathematical	*length*	%
baseline-shift	baseline	sub	super	*length*	%
dominant-baseline	auto	use-script	no-change	reset-size	text-before-edge	middle	central	text-after-edge	ideographic	alphabetic	hanging	mathematical
drop-initial-after-align	central	middle	after-edge	text-after-edge	ideographic	alphabetic	mathematical	*length*	%
drop-initial-before-adjust	before-edge	text-before-edge	central	middle	hanging	mathematical	*length*	%
drop-initial-value	initial	*integer*
drop-initial-size	auto	*integer*	%	*line*

Properties	Values
inline-box-align	initial I last I *integer*
line-height	normal I *number* I *length* I %
line-stacking	*line-stacking-strategy* *line-stacking-ruby* *line-stacking-shift*
line-stacking-strategy	inline-line-height I block-line-height I max-height I grid-height
line-stacking-ruby	exclude-ruby I include-ruby
line-stacking-shift	consider-shifts I disregard-shifts
text-height	auto I font-size I text-size I max-size
vertical-align	baseline I sub I super I top I text-top I middle I bottom I text-bottom I *length* I %

List

Properties	Values
list-style	*list-style-type* *list-style-position* *list-style-image*
list-style-type	none I asterisks I box I check I circle I diamond I disc I hyphen I square I decimal I decimal-leading-zero I lower-roman I upper-roman I lower-alpha I upper-alpha I lower-latin I upper-latin I hebrew I armenian I georgian I cjk-ideographic I hiragana I katakana I hira-gana-iroha I katakana-iroha
list-style-position	inside I outside
list-style-image	none I url(*url*)
marker-offset	auto I *length*

Margin

Properties	Values
margin	*margin-top* *margin-right* *margin-bottom* *margin-left*
margin-top	auto | *length* | %
margin-right	auto | *length* | %
margin-bottom	auto | *length* | %
margin-left	auto | *length* | %

Marquee

Properties	Values
marquee-direction	forward | reverse
marquee-loop	infinite | *integer*
marquee-play-count	infinite | *integer*
marquee-speed	slow | normal | fast
marquee-style	scroll | slide | alternate

Padding

Properties	Values
padding	*padding-top* *padding-right* *padding-bottom* *padding-left*
padding-top	auto | *length* | %
padding-right	auto | *length* | %
padding-bottom	auto | *length* | %
padding-left	auto | *length* | %

Positioning

Properties	Values
bottom	auto | *length* | %
clear	left | right | both | none
clip	*shape* | auto
float	left | right | none
left	auto | *length* | %
position	static | relative | absolute | fixed
right	auto | *length* | %
top	auto | *length* | %
z-index	auto | *number*

Print

Properties	Values
fit	fill | hidden | meet | slice
fit-position	[[% | *length*]{1,2} | [[top | center | bottom] || [left | center | right]]] | auto
image-orientation	auto | *angle*
orphans	*integer*
page	auto | *identifier*
page-break-after	auto | always | avoid | left | right
page-break-before	auto | always | avoid | left | right
page-break-inside	auto | avoid
size	auto | landscape | portrait | *length*
widows	*integer*

Speech

Properties	Values
cue	[*cue-before*		*cue-after*]	inherit
cue-before	url(*url*)[silent	x-soft	soft	medium	loud	x-loud	none	inherit]	*number*	%
cue-after	url(*url*)[silent	x-soft	soft	medium	loud	x-loud	none	inherit]	*number*	%
mark	*mark-before* || *mark-after*
mark-before	*string*
mark-after	*string*
pause	[*pause-before*		*pause-after*]	inherit
pause-before	none	x-weak	weak	medium	strong	x-strong	inherit	*time*
pause-after	none	x-weak	weak	medium	strong	x-strong	inherit	*time*
phonemes	*string*
rest	[*rest-before*		*rest-after*]	inherit
rest-before	none	x-weak	weak	medium	strong	x-strong	inherit	*time*
rest-after	none	x-weak	weak	medium	strong	x-strong	inherit	*time*
speak	none	normal	spell-out	digits	literal-punctuation	no-punctuation	inherit
voice-balance	left	center	right	leftwards	rightwards	inherit	*number*
voice-duration	*time*
voice-family	[[*specific-voice*	[*age*] generic-voice] [*number*],]* [*specific-voice*	[*age*] generic-voice] [*number*]	inherit
voice-rate	x-slow	slow	medium	fast	x-fast	inherit	%
voice-pitch	x-low	low	medium	high	x-high	inherit	*number*	%
voice-pitch-range	x-low	low	medium	high	x-high	inherit	*number*	%
voice-stress	strong	moderate	none	reduced	inherit
voice-volume	silent	x-soft	soft	medium	loud	x-loud	inherit	*number*	%

Table

Properties	Values
border-collapse	collapse I separate
border-spacing	*length length*
caption-side	top I bottom I left I right
empty-cells	show I hide
table-layout	auto I fixed

Text

Properties	Values
color	*color*
direction	ltr I rtl I inherit
hanging-punctuation	none I [first II last II [allow-end I force-end]]
letter-spacing	normal I *length* I %
line-break	auto I newspaper I normal I strict I kepp-all
punctuation-trim	none I [start II [end I allow-end] II adjacent]
text-align	start I end I left I right I center I justify
text-align-last	start I end I left I right I center I justify
text-decoration	*text-decoration-line* *text-decoration-color* *text-decoration-style*
text-decoration-line	none I [[filled I open] II [dot I circle I double-circle I triangle I sesame]]
text-decoration-color	*color*
text-decoration-style	solid I double I dotted I dashed I wave
text-emphasis	none I [[accent I dot I circle I disc][before I after]?]
text-emphasis-color	*color*
text-indent	[*length* I %] II [hanging II each-line]?
text-justify	auto I [trim II [inter-word I inter-ideograph I inter-cluster I distribute I kashida]]
text-outline	none I [*length length? color*] I [*color length length?*]
text-shadow	none I [*length length length color*]

continues

Text (continued)

Properties	Values
text-transform	none I capitalize I uppercase I lowercase I fullwidth I large-kana
text-wrap	normal I unrestricted I none I suppress
unicode-bidi	normal I embed I bidi-override
white-space	normal I pre I nowrap I pre-wrap I pre-line
white-space-collapsing	collapse I discard I [[preserve I preserve-breaks] II trim-inner]
word-break	normal I break-all I hyphenate
word-spacing	normal I *length* I %
word-wrap	normal I break-word

Transform

Properties	Values
transform	rotate(*deg*) scale(%) translate([*x-length*], [*y-length*]) skew(*deg*)

Transition

Properties	Values
transition	*transition-property* *transition-duration* *transition-timing-function* *transition-delay*
transition-property	none I all
transition-duration	*time*
transition-timing-function	ease I linear I ease-in I ease-out I ease-in-out I cubic-Bézier (*number, number, number, number, number*)
transition-delay	*time*

User Interface (UI)

Properties	Values
appearance	normal	inherit	[icon	window	desktop	workspace	document	tooltip	dialog	button	push-button	hyperlink	radio-button	checkbox	menu-item	tab	menu	menubar	pull-down-menu	pop-up-menu	list-menu	radio-group	checkbox-group	outline-tree	range	field	combo-box	signature	password]
cursor	auto	crosshair	default	pointer	move	n-resize	s-resize	e-resize	w-resize	ne-resize	se-resize	nw-resize	sw-resize	text	wait	help url(*url*)
icon	auto	inherit	*number*
nav-index	auto	inherit	*number*
nav-up	auto	inherit	*id*[current	root	*target-name*]
nav-down	auto	inherit	*id*[current	root	*target-name*]
nav-left	auto	inherit	*id*[current	root	*target-name*]
nav-right	auto	inherit	*id*[current	root	*target-name*]
resize	none	both	horizontal	vertical	inherit

Pseudo Classes, Measurements, Colors, and More

Pseudo Classes

Pseudo Class	Description
:active	active element
:focus	element has focus
:visited	visited link
:hover	mouse over element
:link	unvisited link
:disabled	disabled element
:enabled	enabled element
:checked	selected form element

continues

Pseudo Classes (continued)

Pseudo Class	Description
:selection	selected (highlighted) element
:lang	specified language for the element
:nth-child(n)	nth sibling of another element
:nth-last-child(n)	nth sibling counting from the last
:first-child	first sibling
:last-child	last sibling
:only-child	only sibling
:nth-of-type(n)	nth sibling of its kind
:nth-last-of-type(n)	nth sibling of its kind, counting from the last
:last-of-type	last sibling of its kind
:first-of-type	first sibling of its kind
:only-of-type	only sibling of its kind
:empty	element that has no children
:root	root element in document
:not(x)	element not represented by "x"
:target	element targeted in a URL

CSS Pseudo Elements

Pseudo Element	Description
::first-letter	first letter of text element
::first-line	first line of text element
::before	inserts content before element
::after	inserts content after element

CSS Absolute Measurements

Abbreviation	Unit
cm	centimeter
in	inch
mm	millimeter
pc	pica (1pc = 12 points)
pt	point (1pt = $1/72$ inch)

CSS Relative Measurements

Abbreviation	Unit
%	percentage
em	em space = font width
ex	x-height of font
px	pixel
vh	viewport height
vw	viewport width
vm	viewport height or width (whichever is smaller)

CSS Angles

Abbreviation	Unit
deg	degrees
grad	grads
rad	radian
turn	turns

CSS Time

Abbreviation	Unit
ms	milliseconds
s	seconds

CSS Colors

Syntax	Color (Examples)
color name	red, blue, green, yellow, …
rgb (x,y,z)	blue = rgb (0,0,255)
rgb(x%,y%,z%)	blue = rgb (0,0,100%)
rgba(x,y,z,alpha)	blue 50% transparent = rgba(0,0,255,.5)
#rrggbb	blue = #0000ff
hsl(hue, saturation, lightness)	blue=(170,255,255)
hsla(hue, saturation, lightness, alpha)	blue 50% transparent = hsla(170,255,255,.5)
opacity	value = 0.0 (more transparent) to 1.0 (completely opaque)
flavor	Accent color for user interface

HTML Special Characters and Symbols

Sometimes, you'll need to add a character or symbol to your web page that's either not on your keyboard or is one of the funkier symbols that's on your keyboard. You might need to type an HTML entity name or number to insert it. (An HTML entity is any character you can't enter easily on your keyboard.)

The following table lists the most common HTML entities, along with the name and number you need to enter for each.

HTML Character Entities

Character/Symbol	Entity Name	Entity Number
"	&quot;	&#34;
&	&amp;	&#38;
'	&apos;	&#39;
<	&lt;	&#60;
>	&gt;	&#62;
nonbreaking space		
¡	&iexcl;	&#161;
¢	&cent;	&#162;
£	&pound;	&#163;
¤	&curren;	&#164;
¥	&yen;	&#165;
¦	&brvbar;	&#166;
§	&sect;	&#167;
¨	&uml;	&#168;
©	&copy;	&#169;
ª	&ordf;	&#170;

continues

HTML Character Entities (continued)

Character/Symbol	Entity Name	Entity Number
«	&laquo;	&#171;
¬	&not;	&#172;
-	&shy;	&#173;
®	&reg;	&#174;
¯	&macr;	&#175;
°	&deg;	&#176;
±	&plusmn;	&#177;
²	&sup2;	&#178;
³	&sup3;	&#179;
´	&acute;	&#180;
µ	&micro;	&#181;
¶	&para;	&#182;
·	&middot;	&#183;
¸	&cedil;	&#184;
¹	&sup1;	&#185;
º	&ordm;	&#186;
»	&raquo;	&#187;
¼	&frac14;	&#188;
½	&frac12;	&#189;
¾	&frac34;	&#190;
¿	&iquest;	&#191;
×	&times;	&#215;
÷	&divide;	&#247;
À	&Agrave;	&#192;
Á	&Aacute;	&#193;
Â	&Acirc;	&#194;
Ã	&Atilde;	&#195;
Ä	&Auml;	&#196;
Å	&Aring;	&#197;
Æ	&AElig;	&#198;
Ç	&Ccedil;	&#199;
È	&Egrave;	&#200;

Character/Symbol	Entity Name	Entity Number
É	&Eacute;	&#201;
Ê	&Ecirc;	&#202;
Ë	&Euml;	&#203;
Ì	&Igrave;	&#204;
Í	&Iacute;	&#205;
Î	&Icirc;	&#206;
Ï	&Iuml;	&#207;
Ð	&ETH;	&#208;
Ñ	&Ntilde;	&#209;
Ò	&Ograve;	&#210;
Ó	&Oacute;	&#211;
Ô	&Ocirc;	&#212;
Õ	&Otilde;	&#213;
Ö	&Ouml;	&#214;
Ø	&Oslash;	&#216;
Ù	&Ugrave;	&#217;
Ú	&Uacute;	&#218;
Û	&Ucirc;	&#219;
Ü	&Uuml;	&#220;
Ý	&Yacute;	&#221;
Þ	&THORN;	&#222;
ß	&szlig;	&#223;
à	&agrave;	&#224;
á	&aacute;	&#225;
â	&acirc;	&#226;
ã	&atilde;	&#227;
ä	&auml;	&#228;
å	&aring;	&#229;
æ	&aelig;	&#230;
ç	&ccedil;	&#231;
è	&egrave;	&#232;
é	&eacute;	&#233;

continues

HTML Character Entities (continued)

Character/Symbol	Entity Name	Entity Number
ê	&ecirc;	&#234;
ë	&euml;	&#235;
ì	&igrave;	&#236;
í	&iacute;	&#237;
î	&icirc;	&#238;
ï	&iuml;	&#239;
ð	&eth;	&#240;
ñ	&ntilde;	&#241;
ò	&ograve;	&#242;
ó	&oacute;	&#243;
ô	&ocirc;	&#244;
õ	&otilde;	&#245;
ö	&ouml;	&#246;
ø	&oslash;	&#248;
ù	&ugrave;	&#249;
ú	&uacute;	&#250;
û	&ucirc;	&#251;
ü	&uuml;	&#252;
ý	&yacute;	&#253;
þ	&thorn;	&#254;
ÿ	&yuml;	&#255;

Index

X-Y-Z